Brothers Notorious
THE SHELTONS
Southern Illinois' Legendary Gangsters

Taylor Pensoneau

Downstate Publications

Downstate Publications
P.O. Box 320
New Berlin, IL 62670
www.downstatepublications.com
contact@downstatepublications.com

Publisher's Cataloging-in-Publication
(Provided by Quality Books, Inc.)

Pensoneau, Taylor.
    Brothers notorious : the Sheltons : the story behind
    Southern Illinois' legendary gangsters / Taylor
    Pensoneau, author ; Liz Pensoneau, editor. -- 1st ed.
    p. cm.
    Includes bibliographical references and index.
    LCCN 2001118337
    ISBN 0-9710718-0-2

    1. Shelton, Earl. 2. Shelton, Carl (Carl Ray)
    3. Shelton, Bernie. 4. Outlaws--Illinois--Biography.   I.
    Title.

    F546.S54P46 2001   364.15'23'097737
                                  QBI01-700908

Frontispiece: Earl, left, and Carl Shelton. The brothers, along with a
third brother, Bernie, headed the most famous gang in downstate Illinois
crime history. *Photograph courtesy of James S. Zuber.*

In appreciation of my parents, Leslie and Bernice Pensoneau,
who lived life to the fullest
in the times recounted in this book.

Contents

Contents

▼

Prologue

Notorious. That was the word used more than any other to describe them.

They became household names. Carl, Bernie and Big Earl, that is. Some people still quivered at the mention of their names decades after they were gone. They were, after all, central figures in a dark saga that ran beyond a quarter of a century, a captivating tale of murder, mayhem and sordid drama enveloping Illinois from its humblest nooks to the pinnacle of power. Few of the lives caught up in it all, and they were many, emerged unchanged.

The Sheltons they were, and they may or may not have been "America's Bloodiest Gang," as *The Saturday Evening Post* would have had readers believe in an article in 1950. Lawlessness abounded across the country during the Sheltons' reign from the Roaring Twenties through the heyday of gambling in the 1940s. Yet, it was astounding the way attention riveted on the Sheltons and their exploits even as Al Capone set the standard for wickedness most embedded in the state's legacy. When the Sheltons rode highest in downstate Illinois, few would dare to spit on the sidewalks of towns where they held sway, such as East St. Louis and Peoria, without permission from a Shelton.

Like the James boys in the previous century, the Sheltons turned into the stuff of legends and lore. If some who knew them were to be believed, the Sheltons even displayed a Robin Hood touch here and there. Their reputation got so big that Hollywood once took an abbreviated interest in their deeds.

Curiosity about the Sheltons, perhaps it was more fascination, hardly ebbed after their family—what was left of it—disappeared from Illinois early in the '50s. Good riddance many law-abiding folks believed with sighs of relief. The better to obliterate a stain on public morality. Nevertheless, sweeping the Sheltons under the rug is no easy task. Americans love a good yarn, have a penchant for knowing all there is to know about their black sheep. In the Shelton narrative, they have a feast.

For all the raucousness in the family, its grave site in Fairfield's Maple Hill Cemetery, where some but not all of the Sheltons are buried, was serenely peaceful as two visitors viewed the gravestones on a glorious day in southern Illinois in the spring of 1998. Only the whine of a caretaker's mower pierced the silence.

Momentarily, though, the pair caught the eye of an elderly gentleman strolling by. The older man, clad in blue coveralls, his creased face shaded by a baseball cap, stopped and took note of the objects of the two strangers' attention.

"Yep," he remarked softly, "them Sheltons, they was somethin."

Acknowledgments

I didn't realize it back then, but the incentive for this book was born during hot summer nights when I was a youngster in my hometown of Belleville, Illinois. As was the custom in those days, before air conditioning became commonplace, my father and other men in the family spent their evenings in backyard gatherings, where they talked as they sipped cold beer from one of the many nearby neighborhood taverns. The subjects usually seemed to be World War II, politics or gangsters. I'd sit on the grass, swiping at mosquitoes and eagerly taking in the conversations. The gangland stories were the most intriguing, especially the ones tied to the Shelton gang. I never budged when the conversation turned to it—the gang that once ruled our part of the world with an iron hand.

My interest in the Sheltons did not wane as decades came and went, most certainly not in my early years as a *St. Louis Post-Dispatch* reporter, when older staff members who'd covered and even known the Sheltons reminisced about the gang. So, years later, when Gordon Pruett, a friend and expert on southern Illinois lore, suggested I write a book about the Sheltons, I didn't need much time to debate the thought. Within days, I was engaged in research for the book.

I found nothing more gratifying than the readiness of so many individuals to be helpful, including Gordon, who, besides suggesting the project, provided invaluable assistance in getting it under way. Others who came into play included Stephen Kerber, archivist, Bowen University Archives and Special Collections, Southern Illinois University at Edwardsville; Charles E. Brown, reference department head, St. Louis Mercantile Library, University of Missouri-St. Louis; Jean E. Wilkins, director, Illinois State Library, Springfield; Karen Deller and Sherri Schneider, special collections assistants, Cullom-Davis Library, Bradley University, Peoria, Illinois; Barbara DeWitt, librarian, and Evonne Hallam, assistant librarian, Fairfield Public Library, Fairfield, Illinois; Cheryl Pence and Jennifer Ericson of the microfilm section, Illinois State Historical Library, Springfield; M. Cody Wright, an archivist at the Illinois State Archives, Springfield; Mike Crowley, news research department, *St. Louis Post-Dispatch*; Gary Thomas, editor, *Outdoor Illinois* magazine; Illinois State Historian Thomas F. Schwartz; and Robert Fletcher of the Illinois State Police.

Many others granted my requests for help on the book or, in some cases, emerged voluntarily to offer information, such as Robert Granda, a Springfield, Illinois, attorney, legal researcher and old friend. Others included East St. Louis, Illinois, historian Bill Nunes; historical researcher Harold W. Fiebig of Belleville; Lucile Young Bent of Oakland, California; and another old friend, Shelley Epstein, associate editor of the *Peoria Journal Star*.

As for those in the Fairfield area who gave of their time to help make the book as accurate as possible, special appreciation goes to Judith Puckett for sharing her knowledge about her hometown and to attorney Richard C. Cochran, former Wayne County Sheriff Thomas Cannon Jr. and good friends Bill and Kathy Schmitz. And, most importantly, to veteran Fairfield newspaperman Jack Vertrees, who gave me more assistance than any author could expect in helping to make possible a book that Jack felt was long overdue.

Finally, the advice and encouragement from Charlie Birger biographer Gary DeNeal meant a lot to me.

To those reading this book, it is important to remember that many individuals named Shelton have resided in Wayne County. However, the book covers only the story of the family of Benjamin and Agnes Shelton.

1

Good Morning, Mr. Shelton

Carl Shelton seemed on the verge of living like a country squire. As many a farmer, he was out and about early on the agreeable morning of October 23, 1947. The hour of eight o'clock found him driving an army surplus jeep, riding alone in the vehicle that was headed north on Pond Creek Road, a few miles east of the Wayne County seat of Fairfield. The gravel and dirt road lay near part of his farmland, meaning he could have driven it blindfolded since this was his backyard, the countryside in which he had grown up and where his octogenarian mother still lived in the family farmhouse.

For many other Illinoisans, this was the time of day when they were scanning morning newspapers, catching up on things.

Just yesterday, actor Robert Taylor had urged members of the House Committee on un-American Activities to support the deportation of motion picture workers exposed as Communist Party followers. Hollywood, it appeared, was a prime target of Red hunters. Violent labor strikes were rampant in Ohio and elsewhere, and out along the Potomac there was the debate on the drafting of the Marshall Plan intended to aid war-ravaged Europe. Forest fires were sweeping New England; flames were so fierce at Maine's Bar Harbor that hundreds were facing evacuation from the resort island on any and all available crafts.

Most of this was light years away from Wayne County and its most widely known resident. Precious few in the county had firsthand knowledge of Hollywood Commies or tony Bar Harbor.

Whatever Shelton had on his mind that morning, he did not forget to beep, wave and yell "Hi, Boy!" to Harvey Wagner. Harvey had a farm along Pond Creek Road, and the jeep passed him as he stood outside his house, three miles or so south of where the thoroughfare reached State Highway 15. The two occupants of a truck trailing the jeep also waved to Wagner.

One was Earl Benjamin Shelton, a twenty-eight-year-old nephew of Carl Shelton known as Little Earl so as to avoid confusing him with another one of his uncles, Earl Robert Shelton, the Big Earl of Illinois gangster lore. The other fellow in the truck was Ray Walker, a tough hoodlum from Herrin who was a trusted lieutenant and bodyguard of Carl Shelton.

Carl might have had earmarks of a gentleman farmer, but he seldom went anywhere without protection or taking extreme caution. On this morning, as was always the case, he was armed. His .44 caliber revolver was beside him.

Only the naivest individuals really believed Shelton was disassociated completely from his past activities. Many law enforcement officials assumed that Carl had relinquished day-to-day supervision of the Shelton gang's still ongoing underworld activity in the Peoria area to his brother who resided there, the rough-and-tumble Bernie. Yet, the word was that Carl surely had his hand in, his imprint on, most gambling enterprises worth their salt, especially dice games, in the stretch of the gang's old territory running north and south through the lower part of Illinois and on into bits of southern Indiana and Kentucky. If not, why the persistent rumors that crime syndicate figures in the St. Louis area had aligned with Chicago's old Capone mob to take over what remained of the Sheltons' traditional gambling stamping ground?

Gambling may have been illegal in Illinois, but casinos and an assortment of gaming joints were operating at full throttle through much of the state. Law officers carried out token raids on some of the places periodically, but by and large the wagering proceeded with impunity as officialdom, from the governor on down to sheriffs and city cops, either looked the other way or pretended to be ignorant of what was going on. Many officials were blind to the situation because of payoffs from gambling chiefs, which turned out to be even more widespread than most folks figured. Nobody knew more about these machinations than Carl Shelton, who as an old grand master of downstate gambling had laid down the rules by which so many in the dangerous but very lucrative wagering business played.

No, Carl Shelton never could be too careful. A man who'd earned his bread the way he did always had to look over his shoulder because he'd compiled a laundry list of enemies, a fair share of them going back to his wild and infamous bootlegging escapades in Williamson County two decades before.

Quite likely, Carl may have learned about an ominous tip to St. Louis police a week or so ago. Word had it that one of four well-dressed men visiting the Plantation Inn Tavern over near Fairmont City, Illinois, was heard offering to bet the bartender a roll of bills that "they would get Shelton within a few weeks."[1] Carl had a knack for picking up those kinds of tidbits. Working to his advantage, this sixth sense time and again had steered him away from traps or other setups where he was the intended victim.

The fall of 1947 also happened to be a time in which Carl Shelton was feuding with some of the other farmers in the Pond Creek area over this or that. Ill feeling in particular had erupted with a family tied to Charles Harris, a former convict once a cohort of Carl. But Harris was now on the outs with the Sheltons. And, besides the Sheltons, this man Harris—Black Charlie they called him—was the Wayne countian most people feared to cross.

In the eyes of many, Carl Shelton had been living on borrowed time. It was miraculous that he had reached fifty-nine years of age. Still, as long as he kept to his home ground of Wayne, it was reckoned, getting rid of him was no easy task. He simply knew the lay of the land too well. Anyway, he didn't advertise his movements ahead of time.

Moments after passing Harvey Wagner, Carl's jeep and the following truck approached a small bridge on Pond Creek Road.[2] When the jeep got there, all hell broke loose.

A volley of gunfire exploded out of dense brush and trees on the west side of the bridge. Carl toppled out of the jeep. Little Earl and Walker, who were not armed, leaped from the truck and scrambled into a ditch near the bridge. On the way, they caught a glimpse of a car, enough to later describe it as a black Ford sedan, perched in a side lane near the underbrush from which the shots rang out.

After hitting the ditch, Walker heard the voice of Carl Shelton pleading: "Don't shoot me any more, Charlie. It's me, Carl Shelton. You've killed me already."[3]

The only reply was another burst of gunfire echoing through the lonely countryside.

2

Ben and Agnes

From the beginning, the Sheltons and guns were inseparable. Learning to shoot was a rite of passage for the boys of Ben and Agnes Shelton, something that came naturally. The same was true for most of the other farm families in the rolling terrain of Wayne County east of Fairfield. Life was a cakewalk for very few of those folks, and the Sheltons weren't the only ones often having to rely on good marksmanship to put meat on the table at night.

Many a time the children of Ben and Agnes heard their mother, in planning for dinner, order her husband, "Pa Ben, go get me some squirrels." Pa Ben was what Agnes and other family members called Benjamin Marsh Shelton, a respected if hardly affluent man.[1]

Pa Ben was a fellow of good attributes. As a family history put it, he was "well thought of in his own neighborhood and...a church man."[2] Actually, for a person who sired sons of such great notoriety, Ben walked a very conventional life path for his time and place in the world.

Born in 1861 in Kentucky, one of eight children produced by the marriage of Wilson Albert Shelton and Paulina Johnson, Ben was among the numerous Sheltons whose families moved from Kentucky to Wayne County in the nineteenth century.

In many respects, the migration to southern Illinois by many families from Kentucky, Tennessee and other points south was a natural progression. Most were hill people who found the lower region of Illinois to be a lot like the places they had left. Farming was a challenge because of the often weak condition of the soil, but fish and game were as plentiful as they had been in the wooded parts of the southern states, maybe even more so. Prosperity still eluded a great number of those who moved, but that did not diminish their prideful stubbornness. They continued to insist in their new homeland on raw, simple rules for conducting their lives in which individualism was tempered only by strong allegiance to family. Government was regarded with suspicion by these individuals who often persisted in settling disputes on their own instead of through authorities. Independence was cherished.

The move to Illinois by the family of Wilson Albert Shelton came in the period following the Civil War. Getting settled in Wayne County was not easy for Wilson and his progeny, if family historians were right. According to one, "Wilson would load up the brood and mother said she could see them coming down the road, a wagon full to stay a week and she did not know what to do with this many."[3]

Various roads would be taken by Wilson's children. Ben's oldest brother, Joseph, for one was said to have gone on to respectability in the Wayne County area as a postmaster and "small country" undertaker. On the other hand, Ben's younger brother Albert was depicted as having become a professional gambler, perhaps a sign of things down the line with Ben's sons. As for Ben himself, the hard path for his father's family led him to live as a young man with relatives for a spell.[4]

However, the relationship that would define Ben for most of his eighty-two years of life began when he met Agnes Gaither, a large-boned daughter of a Wayne County farmer. If some remembered it correctly, Ben and Agnes became close as youngsters during a time when both attended the same log schoolhouse. Whatever, they were married in 1882.

Like so many others in Wayne County, the family of Agnes Fantroy Gaither had southern roots. Her father, Belia Gaither, may have been a Union Army veteran, but he was from Alabama. The mother of Agnes, Cornelia Parkinson Goodall, was born in Tennessee. The year of Agnes' birth, depending on the source of information, was either 1862 or 1866, or sometime in between.[5]

One thing about Agnes was quite clear, though. She was a holy terror when upset—a woman given wide berth by Ben and others as she struggled for years to keep her family's head above water. She and Ben would see better days financially later in life, but not in their first decades together.

For many years, the Sheltons were tenant farmers in a land still dominated by agriculture, muddy roads and horse-drawn buggies. They worked their share of largely unproductive tracts around the little village of Merriam, five miles east of Fairfield, and they also tilled rich acreage in or near river bottoms in the area. However, that land was prone to flooding.

In 1883, the year after her marriage, Agnes gave birth to her first child, Nora. She died in 1897. Two other children of Agnes and Ben died in infancy. Of the offsprings who lived to adulthood, the oldest was Roy, born in 1885. Next came Carl Ray. He was born February 7, 1888, on a farm in Massilon Township in the eastern part of Wayne County. He was followed by Earl Robert, born in 1890, and then Dalta in 1893, Bernard in 1899, Hazel Katherine in 1904 and Lula in 1909.

Although acquaintances of the family did not remember the Shelton sons as the hardest working boys around, they were credited with helping their father with farm chores. Their lives had a touch of Huckleberry Finn's lifestyle as they prowled the countryside for game and nuts—and, some folks recollected, neighbors' chickens and corn and just about anything else they could get their hands on. They rode horses when they had the opportunity, as well as the mules that Ben kept. Years later, horses and mules remained an important part of Shelton family life. The boys caught catfish and scavenger fish in the Little Wabash River and other nearby sluggish streams. When they were grown, the brothers still maintained a rough shed with a lean-to roof over on the Little Wabash for fishing, hunting, trapping and, of course, shooting. They never tired of the endless shooting matches with guns from their private arsenal.

Schooling, a luxury for many from southern Illinois farm families in the late 1800s, was not ignored entirely for the young Sheltons. Carl made it through the sixth or seventh grade and, despite his failure to master reading and writing, was never considered a slow learner. As for Bernard, or Bernie, he couldn't get the hang of school and quit after a couple of grades. Nor was religion ignored. Protestants like most everybody else in Wayne County, the Shelton boys spent Sunday school time at the

Methodist church at Merriam. Carl even tried his hand at teaching Sunday school and playing the church organ.

As the years progressed, Fairfield was always the hometown listed for the Shelton boys, but Ben and Agnes truly were members of the Merriam community. This was certainly the case when—after a flood destroyed their crops about 1908 and they ran a country store for a year or two—the family managed to buy a little more than twenty acres a half mile north of Merriam. Right where the Merriam Road crossed State Highway 15.

The Shelton property at that intersection, known appropriately as the Merriam crossroads four miles east of Fairfield, became the home for Ben the rest of his life and for Agnes until her departure from Illinois. At least by most accounts. Shortly before his death in 1998, Little Earl Shelton recalled that Ben and Agnes, his grandparents, lived or stayed for a time in or near Herrin in the late 1920s (possibly at one of the houses or quarters kept in that area by their then bootlegging sons).

Nevertheless, memories of Ben and Agnes were always associated with the Merriam crossroads. In the years after the Shelton boys made their name, inquisitive passersby on Highway 15, slowing their cars, would point to or gawk at the unpretentious farmhouse on the property with morbid curiosity. Quite often, particularly if they turned down the Merriam Road, they might see white-haired Agnes Shelton sitting on a swing on the front porch of her one-story home, quilting. Working up the nerve to stop could have taken some doing, but in event one did Agnes normally would have been very approachable. Bums and hoboes certainly were not bashful around her.

James Shelton Zuber, a grandson of Agnes and Ben who spent a good part of the first two decades of his life living with them and his mother, Lula, at the Merriam Road house, remembered the bums and hoboes well. "Grandma Agnes fed all of them," he said. "She claimed there wasn't one who didn't know where she lived. With some of course, she'd have them split firewood or do other chores."[6]

His poignant memories of those days in the 1930s and early 1940s began with the vast amounts of food prepared by Agnes before daylight every morning to sustain the comings and goings of his uncles, if they were around, along with others crossing her modest threshold.

Cooking over an oil stove, Agnes laid out breakfasts that could have fed a battalion. Heaping platters of eggs, bacon, ham, tenderloins, sausages and, of course, biscuits and corn bread and even potatoes and gravy. Pies too. She'd bake two or three of them each morning. Carl Shelton was one of Jim Zuber's uncles frequently present at Agnes' home in those years. Oftentimes Jim's first sight in the morning was of Carl devouring an Agnes breakfast and then topping it off by dunking his mother's biscuits into coffee, one of his favorite habits.

In the best tradition of farm life, Ben and Agnes were pretty self-sufficient on their twenty-two acres. Apart from the residence was a tin-roofed summer kitchen where Agnes stored the pickles, peaches, homemade ketchup and the other vittles she canned. They raised everything they consumed, much of it from a garden nurtured by Agnes after Ben set it out. The family slaughtered its own meat. When a hog was butchered, the first part eaten was the liver, a delicacy in the eyes of the Sheltons. Ben even maintained three or four small ponds on the farm, which he stocked with deep-voiced bullfrogs. For all things, there was a use and a place.

When the gangster sons of Ben and Agnes were riding high, they never hesitated to flaunt their ill-gotten wealth by purchasing big houses, fast cars and flashy jewelry. But the farm at the Merriam crossroads never reflected any of this.

The farmhouse only had one closet, Zuber recalled. But, he added, "When you just had two suits of clothes, you didn't need a lot of closet space." The place did have electric lights, but indoor plumbing didn't make it to the residence until World War II was ending. Before then, Ben would clean out an old horse trough on the property for himself and young Jim to bathe in on Saturday evenings once the sun went down. A small congregation of barn owls usually gathered to watch. (The women washed in the house.) Water in the pre-plumbing years was supplied by a brick-bottom cistern near the summer kitchen, and its cleaning became one of Zuber's earliest and most unpleasant chores.

A task not assigned to Jim was cutting the grass. Ben and Agnes did not have a lawn mower. The job got done, Zuber explained, when "Grandma Agnes would tell grandpa, 'Pa Ben, I want you to get this grass cut down.' So, he'd go put the sheep in the yard to eat the grass. Which they'd do in a hurry. Still, she'd come out and stand there with a stick so the sheep wouldn't eat her flowers."

Ben Shelton never mastered another convenience of modern life, a car. Although his sons could drive rings around many law enforcement types, Ben never learned how to drive. That's where Ben's mules—especially old "Jimmy John"—came into play. To get to the church in Merriam or to go just about anywhere else, Ben hitched a mule to a hay wagon. Pa Ben took a stab once at building an auto garage on the farm. He constructed it too small, though, for any of the cars at the time to fit in it. According to others in his family, the garage was "a poor carpenter's job."

Since the hamlet of Merriam was the center of Agnes and Ben's social life, they hardly needed a car. After all, Merriam housed not only their church but also a small grocery store and a blacksmith shop. Ben and his sons, who had not abandoned farming in spite of their other enterprises, beat a steady path to the smithy to get plowshares sharpened.

Zuber's memory of the blacksmith did not fit the bucolic image of poet Henry Longfellow's smithy standing under a spreading chestnut tree. "Although the blacksmith's shop was a meeting spot," said Zuber, "the old forge was a hot, dirty place. The smithy had a real long beard, so long, going down to his waist, he'd have to tuck it into his bib. Still, you'd stand there and smell hair burning from his beard. It was just a nasty place."

Remembrances of Merriam also included the cake and pie suppers to raise money for the church. The way it worked, Agnes and the other women baked pies or cakes for auctioning off to the men in the church, marrieds as well as bachelors. A fellow got to eat with the woman whose offering he successfully bid on. Plenty of times, Zuber noticed, men bid more to get the baked goods of pretty girls than what their wives had brought. "A few of the women really could not believe their husbands couldn't even recognize their own wives' pies," Zuber noted, "but I was told that those fellows knew exactly what they were doing."

Carl and one or two of his brothers might join in the suppers if they happened to be hanging around. They'd still attend services at the church, too, on occasion.

Years after the surviving members of Ben and Agnes' family had departed Wayne County, the clannishness of the family still stuck in people's minds. But, then again, that was a trademark of so many of the hill families that had migrated to Wayne from Kentucky and Tennessee. A distinct impression remained of Ben Shelton as an honest, forthright person; an individual who disapproved strongly of the sordid doings linked to four of his sons. He did not feign his disappointment.

Agnes was another story. True-blue in her unswerving loyalty to her sons, she doted on them when they came home, never paying heed, or at least giving credence, to their bad image. Her boys could do no wrong in her eyes. To hell with what the big city newspapers and popular magazines wrote. A lot of that stuff never made it to Wayne County anyway. Ben could think what he wanted. She'd have none of it.

Decades afterward, Jim Zuber recalled Pa Ben. "He may have been dirt poor," Zuber said, "but he was a proud man." Zuber mentioned that, as a young man, Ben had two or three fingers sliced off in a sawmill mishap. "But," Zuber added, "they were sewed back on, and they did function again, even though they were real stiff. I could always still see him milking cows with those fingers."

Another story stuck in his mind from the time when Benjamin was a kid, and he agreed to work nine months for a man to get a horse from him. During the seventh month, the horse died, Zuber said. "Nevertheless, Pa Ben labored for the man for two more months because he had given his word."

Thinking of his grandpa struck warm chords in Zuber, even when remembering occasions that some persons might wish to forget. Like the time Zuber encountered a skunk when he was seven or eight years old.

"I saw the skunk in the chicken house at Ben's farm," related Zuber. "I ran back into the house and told grandpa about it. He told me to go shoo it out. So I grabbed a stick and tried to hit the skunk. Well, the thing turned its rear end to me and let me have it with spray. It only took an instant. About then, grandpa had come on down with a shotgun. He smelled me right away. Well, first he shot and killed the skunk. Then he ordered me to get to the nearest pond and get undressed and get on in the pond. Then he yelled back to grandma to fetch a bunch of tomatoes, which she did. Then he brought me the tomatoes at the pond, and helped me squash them all over me. He just kept saying: 'Dumb, dumb, dumb.' He then burned my clothes. The family all claimed the smell on me didn't go away for a week."

The rank case of the skunk not withstanding, Pa Ben seldom raised his voice about anything or to anyone. He was not easily provoked. "When grandma would get on Pa Ben," Zuber noted, "he'd just go out behind a barn and sit there quietly in the sun." Yet, he could get riled— even at little Jim.

"He spanked my tail a time or two," Zuber said with a wince. "Once it happened when we'd hitched up the mule to a wagon and gone to an auction. Without telling grandpa, I bought fifty baby ducks for a quarter. On the way home he noticed them in the back of the wagon, and he gave me a whipping for buying them. He said he didn't want those filthy, nasty ducks around."

The grown sons of Pa Ben still could test his reserve too. Zuber never erased one particular incident from his mind that gossip columnists, had they known about it, would have found juicy. It occurred around 1940 when Bernie, the Shelton gang's hotheaded muscle, its brawler, was making his customary Christmas visit to Ben's home. As usual, Bernie had fun making snowballs and throwing them at Zuber and his cousins. But following that, Zuber related, "Uncle Bernie and Ben got into it over something, and Ben just hauled off and punched Bernie. Ben had to be pushing eighty, but I tell you Bernie went down, got knocked down in the snow. And Ben yelled to him in no uncertain words, 'You don't ever talk to me like that!'"

Not too many years afterward, in 1944, Ben died of cancer in a hospital in Evansville, Indiana. As he was laid to rest in Maple Hill Cemetery at Fairfield, the first in his family's plot, what this unadorned man had bequethed the world filled police blotters and pulp magazines to overflowing.

During the last thirty years of his life, one or more of his sons had been charged with murder, bank robbery, burglary and larceny, auto theft, violations of the Prohibition law, kidnapping, mail robbery, tax evasion, assault, vagrancy and disturbing the peace. On the other hand, outside of the oldest son, Roy, the boys spent considerably little time in prison or jail, mainly because the countless charges against them were not always followed by convictions, or at least convictions that held up.

If the memories of some Wayne countians were on target, the Shelton boys earned a reputation as troublemakers and bullies when they were youngsters. In the words of one Fairfield old-timer, "The other farm families that lived around them said the boys would steal anything they could get away with." But, he added, "it was more than that. They were mean ruffians. People tried to stay out of their way...hoping they'd leave the area to look for greener pastures elsewhere."

Scatter they did, to some extent. After an early marriage ended with his wife's death, Carl wound up in St. Louis in the years before World War I, clerking in grocery stores for a while and then driving a taxi for the Columbia Cab Company. Earl got behind the wheel of cabs, too, during extended visits with Carl in the bustling big city 110 miles west of Fairfield.

But Earl had not given up on Wayne County. He married a local girl from a respected family and tried to make a go of it in farming. However, he fared no better than Carl in that Earl's wife also passed away. A widower in his early twenties, Earl began hanging around the courthouse square in Fairfield, shooting a lot of pool. Now, everybody knew that was often considered a bane for young men. Earl appeared to be courting trouble, the townies warned. They were right.

3

Destined for Trouble

Big Earl Shelton embroiled himself in the first serious criminal imbroglio of record involving his family in 1915. By the time the untidy affair played out, those who took notice had a pretty good idea of what to expect from the Shelton boys in the future.

On the evening of March 20 of that year, a Saturday, Earl was riding home as he often did with a neighbor, Cloyd Wilson, in Wilson's horse-drawn buggy. Earlier in the evening, Earl had borrowed five dollars from Wilson, which unbeknownst to Wilson was used by Earl to buy a gun. Subsequently, as Earl and Wilson made their way along a fellow stepped out on the road at a cemetery bridge, grabbed the horse and announced a holdup. The man, brandishing a gun, snatched Wilson's money, gold watch and ring before letting Earl and Wilson proceed.

The following day, a chap named Thomas Draper, who fit the robber's description, was arrested with a gun in his possession. Wilson identified him as the stickup man, but Earl argued otherwise. However, a local individual recognized Draper's gun as the one he'd sold to Earl the previous evening for five dollars. Earl and Draper were indicted by a grand jury for robbery and conspiracy. Each was released on $400 bond.

An interesting chain of events followed.

According to Wilson, Earl approached him and offered him a sum of money to drop the charge. Wilson refused. Next, Carl came home from St. Louis and threatened Wilson. That didn't work either. So the Sheltons asked a couple of tough guys from St. Louis to work over Wilson. Agreeing, they checked in at a Fairfield hotel as book salesmen. Wilson was alerted to their presence, though, by a relative in St. Louis, Frank Crews. The wife of Crews, it turned out, somehow had gotten wind of what the Shelton brothers were up to. The bruisers from St. Louis were arrested in Wayne County, but not charged. Back in St. Louis, Crews' wife was threatened with death by the Sheltons if she did not leave the city. An alarmed Crews informed the St. Louis police of what was happening, which led the cops to accuse Carl and Earl of compounding a felony. Furthermore, Crews informed the police that Carl also had stolen an auto in St. Louis. This led to a charge of grand larceny against Carl.

Nevertheless, the Sheltons weren't about to give up on Crews. Conspiring in St. Louis, Earl and Carl offered a black man a wagon and a horse if he would lie to the police by saying Crews had made off with a ring of his. When the fellow did so, a bizarre development was triggered. As detectives approached Crews for questioning, he mistook them for Shelton allies and proceeded to shoot off a finger of one of the cops. In turn, the police shot Crews through a lung before arresting him. However, Crews was set free after the black St. Louisan admitted he was part of a trumped-up charge.

The Shelton boys still refused to just hunker down. As the criminal cases against them were continued, they tried to poison Wilson's livestock. Agnes even entered the picture by contending that Wilson's mother attacked her with a knife. Wilson himself repeatedly was asked if he feared the Sheltons might kill him. His stock reply, based on written and verbal accounts, was "if they shoot me, they will do it from behind a tree and not out in the open because I know them too well."[1]

In the end, Wilson and law enforcement authorities were not to be deterred. Seven months after the robbery of Wilson, Earl Shelton went to trial in Wayne County Circuit Court. (Thomas Draper had already been convicted for his role in the crime against Wilson three months after its commission.) Earl was convicted of robbery and sentenced on October 25, 1915, to an "indefinite" term (but not to exceed fourteen years) in the Illinois State Reformatory at Pontiac. The following month, Carl pled guilty in St. Louis to a reduced charge of petty larceny and was sentenced to a year in the city workhouse.

Upon entering Pontiac four days after his sentencing, penal officials recorded the following profile of Earl: "Age: twenty-five. Occupation: farmer. Pecuniary condition: poor. Religion: Methodist. Education: fourth grade (but can read and write). Drinks intoxicating liquors: no. Chews or smokes tobacco: no. Profane: yes. Previous imprisonment or arrest: once (disorderly conduct)." The file also stipulated that Earl had "good" associations and was rated "fair" in his physical condition, moral "susceptibility" and mental "natural capability."[2]

Turning out to be a model prisoner, Earl was paroled May 15, 1917, to an acquaintance in St. Louis. He was released from parole the following November 29.[3] By that time, he had joined Carl—who had survived his brush with the law in St. Louis—in the taxi business in the Missouri city.

Hacking around the town, negotiating its congested and frequently narrow streets, the brothers became experts at wheeling in and out of tight spots. Good training it was for their days to come. Their younger brother Bernie, although still a teenager, also had surfaced in St. Louis. Before the end of 1917, he too found trouble by being arrested in a stolen vehicle. There was no record, though, of him serving any time in jail. Nevertheless, and not surprisingly, the St. Louis police had their eyes on the Sheltons as dubious characters, hardly welcome additions to the large number of homegrown thugs running around the city. If the memories of reporters who later covered the Sheltons were accurate, the brothers were convinced by authorities to exit St. Louis.

Subsequently, in the period after World War I, Carl and Earl surfaced in southern Illinois coal country. They spent most of their time at Carterville, a city of 3,500 persons described by historians as the site of the first mine in Williamson County. Jobs were plentiful in the collieries because coal production in Illinois had soared in 1917-1918 to boom levels while World War I raged in Europe. And, by then, a good number of the more than 300 operating mines in the state were in Williamson and other coal-rich counties south of Wayne. After the United States entered the war, many a young man from southern Illinois was likely to be found either underground in a mine or in a trench in France.

When the United States declared war, the size of its armed forces was not large. However, the challenge of building a sizable and effective fighting machine was met in impressive fashion. The Selective Service Act of 1917 required all men between the ages of twenty-one and thirty to register with locally established draft boards. Later, the minimum age was lowered to eighteen and the maximum upped to forty-five. More than 24 million men registered for the draft, out of which about 2.8 million were inducted into the army. Close to 2 million men voluntarily entered the army, national guard, navy or marine corps.

As for the Shelton boys, only Earl was known to have worn a uniform during the war. Although it remains unclear whether he was drafted or volunteered, Earl was in the army and headed for France when the fighting ended in November 1918.[4]

Carterville had established a reputation as a hotbed of mine strike violence before the Sheltons arrived, but Carl and Earl found their days in mining anything but exciting. Earl for one viewed the digging of coal as not only oppressive but also frustrating, saying later in life that "you almost couldn't make any money in a coal mine."[5] In addition to Earl and Carl, their brother Roy also toiled in the mines in the years after the war. If some remembered it right, Bernie did too. When Roy ran afoul of the law in Williamson at the start of the 1920s, the words "mining, Carterville, Ill." were written alongside his name on state prison records.[6]

At the time of Carl's death, his family stated in his obituary that he had served as chief mine inspector for the state in the southern counties of Illinois. This could not be confirmed by records of the Illinois Office of Mines and Minerals, but they did reveal that one Carl Shelton, residing at Carterville, received a certificate for the highly responsible position of mine examiner on May 9, 1921, when he was thirty-three.[7] By then, though, or very soon thereafter, Carl, Earl and Bernie had shifted the focus of their attention from the coal fields to East St. Louis, a city with which the trio would be linked well into the 1930s.

Roy Shelton also spent time in East St. Louis in between the periods he sat in prison. The other Shelton brother, Dalta, stayed home, never becoming part of the gang headed by Carl, Earl and Bernie. For that matter, Roy was never considered a member of the Shelton gang, if for no other reason than that he resided so much of his life behind bars.

Roy's history of incarceration went back to April 23, 1922, when he became No. 5441 at the Menard state prison for committing burglary and larceny in Williamson County. Although sentenced to a term of one to twenty years, he was paroled a few years after entering prison. But he violated his parole, and after a spell as a fugitive was sent back to the pen. He was paroled again in 1931.[8] Two years later he was back in prison, convicted of robbery and kidnapping. Sentenced to an indeterminate term of from one year to life, he was not released again until the ensuing decade.

The gravitation of Carl, Earl and Bernie to East St. Louis led to the real beginning of the Shelton gang story.

No city could have exhibited a more opportune backdrop for the talents that the brothers would display. Scribes often had to strain to find sufficient adjectives for describing East St. Louis. More than a few went overboard, like a crime writer named Charles Remsberg who characterized the town as "a grimy, bawdy suburb of Hell." To the thousands of upstanding individuals taking pride in East St. Louis during the colorful stages of its history, comparing the place to hades was not fair. It was just that East St. Louis had never been equated with gentility, starting with the hardy souls who struggled mightily to build the city on the swampland of the Great American Bottom across the Mississippi River from St. Louis.

For a balanced view of East St. Louis, one had to look no further than the writings of distinguished journalist Carl R. Baldwin. Baldwin, who spent much of his boyhood in East St. Louis and went on to become a top-notch reporter for the *St. Louis Post-Dispatch*, knew the East Side like the back of his hand. Writing in *St. Louis Commerce* magazine in 1982, he painted a portrait of East St. Louis shortly before its adoption by the Sheltons.

"East St. Louis," wrote Baldwin, "seemed to be sitting on top of the industrial world in 1920. It ranked No.1 in the sale of horses and mules, and was near the top in hog sales. It was the world's largest aluminum processing center, the second largest railroad center (behind Chicago), and led the country in the manufacture of roofing material, baking powder and paint pigments. It was the third largest primary grain market and had the cheapest coal in the world. Its population was over 75,000."[9]

However, Baldwin also chronicled problems facing the city, such as its low income from taxes, blatantly corrupt politicians and the railroads—their tracks everywhere—choking the city. Baldwin was no more blind than others to the city's image, even in good times, of a town smothered by smoke and the putrid smells from the stockyards and factories.

East St. Louis also suffered from the shock waves emanating from a violent race riot in the city in the summer of 1917, one of the worst in United States history. A congressional investigating committee found that at least thirty-nine blacks and eight whites were killed.[10] Other sources put the numbers higher.

St. Louisans especially looked down their collective noses at East St. Louis. Everybody knew when the Missourians referred to it as the East Side they intended it as a put-down. But then, what else was new? Having their city's reputation thrown in their face was a fact of life for East St. Louisans like Bill Nunes or Harold Fiebig. Nunes, a retired educator and extensive writer on the city in which he was born and raised, traced what he saw as the "distorted image" of East St. Louis to "the filtered perspective of a news media obsessed with sensationalism."

It was quite obvious to Fiebig that "when you went somewhere and said you were from East St. Louis, people backed away. They feared you." However, he added, "this never really bothered me. I let it work to my advantage. But, the thing about it was that you never saw it as a tough town living there."

A look at Fiebig revealed his life odyssey to be typical of many twentieth century East St. Louisans. Born in the city in 1926. Mother was Polish; father German, a molder in an iron foundry. Grew up in the neatly maintained working class neighborhood around Cleveland Avenue. Served in the air force. Married another East St. Louis native, Emily Kobzina, in St. Peter's Lutheran Church in the city in 1953. Employed as a telephone repairman until retirement in 1984, by which time he was living in Belleville. Since retirement, engaged in historical research, specializing in East St. Louis.

As Fiebig's family helped show, East St. Louis was a true melting pot in which very few ethnic groups were not represented. In the words of Nunes, the city was "a rich tapestry, woven with the lives of those simple folk who migrated here from all over the globe to earn a living and to make a life for their families." At the same time, Nunes categorized East St. Louis before its economic decline in the latter part of the twentieth century as "perhaps the most complex small city in America," a hodgepodge of contrasting neighborhoods with names like Goose Hill, Pearl Harbor and Whiskey Chute. Nunes didn't argue that his hometown exhibited contradictions, readily admitting that "good and bad were juxtaposed."

Carl Baldwin had as much affection for East St. Louis as Nunes and Fiebig, but, as the main *Post-Dispatch* reporter for many years on the East Side beat, he was paid to focus on the crooked officeholders, ladies of the night, gamblers and mobsters who gave East St. Louis such a wicked underbelly. In his early reporting days, Baldwin covered doings in the city by the Sheltons. He eventually came to know some members of the family. Although he never got to it, he considered late in life (Baldwin died in 1994) writing a book on the Sheltons and their era.

So, what did the Sheltons do when they went to East St. Louis? They opened and operated a saloon. As did many others in the town. At the conclusion of World War I, East St. Louis and its environs contained an incredible number of saloons for an area its size. (In East St. Louis alone, some 375 drinking establishments were licensed in 1917, a year before the war's end.) The coming of Prohibition in the years after the war hardly derailed the conduct of business as usual by East St. Louis saloon keepers, including the Sheltons in their new bar at Nineteenth Street and Market Avenue.

To fully grasp the deep rootedness of the love for beer alone in cities like East St. Louis and neighboring Belleville, one had to be aware of rituals in those places such as the "terrific bucket trade." Harold Fiebig recounted the way it worked in his neighborhood, which was the standard operating procedure. The routine seldom varied.

"When the five o'clock foundry whistle blew," Fiebig related, "all the kids in the neighborhood would run home, get their dad's beer bucket and ten cents, and run to the nearby German Hall. They'd throw the buckets on the bar, and the bartender, who knew everybody's bucket, filled them up. So that way the kids would have beer waiting for dad when he came home from work. If you didn't have dad's bucket filled when he got to the house, you'd get your fanny kicked."

While Prohibition did not put a clamp on drinking in East St. Louis, it could not be ignored. Consequently, the Sheltons and other dramshop owners quickly became adept at paying off the right public officials, the ones who could ensure that the illegal sale of alcoholic beverages could proceed unimpeded. Carl in particular perfected the practice of bribing officials so skillfully in his early days in East St. Louis that he earned a reputation as a master of the fix. From then on, getting to the key people with payoffs was an important part of his modus operandi.

If not for Prohibition, the Shelton gang might never have gotten off the ground. Without question, the history of organized crime in the country would have been far less recognizable.

The Eighteenth, or Prohibition, Amendment, prohibiting the manufacture, sale or transportation of intoxicating liquors, was approved by Congress in December 1917. Ratification by the required number of states was achieved by early 1919. The Volstead Act, passed over President Wilson's veto in October 1919, provided the machinery for implementing the Eighteenth Amendment. Prohibition officially began January 20, 1920, culminating a highly idealistic temperance movement that had persisted doggedly with unbridled optimism.

A great social experiment it was, Prohibition, and Illinois certainly had played its part in bringing it about. Strong efforts to restrict or curtail the availability of alcoholic liquors ignited social and political controversies throughout much of the nineteenth century in Illinois. As far back as the 1830s, certain Protestant church groups and other temperance advocates succeeded in getting fourteen counties to petition the state legislature to repeal laws authorizing the sale of strong distilled liquors. One result was a local option law permitting a majority of voters in a town to petition county officials to prevent the licensing of places selling wine and liquor in small quantities. But the legislation was repealed in 1841. However, in the early 1850s, the Illinois Supreme Court in ruling in favor of a Jacksonville ordinance decreeing the sale of liquor to be a nuisance supported the principle of local option. Later in that decade, the legislature, following the example of Maine, approved a law for complete prohibition—as long as it also was approved in a popular referendum. In the ensuing campaign, the liquor crowd countered the dry forces by insisting that drinking could not be curtailed by legislation and that prohibition would limit farmers' markets. The voting produced a large turnout. Although the drys swept much of northern Illinois (but not Cook County), the vote in the southern counties against the prohibition law was large enough to keep it from going into effect.

After the Civil War, the temperance folks were at it again in Illinois. Many in the Republican Party wanted to halt the sale of intoxicating drinks. The Prohibition Party kept the heat on even though it failed to get candidates elected to state office late in the century. Then there were the women. Often organized, they pursued the shuttering of drinking establishments with increased zeal. And in Illinois, they had a home-based patron saint, Frances Willard of Evanston.

Willard, a tireless reformer and feminist, made the Woman's Christian Temperance Union a dynamic force after becoming its president in 1879. Traversing the country, a familiar figure with her pince-nez eyeglasses and short-cropped hair, Willard strove with great success to rally crowds in every state to support her frequently stated goal to reach "that day when mothers and daughters of America shall have a voice in the decision by which...the rum-shop is opened or shut beside their homes." When the Democratic and Republican parties refused to include temperance in their platforms, Willard sided with the Prohibition Party. In the mid 1880s, Willard involved women around the globe in the temperance crusade by penning the Polyglot Petition, which beseeched heads of state to halt trafficking in alcohol, drugs and tobacco. A decade later, 7.5 million signatures had been gathered on the petition by women throughout the world. Although Willard died in 1898, her efforts unquestionably built part of the foundation for the Eighteenth Amendment. So formidable was Frances Elizabeth Caroline Willard that a statue was dedicated to her in the United States Capitol. However, by the time Prohibition had run its course, bootleggers and their allies also might have justified a statue in her honor.

For them, Prohibition opened a cornucopia of sterling opportunities. The Eighteenth Amendment may have been a noble thrust for the moral high ground, but there would be no quenching of the insatiable demand for booze in the big cities, and in many of the smaller towns too. Some people just made their own; distilling in a home only required a bathtub and a few other things. For the most part, though, the far-flung market for liquor triggered illegal production and distribution systems blanketing virtually every part of America. Lawless or not, these operations turned profits like any other large business, only often greater. Of course, most of the dough ended up in the pockets of organized crime, which wound up pretty much running the whole illicit show.

East St. Louis was far from the only place where bar after bar continued to conduct business as usual during Prohibition. Only in East St. Louis minimal effort was exerted to camouflage the flouting of the law, as opposed to towns where thirsty patrons had to know a code word and pass a peephole test before admittance to a speakeasy. Hidden bistros were most often the norm, and they were found everywhere, not just in the back of restaurants but also in shops and other unlikely spots.

Simply put, Prohibition turned an amazingly large number of Americans into lawbreakers for the first time. Many just found it exciting, kind of like the decade of the twenties itself, a period of great energy in the economy as well as in society. Change was profound. With the mass production of material goods, ordinary people—buttressed with greater buying power resulting from higher wages—could satisfy their wants as never before. The country took on the look in the twenties that it would retain for the rest of the century. Higher buildings were shooting up on the skylines of the big cities, to which people from rural areas were flocking to live. Paved roads, motels in the countryside and gas stations were suddenly everywhere, all because cars had become as commonplace as Sunday chicken dinners.

Old restrictions were cast aside, most evidently in the larger towns. Victorian morality went down the drain, supplanted by Jazz Age flappers in abbreviated dresses dancing the Charleston. The flappers strikingly represented the era's freedom from the past. Abandoning corsets and long skirts, they swirled around with hair cropped short, faces all made up and cigarettes in hand. Taboos of the previous century turned pleasurable in the 1920s. Business and fun came first, not always in that order.

In thinking of businesses, the most riveting in the public eye had to be bootlegging and speakeasies, the black sheep by-products of the Eighteenth Amendment. If the twenties really did have the aura of one long binge, the well-known bootleggers especially could not escape the status of celebrities, infamous to some persons but heroic to others. After all, the nation needed somebody to service its toot, and the bootleggers filled the void with gusto, even if it meant smuggling in liquor from other countries.

The bootleggers well could have taken their cue from that legendary and corrupt leader of New York's political Society of Tammany, George

Washington Plunkitt, the fellow who said, "I seen my opportunities and I took 'em."

Carl Shelton would get a good ride through the years in those old crime magazines printed on cheap pulp paper, the ones his mother disdained. Whether he really said all the things attributed to him was questionable. However, one quote put in his mouth back at the start of Prohibition, though not verifiable, couldn't have been too far off base.

"There ain't a little town around here that's not gonna miss its whiskey," Carl was said to have told his brothers in East St. Louis. "These farmers may vote dry on election day, but they drink wet on Saturday night. We can run enough rum up here from the Bahamas to flood all of Little Egypt (a nickname for southern Illinois). And if some day comes along we can't, we'll hijack a load from the big boys across the river in St. Louis."

For the Sheltons, for Al Capone in Chicago, and for many others, Prohibition was their gold rush. The twenties and Prohibition would end, but its scars would remain. None more vividly than crime, which did an about-face during Prohibition. It went big time.

Three decades after the onset of Prohibition, the report of a special Unites States Senate committee to investigate organized crime, chaired by Senator Estes Kefauver of Tennessee, had the following to say in analyzing the history of crime in the Sheltons' part of the world.

"At the close of World War I, all areas of the Midwest proved to be lucrative for the furtherance of gangland activities because of the advent of prohibition. Prior to the war, organized gangs were practically nonexistent, and hoodlums operated largely on an individual basis. When it became evident that illegal manufacture and distribution of liquor carried with it great financial potentialities, gangs began organizing and competing for this lucrative business."[11]

They sure did.

4

Bootlegging—
The Farm Boys Hit Their Stride

To paraphrase an old refrain, gang wars and the Roaring Twenties went together like a horse and carriage. The whole world was painfully aware of Chicago. But the bloodshed in Chicago, or in New York for that matter, hardly was more sensational than the gang violence that erupted with astonishing ferocity in southern Illinois and St. Louis during the decade.

In fact, the Kefauver committee minced no words in concluding that the gang battles in southern Illinois and St. Louis during the 1920s "reached a peak in bloodiness unparalleled in United States crime history."

The focus of the Illinois carnage, the panel pointed out, "was in the coal-mining districts of that state, and the center of the war was in Williamson County, which finally became to be known as 'Bloody' Williamson County."

As the committee report put it, central and southern Illinois "furnished" two major gangs, one headed by the Shelton boys and the other by Charles Birger. The Sheltons received the marquee billing. "The Shelton gang," the committee stated, "was headed by Carl Shelton who, with his brothers, Earl and Bernie, started the bribing of public officials in Illinois and ultimately controlled all of the bootlegging and organized gambling in Illinois, save Cook County."[1]

However, in the early days of Prohibition, the Sheltons controlled little but their tavern in East St. Louis. That would change, though, as the brothers displayed a ready knack for running liquor up from the south not only for their own place but for other saloons as well. To some of their fellow barkeeps, the farm boys from over in Wayne County were reliable to do business with and, although tough, more than a tad likable. Well, Carl and Big Earl could be pleasant. Their younger brother Bernie was another story. Surly and armed with a hair-trigger temper, Bernie revealed early on a proclivity for putting the fear of God in those with whom he dealt. Bernie rightfully shouldered a good deal of the credit for expanding the brothers' business by convincing many of the saloon keepers they supplied to also buy protection from the brothers—protection from the law as well as from other bootleggers as ambitious as the Sheltons.

While establishing themselves in East St. Louis, the Sheltons resided downtown for a spell at the Arlington Hotel at 200 Missouri Avenue, a lodgment which was part of a small hotel row near city hall and not far from the train passenger station down at the end of Missouri. In a city rife with dubious establishments, the Arlington stood out on the list. The clientele included gamblers, whores and an assortment of criminals. The hotel's short, slender proprietor fit in well with this rogues' gallery. His name was Art Newman. Calling him a gambler, a thief and, as time would show, a killer was only part of the rap on Newman. He befriended the Sheltons, finding they had common interests, of which one was bootlegging. Seemingly overnight, their lives became intertwined. After several years, their early comradeship would dissipate, replaced by mutual hatred, the deceitful and murderous kind. The weasel-like Newman would haunt the Sheltons, and they him.

Now Bessie Newman, Art's wife, harbored a dislike for the Sheltons from the beginning. At least the Sheltons thought so when they laid the blame for their split with Newman at her feet.[2] Blonde Bessie, of course, was no innocent herself. She operated, or certainly had a big hand in running, one of the best bordellos in the infamous "Valley," East St. Louis' internationally known vice district centered on Third Street just a block north of city hall.

The Valley was a dark world of brothels, gambling joints and saloons crammed together for the easy use of its customers, including tourists from afar. Sunday blue laws in Missouri drove St. Louisans to the Valley in droves; for many young men in towns near the East Side, a visit to the Valley was part of the rite of passage to manhood.

One reason the Valley sprung up was that a mean flood in 1903 forced many residents to leave homes around Third Street. When a number did not return to their houses, the madams moved in. The Valley was home to black as well as white prostitutes, but they were segregated. Nevertheless, one and all, along with their employers, were protected from harassment by paid off politicians and police. From an economic standpoint, the Valley provided a shot in the arm for East St. Louis, and even many in the city professing abhorrence at the Valley didn't deny that its enterprises lined the pockets of a good number outside the tenderloin. Predictable outcries by concerned citizen groups against the Valley would result in real or purported crackdowns by reform-minded mayors or put-upon law enforcement officials. However, any cessation of the action proved to be only temporary. The Valley flourished until World War II, when military authorities, threatening to declare the entire city off-limits, finally prompted the district's death.

If Art Newman was to be believed, he was an early benefactor of the Sheltons. He relished telling people that the Sheltons were flat broke when they became acquainted, but that he granted their request for a loan because he saw promise in the smooth-spoken Carl and his rustic brothers. His intuition was on target because the Sheltons quickly were on their feet financially.

According to Newman, they "soon were rolling in bucks. Their main business was liquor running, but on the side they knocked over gambling joints, stole automobiles and blew up stills of rival bootleggers, thus stabilizing the liquor market."[3]

Along with their success, Newman added, the Sheltons grew arrogant. They'd strut with a pompous air around the Arlington, flashing their firearms, or even cleaning them and peering into the barrels in an obnoxiously self-assertive manner. To make matters worse, they began to hurt business.

As Carl Baldwin recorded it, "Gents who came to the hotel to purchase the mercenary love that Bess and her girls peddled would lose their ardor when they peered into the lobby and saw the Sheltons furbishing their weapons and squinting down the gun barrels."[4]

Yet, overbearing or not, the Sheltons were accorded a wide berth because their background and contacts made a few years earlier in southern Illinois allowed them to cultivate a broader base for their bootlegging activity than was available to many of the longer established gangsters in East St. Louis. As opposed to the big city guys, the Sheltons talked the lingo of the local thugs, dicers and bootleggers in the coal towns of southern Illinois. And then, in addition, when the Sheltons brought to the table in those places a demonstrated connection to tough East St. Louis, the brothers had a definite leg up in the early 1920s toward the attainment of authority over the distribution of liquor in a broad terrain. To shore up their standing in southern Illinois, the Sheltons opened a roadhouse near Herrin and maintained lodgings in the area.

The southern Illinois coal belt was as ripe for the bootleggers as any other place. Drinking was an intrinsic part of its life. Those who came up from Kentucky, Tennessee and other southern states left a culture infused with intoxicating liquor, a lot of it moonshine. Immigrants to southern Illinois from Europe carried with them their old world fondness for wine and beer. Coal towns usually revolved around two institutions that often didn't see eye to eye, saloons and churches.

For persons with long memories, historian David Conrad hit it on the head in noting poignantly that in coal towns the saloons "could be anything from a dingy hut run by a miner's widow to a full-blown establishment with swinging doors, sawdust on the floor, and paintings of chubby, reclining nude women behind the bar."

"It was common," wrote Conrad, "to have what was called a 'free lunch,' a spread of highly seasoned salami and bologna, pretzels, beans and Limburger cheese. The smells of the free lunch, combined with the clouds of tobacco smoke and the ever present scent of beer and sweaty bodies, provided an atmosphere that was not for the delicate. Women and children never entered saloons. These were places where men could relax and forget the hard work and dangers of the mines." A saloon, Conrad concluded, was "an oasis for the miners."[5]

As their reputation spread in the coal belt and elsewhere in the early 1920s, so did the Sheltons' acquaintanceship with others making their mark in the mushrooming illicit liquor trade. One in particular was Charlie Birger. Birger—an enigmatic figure overly imbued with Jekyll and

Hyde qualities, a man seven or eight years older than Carl Shelton—had emerged as the underworld chief of Saline County in southeastern Illinois. He had earned a reputation, quite well deserved, as a person not to toy with. The kind of image Carl and his brothers were rapidly working to successfully build. It was inevitable that the Sheltons and Birger would meet, as the bigger fish surely do in a small pond. Southern Illinois was not, after all, that big. Too, Birger got up to East St. Louis, where he knew the lay of the land and even some of the right people.

Born in Russia, Birger, a Jew, lived as a youngster in St. Louis, where he learned to defend himself in the scrappy street world of newsboys. He later lived as a young man in the Madison County coal mining village of Glen Carbon northeast of East St. Louis. Following a stint in the West with the United States Cavalry, where he was introduced to wild horses and was able to shoot to his heart's content, Birger killed more time living in the East St. Louis area among other places before making his way to Saline County in 1912 or 1913. Along the way, he tried coal mining and concluded, as did the Shelton boys, that less backbreaking methods of turning a dollar had much greater appeal. While at another stop on the path to Saline, a sort of no-man's-land between East St. Louis and Belleville called Edgemont, the first killing of a man by Birger was recorded. The year was 1908, and the victim was a local ne're-do-well who lacked the common sense to avoid attacking Birger.[6]

As fateful as the meeting of the Sheltons and Birger would be, its time and place as well as circumstances were always subject to conjecture. Was it during one of Birger's visits to East St. Louis? Did Art Newman, who'd end up having a long history with Birger along with the Sheltons, serve as a go-between? (There were also persons who insisted Carl Shelton introduced Newman to Birger.) Or, did the get-together of Birger and the Sheltons occur as the brothers were spreading their wings in the lower part of the state?

If Birger was believable, they met in 1923 in southern Illinois. Testifying against Carl, Earl and Bernie in a trial in 1927, Birger related that he met the trio when they called on him in a Herrin hospital November 23, 1923. "I had been shot, and they came down to see me to talk about a diamond robbery which had got Bernie and Charlie Briggs into trouble," Birger testified. Briggs was a gangland buddy of the Sheltons.[7]

By the time of that 1927 trial, the Birger-Shelton enmity was the hottest crime story south of Chicago, lacking none of the unrestrained violence of the murderous warfare between rival gangs in the Windy City. At first, though, the relationship between the Shelton and Birger camps, while not exactly a match made in heaven, reflected mutual tolerance by each side of the other.

Again, back to that 1927 trial, Birger testified that at one time "Carl was my friend...I helped him when I could, and he helped me. I wanted to help him with the whiskey running, and if he had made a million it would have been all right with me."[8]

In some ways, Carl Shelton and Birger were like two peas in a pod. Birger, as did Shelton, effected a winning folksiness when he wanted to. Both fancied themselves as ladies' men. Like Shelton, Birger ingratiated himself with many law officers in his territory—not just with payoffs but also through a demonstrated ability to preserve order among other lawless elements around, thereby curtailing loose ends otherwise spelling trouble for sheriffs and local cops. The truth of the matter was that most of the lesser lights in lawbreaking dreaded Birger or the Shelton brothers in the 1920s more than the fellows with badges.

Respect for the law was at a low ebb anyway in many of the places frequented by the Sheltons or Birger. Williamson County easily came to mind. The Herrin Massacre had astounded the country by claiming twenty-three victims, the bulk of them mine guards and strikebreakers slaughtered by striking miners and their sympathizers on June 22, 1922. Prosecutors did not obtain convictions of any of those individuals indicted in the killings. As a result, regardless of where residents of Williamson placed the blame for the massacre and the events leading up to it, the images of the county and Herrin and union labor were brutalized by outsiders ranging from President Harding to newspapers across the nation. Williamson couldn't get a break anywhere, it seemed, not even from the Illinois State Chamber of Commerce. Several months after the massacre, Williamson was highlighted on the cover of the chamber's magazine as a dark spot on the terrain of Illinois. Wording on the cover asked what could be done to remove the stain.

Although many of the leading citizens of Williamson considered attacks like the chamber's to be unduly harsh, the incursion of the bootlegging Sheltons into Williamson and some neighboring counties in the early 1920s came across to many as anticlimactic. Not all that earth-shaking, just as long as large-scale violence was avoided—stuff beyond the roughing up of would-be local competitors. None understood this better than the Sheltons and Birger as they maneuvered, at least tacitly, to keep the peace. When their illicit activity finally did trigger big-time violence, the brothers and Birger remained allies, more or less. They had little choice because they faced a common enemy. A formidable one. The Ku Klux Klan.

The KKK, a secret society organized in the South after the Civil War to reassert white supremacy, had been resurrected with renewed vigor in the twentieth century—starting in 1915 in Georgia. There, according to a widely accepted account, an Atlanta entrepreneur named William J. Simmons revived the Klan, named himself imperial wizard and proceeded to make a fortune selling to members robes and various mementos, including Confederate States of America symbols (which the Klan previously had not used).

Another thing. Although the earlier Klan courted all whites, the Simmons version excluded all but native-born Protestants in making clear a perhaps once quiescent but now undisguised distaste for Roman Catholics and Jews as well as blacks. With the onset of Prohibition, the renewed KKK grew fast, becoming a national fraternity with surprisingly more members in the North and other places away from the South. By the mid 1920s, membership peaked to as many as 5 million men, some of whom were public officials. Soon thereafter, though, beset by negative publicity and internal scandals, the Klan's membership and influence dwindled in Illinois and elsewhere.

However, it did not pass completely from the scene. For instance, the Klan surfaced again in the 1960s when the civil rights movement ran counter to the KKK's historic opposition to advancement by blacks. But, that was a paltry comeback in comparison to the Klan's revival in the early part of the century. The decline of the group in Illinois was underscored by a probe of it in the mid-1970s by the state's Legislative Investigating Commission. In a report to the General Assembly, the commission said that undercover agents infiltrating the Klan found it to be a "comic strip" organization posing no threat to anybody. The Klan was surviving in Illinois only as "a name which a handful of individuals have fastened upon their desperate desire for attention," the commission concluded.[9]

Comical was not a word to describe the Klan in Illinois through much of the 1920s, though. Certainly not in downstate, where the organization attained considerable influence and notoriety virtually overnight—much like the bootleggers and their cohorts, principal targets of the Klan's ire.

KKK rallies became familiar sights in numerous towns, where the atmosphere was ripe for acceptance of the Klan's espousal of "pure Americanism." As the Klan saw it, true adherence to the ideals, traditions and interests of the United States was darn near impossible for Jews, Catholics, most immigrants and Communists. And of course blacks. It was hardly coincidental that KKK membership grew as the country suffered a seditious anxiety in the aftermath of World War I. This was evidenced most noticeably by the Red Scare in 1919 and 1920, when the federal government rounded up and deported hundreds of immigrants with radical political views. Thanks to the Russian Revolution, fear of subversion in this country by Communists was rampant. Nativism in America was again raising its head.

Following past practice, the Klansmen paraded around in white hoods and robes to prevent disclosure of their identities. Ostensibly, the outside world only was to know that each Klansman was an American-born white Christian, almost surely a Protestant. In many places, though, the secrecy was just a cut above a charade. The leaders, brandishing titles through the years such as Grand Dragon, Grand Cyclops or Imperial Wizard, openly discarded anonymity through public pronouncements and the like. Even the names of rank and filers often were common knowledge. The faces behind the hoods well might be those of some of the most highly regarded members of the communities.

Indeed, the Klan's bent to seek respectability in the Roaring Twenties took some strange turns. One of the more bizarre occurred in Springfield, where local chapters of the Independent Klan of America got behind a move in 1925 to set up an African-American auxiliary of the national group. Black leaders in the state capital turned thumbs down on the idea, saying in a resolution that the Klan could only "serve to stir up hatred, strife, envy, jealously and ill will in the land where dwells a spirit of fair play, justice and charity."

Nevertheless, while the antagonism of the Klan was focused on blacks in the years following the Civil War, much of its wrath was aimed in the 1920s in Illinois at individuals defying Prohibition. This coincided nicely with the Klan's imperious attitude toward foreign-born persons in that frequent violators of Prohibition in many towns certainly included immigrants from countries where the culture meshed with drinking.

Williamson and surrounding counties were fertile ground for the KKK. Besides being predominantly Protestant, the area prided itself on patriotism. In spite of the indifference of many law enforcement officials, numerous civic and other groups demanded strict upholding of the Volstead Act. Nothing less was to be tolerated.

At first, the KKK showed up in a somewhat auspicious fashion, appearing suddenly at Protestant services in southern Illinois, handing the ministers notes and money and then departing quietly. The notes frequently spelled out the Klan's affinity for white Christians attending Protestant churches, public schools and law and order, and also the society's opposition to immoral women. Pretty soon, though, the Klan was showcasing its burgeoning following in massive rallies that hardly were clandestine. In May 1923, thousands of Klansmen gathered by a flaming cross in a field near the Williamson seat of Marion to initiate two hundred new members. The scene was repeated several months later near Carterville, and a few weeks afterward at West Frankfort. As for the rally by Marion, the reporter covering it for the *Marion Daily Republican* found those present to be "a refutation of the charge sometimes made that the Klan is nothing but a bunch of hoodlums."

No doubt, many Klansmen were present without their hoods on August 20, 1923, at a public meeting in Marion at which several thousand persons, at the urging of Protestant clergy, protested the open, widespread vice and corruption in Williamson. The Reverend P. R. Glotfelty, a Methodist minister in Herrin, set the tone of the rally under a blistering sun by pledging that Williamson would be cleaned up "if we have to do it ourselves." He made it clear he was talking about the flood of roadhouses and saloons in the county, many of them supplied by the Sheltons, along with uninterrupted gambling and prostitution.

The spring of 1923 also saw the Klan on the march in the East St. Louis area.

The organization well may have peaked in that region in May of that year when some 10,000 Klansmen gathered by a fiery cross on a farm near the large prehistoric earthwork known as Monks Mound outside East St. Louis. However, what happened after that meeting illustrated the absence of a free pass for the KKK in territory more ethnically diverse than in deep southern Illinois. Dispersing from the Monks Mound area, 100 or more carloads of Klansmen, with white handkerchiefs tied to the left sides of the autos, embarked on a midnight tour of downtown East St. Louis. The city had a heavy Catholic population, which was wary of the Klan and also well represented on the city's police force.

Consequently, the Irish cops got indignant when the Klan parade passed police headquarters. Two good sons of the old sod, patrolmen Willie Walsh and Mike Cullilane, thought they'd seen enough and tried to stop the entourage as it moved past Collinsville and Missouri avenues. The drivers refused to halt when the officers whipped out their nightsticks, but when pistols were drawn one driver did slam on the brakes. The six occupants of that car were arrested and charged with disorderly conduct to help assuage the tender feelings of the arresting officers. Each in the car was fined five dollars and costs by a justice of the peace who was another Irishman.[10]

The Klan's impact on the East Side was not as violent as in Williamson County. Although anti-Klansmen in and around East St. Louis were hard pressed for a time to keep KKK followers out of public offices, the Klan's cleanup efforts proved to be no match for the entrenched politicians in cahoots with the Sheltons and other bootleggers. Actually, one discernible result of the Klan's presence in East St. Louis in the 1920s was to boost the stock of Carl, Earl and Bernie with many in the city, especially Irish Catholics. Of course, the Sheltons did not object to the Klan for the reason that Catholics, Jews and blacks did. To the Sheltons, the Klan simply posed a roadblock to their very prosperous business interests.

The KKK didn't beat the Sheltons in southern Illinois either. But it was a heck of a lot bloodier down there.

5

Flies in the Ointment—
S. Glenn Young and the KKK

The Shelton boys may not have been household names before 1924, but they sure were by the end of the year. The KKK in Williamson County made certain of that. It was nothing short of a battle royal.

To fully grasp the events of 1924, one had to be aware of several developments unfurling in the waning months of 1923. Frustrated by the reluctance of Williamson sheriff George Galligan and other law officers to eradicate bootlegging and gambling in the county, which meant taking on the Sheltons, the KKK-dominated Williamson County Law and Order League sought outside help from the governor of Illinois, Len Small, and from Washington.

Republican Small, who was from Kankakee in the northern part of the state and who was busy building a good hard road system in Illinois, told the League to work to elect a sheriff who would enforce the law. League members also felt they received a runaround in Washington, except for one thing. While there, they met S. Glenn Young.

Young, a former Prohibition officer of extraordinary zeal, was asked, so it was said, to come to Williamson to clean it up. He accepted the offer with relish. The League might as well have enlisted a whirlwind.

Just how much about Young the League, the Klan or anybody in Williamson knew ahead of time was never clear. Young's track record up to then—he was in his late thirties when he arrived in Williamson at the start of November 1923—was full of numerous disparities, more than enough for ten men. For sure, Young went through life being admired or hated; there was no middle ground. Some truly believed a claim in his biography that he was "the greatest law enforcement officer in America." Others saw him as an egomaniacal killer.

Seth Glenn Young was canonized in *Life and Exploits of S. Glenn Young,* a 1925 biography reprinted in 1989. The author, although anonymous, was an admitted friend and ardent admirer of Young.[1] Judging by the book, Young had a rip-roaring life from the start. Born in 1884 or 1886 or possibly 1887 (sources vary on the year), he was raised on the western Kansas plains around the town of Long Island, a son of George Buchanan Young, a rancher from Iowa, and his wife, a woman named Eva Albin McClellan from Illinois.[2] Glenn was reared with a pistol in his hand, astride a saddle, feeding and herding cattle. Short but sturdily built, his legs were bowed, a result, it was held, of all his time on a horse.[3]

More on Glenn Young as a youngster was provided by a brother, Leo, in a Young family history. Glenn was "a dead shot," Leo was quoted as saying. "He seemed to enjoy shooting. He was mean. He was always getting into trouble in school. Very, very smart, (he) would read over something and then he had it. Had a photographic memory. Then he'd get into trouble. He played baseball and football and played crooked. Always getting into fights—loved fights."[4]

For a fellow so in love with guns and fighting, Young made an appropriate move at the age of twenty-one, according to his biography. He hooked up with the Texas Rangers. Chasing cattle rustlers in the Lone Star State, the text romanticized that Young became known as "lightnin' on the draw," a man so accurate when he "cut loose" with a gun that "the figger on the ace of spades would cover his cluster of bullet holes." His days in Texas were followed by similarly harrowing undertakings, all revolving around guns and Young's lifelong crusade against lawbreakers.

The biography detailed in glowing terms a two-year stint by Young as a deputy United States marshal in Oklahoma, as well as his foiling of an attempted robbery of him in DuQuoin, Illinois, by three young ex-convicts. That incident was said to have occurred while Young was maneuvering in southern Illinois as an undercover federal officer (surely at some point prior to his coming to Williamson to enforce Prohibition). His early claim to fame, though, came during World War I when Young, working as an agent for the Bureau of Investigation in the Department of Justice, brought in hundreds of army deserters and draft dodgers who'd sought refuge in the mountains of southern states. Young often tracked these individuals alone, accompanied only by "Pal," his trusted Belgian police dog. Many times the quarries of Young did not surrender without a fight. In October 1918, during a battle with deserters, he reportedly did kill at least one fugitive. Even after the war was over, Young still was tracking down what his biographer called murderous "feudist" gangs in the Blue Ridge Mountains and other backwoods parts of the South.

In 1920, Young secured an appointment as a special agent in the Treasury Department's new Prohibition Unit, set up to enforce the Volstead Act. Assigned to southern Illinois, he soon succeeded in garnering favorable publicity as a nervy and successful operative. Before the end of 1920, though, he got into trouble. During a raid on a house with a still in the city of Madison near East St. Louis, Young shot and killed a man living next to the house that was raided. The victim tried to shoot Young first, but his pistol misfired. Young then drew his gun and shot the man.

Young was exonerated by a coroner's jury, but indicted for murder by a Madison County grand jury. Since he was a federal officer, the case was tried in federal court at Springfield. There, a jury found him not guilty of the charge in June 1921. However, he was out of a job by then. After the killing in Madison, the Prohibition Unit had suspended him until the outcome of its own investigation. That inquiry turned up various incidents of allegedly improper, immoral and arrogant conduct by a government officer during the exercise of his duties. Consequently, Young had been dismissed as a Prohibition agent several weeks before his acquittal on the murder charge.

One thing was apparent. The shooting in Madison added fuel to the image of Young as a man too quick to kill. That impression was abetted further by Young's reported slaying late in 1923, just before or after his arrival in Williamson, of two Pope County bootleggers, a father and his notorious son. Years later, in his family's history, Leo Young said matter-of-factly that his brother Glenn killed twenty-one men in his lifetime, but added that Glenn "always said he never pulled a gun first."[5]

As far as Glenn Young's history in Illinois went, his detractors always insisted that he had been employed as a guard in 1922 at the Lester mine, the one associated with the Herrin Massacre. However, Young's biographer contradicted that. "Right here let it be said once and for all," he or she wrote, "that S. Glenn Young was not involved in any way in the events of the Herrin Massacre."

That was the way it was with Young. Separating truth from fiction was not easy for people, beginning with most of the 70,000 or so residents of Williamson. Actually, the specific legal authority behind Young's crusade in Williamson remained sort of murky. In spite of his dismissal from the Prohibition Unit, a Klan newspaper asserted that Young was recommended for the Williamson assignment by Roy A. Haynes, the nation's Prohibition commissioner. Other backers of Young insisted that, after Young took back to Washington late in 1923 evidence of the hard liquor being served at "soft drink parlors" in Williamson, the Prohibition commissioner was persuaded to deputize Young and individuals of his choosing to raid the illegal outlets. However, as events of 1924 played out in the county, Haynes contended in a telegram to a St. Louis newspaper and at other times during the year that he neither dispatched nor recommended Young to anybody at any time.

Nevertheless, Haynes' denial did not rule out federal involvement, at least in Young's early offensive in Williamson, because there was some. While the thoughts of many individuals were on the Christmas season, Young secretly was organizing for his first big raid, his D day in Williamson. By December 22, 1923, the day of the raid, Young had recruited about 500 men, most of them Klansmen, to carry it out. When this small army reconnoitered in Carbondale shortly before the start of the raid, three federal agents were present at the direction of Haynes, and one administered an oath to the men on hand deputizing each as a federal officer for the conduct of the raid. As the raiders spread out to hit their targets, they were well supplied with federal search warrants signed by U.S. Commissioner William Hart of Benton.

With such a high number of people involved, it was hard to believe that the raid caught so many by surprise. But it did. No fewer than a hundred roadhouses and bootlegging operations, mainly in Herrin and Marion, were hit. Following careful planning, the raiders approached each place with drawn guns and demanded entrance by authority of the federal government. The undertaking reaped a bonanza of arrests, primarily proprietors and bartenders at establishments openly selling liquor. Since those apprehended were transported to Benton for arraignment before the U.S. commissioner, the city's square became a mob scene by midnight as thousands gathered to gawk at the cars arriving with the raiders and their prisoners. Those who couldn't make bail went to jail, a number so large that some had to be confined at Herrin.

The evening of December 22 was replayed on the night of the ensuing January 5 as raiders, deputized by federal officials and led by Young, took into custody enough supposed Williamson law violators to once more stuff jails at Benton and Herrin. Then, two days later, Young's men struck again, this time going into more of the little towns in the county. Williamson was now enmeshed in a state of violent commotion and uncontrollable excitement. The attention rapidly focusing on the county had shades of the spotlight on Williamson after the Herrin Massacre, which was still on everybody's mind. Newspersons trying to keep up on events had more than they could handle.

By this time, one of the more heated disputes growing out of the raids dwelt on the number of hits on private homes in addition to illegal businesses. Ugly renditions made the rounds of beatings and other unsavory conduct, even stealing, by the raiders in the residential stops. Far from unexpected, many of the homes invaded were those of wine-drinking Italians or immigrants from other countries, prompting Italian and French authorities to protest to the Department of State.

However, Young and his men disavowed any untoward conduct in the raids, whether at homes or saloons. If anything, he and his followers saw humor in some stops, a bit of which was related in flowery prose in his biography.

Take the visit to one target at Paulton, a mining hamlet near Marion. Young's troops "were given entrance to a home and asked for a drink, saying that they were peaceable friends," the biographer wrote. "The owner was delightfully hospitable, seated them comfortably, went to the kitchen and returned bearing with him some whiskey glasses and a bottle of the stuff that makes a mouse feel big enough to fight an elephant. He filled the glasses with Sunday measure and told the company to 'drink hearty.'

But, 'there's many a slip twixt the cup and the lip.' One of the officers remarked to the man, 'That's enough—stick 'em up.' And the episode closed for the time being when the liberal dispenser of alcoholic good cheer 'raised 'em,' and was escorted to the Benton jail...to meditate upon the ingratitude of his fellow men, and to lament 'love's labors lost.'"

Another stop was described as follows: "At another questionable place the owner's conscience being very tender prompted him to fly, and through the morning gloom he glumly glided toward a creek which slowly meandered not far away. When his pursuers arrived at the creek they failed to see him, until, looking about more carefully they discovered a pair of feet and ankles encased in boots, sticking out from a brush pile. An enthusiastic pull brought out the remaining parts of Mr. Bootlegger, who like the foolish ostrich, evidently thought that if his head and body was (sic) hidden, he would escape detection."

As for one other raid, the biographer admonished readers to "listen, ye thirsty sons of Bachus (sic), at one place twenty barrels of good, tasty, sparkling wine were found."

Central to everything occurring was Young, who became overnight a controversial man of the hour in Williamson. In the eyes of many, including a share of middle-of-the-roaders not sympathetic to violators of Prohibition, Young's drive in the county seemed to have as much to do with his own self-aggrandizement as with the expulsion of bootleggers. Quickly dubbed the "little Napoleon" of Williamson, even his appearance was attention-getting. His puttees and other military-like garb, pearl-handled sidearms, the submachine gun often in his clasp. Overriding it all, though, was his arrogance. It detracted from his mission. More than that, it got him into real trouble.

After the first major raid, a restaurant operator in Marion was beaten up in an altercation with Young and several of his followers. Consequently, Young was arrested on an assault and battery charge. When the case was heard January 8, 1924, by a justice of the peace, Young and his followers strutted into the courtroom heavily armed. The jury took no time at all to acquit Young. Nevertheless, the trial, abbreviated or not, convinced Sheriff Galligan, mindful of the tension preceding the Herrin Massacre, to wire Illinois Adjutant General Carlos Black for troops. Black responded promptly, and soldiers soon were walking the streets of

Marion. Klansmen protested their presence, with Sam Stearns, chairman of the Williamson supervisors' board and Exalted Cyclops of the Klan in that neck of the woods, insisting that most in the county wanted Young's raids to continue.

Nevertheless, the smooth sailing of Young was now threatened. Young, along with a handful of Klansmen, also was facing charges filed by individuals stating they were abused by Young's raiders. Furthermore, a Prohibition official ordered a halt to any more raids in Williamson unless circumstances changed. Too, Galligan was doing his best to get Klan leaders to dump Young, an effort at first tantamount to the sheriff banging his head against a brick wall.

For his part, Galligan, an amiable Irish Protestant, did attempt to defuse the situation by ordering his deputies to carry out some liquor raids, by directing other saloon operators to dispense with liquor sales and by moving to disarm residents of Herrin, where hundreds of gun permits had been issued to Klansmen. Although each of these initiatives produced meager results, Galligan agreed to the removal of the toops in mid January, about a week after their arrival. He may have felt, or believed, the Klan would get out of the law enforcement business.

No way.

Sunday, January 20. Klansmen, trailing Young, raided thirty-five places, primarily in mining locales, resulting in sixty-six arrests.

Thursday, January 31. Speaking to the Marion Rotary Club, Young pledged that the raids would continue until the bootleggers, gamblers and "other undesirables" were driven away.

Friday, February 1. Carrying state warrants issued by justices of the peace, more than 1,200 Klansmen raided stills and other spots throughout the county. Arrests totaled 125. Marshaled to Benton for arraignment, the prisoners were marched by Young to the public square. Thousands of spectators watched the procession. Afterward, cries of persecution against the raiders again were raised by Italians and French.

Chaos appeared to be enveloping Williamson. In Herrin at least, civil war loomed between Klansmen and anti-Klansmen. And, erupt it did, on Friday, February 8, 1924. The Sheltons were in the middle of it.

First, though, a little backtracking. The arrival of Young obviously had shattered the stability in Williamson cultivated by the Sheltons and other bootleggers. Their cozy live and let live relationship with the local law enforcement community no longer saved the day because Young and his Klansmen conspicuously excluded Galligan and other local law officers from the planning and execution of the raids.

Up in East St. Louis and elsewhere, the Sheltons recruited gunmen to their ranks when it became evident that Young could not be bought or controlled. Charlie Birger was doing the same in his backyard. In addition, when the KKK was emerging as a significant force in Williamson, an anti-Klan group surfaced under the intriguing name of Knights of the Flaming Circle. Its adherents, although fewer in number than the Klansmen, pretty soon if not right at the beginning included the Shelton brothers and others standing to suffer from the KKK's intended war on the liquor business. One of the others was Ora Thomas, a wounded veteran of World War I, erstwhile bootlegger and impassioned foe of the Klan, a person whom many assumed to be an organizer of the Knights. With dangerous men like the Sheltons and Thomas tied to the Knights, violent confrontation with the KKK seemed inevitable.

There was another matter to be kept in mind in examining the prelude to February 8, 1924. In one of Young's raids, a Shelton roadhouse was hammered. Humor was hard to find in that raid, led by Young himself and Caesar Cagle, a Herrin constable who'd gone from bootlegger to Klansman. Earl Shelton happened to be present when the raiders called. After the roadhouse was damaged by the intruders and a $700 crap game bankroll confiscated, they lined Big Earl up against a wall, trained weapons on him and ordered him to tell them whom the Sheltons were paying off. When Earl refused to oblige, Cagle slugged him with a pistol. Earl fell. Then Cagle pistol-whipped him, a put-down no Shelton could let go unanswered. The brothers would remember Cagle. His day would come. Indeed, it turned out to be February 8, a day of lethal hubbub.

The commotion that Friday night started with a meeting of angry and heavily armed anti-Klansmen at the Rome Club hall in Herrin, an assortment that included the Shelton boys, Ora Thomas, a Shelton ally named Jack Skelcher and others. Smelling trouble in the air, Galligan hastened to the gathering, taking along his chief deputy, John Layman, a Klan hater. As Galligan sought to keep the meeting from getting out of hand, the atmosphere reached fever pitch with the arrival of John Ford, the pro-Klan police chief of Herrin, and one of his officers, Harold Crain. Galligan's fear was quickly realized. The two policemen were disarmed, and Ford was roughed up by Layman. With the situation on the verge of a melee, Galligan moved to preserve order by taking Ford and Crain into his protective custody. Suddenly somebody fired a shot. It hit Layman. The wounded man went for Ford, accusing the police chief of shooting him. Ora Thomas tried to assure the crowd that Ford couldn't have fired the shot since Thomas had his guns. Nevertheless, Galligan, sensing that those assembled might become a lynch mob, brusquely escorted Ford and Crain as his prisoners out of the club, along with another Herrin officer just arriving. After making the escape, the sheriff was back on the phone to the state adjutant general, asking that troops be sent to Herrin as soon as possible. To guarantee the safety of the Herrin policemen, Galligan had them incarcerated over in Murphysboro before the night was out.

Galligan erred, though, if he believed the dispatching of the city cops put a lid on the evening's excitement.

On the heels of Galligan's departure from the Rome Club, the night turned deadly. The anti-Klansmen, still riled, spilled out of the club onto the street, and began milling in a pack headed by Carl Shelton and Ora Thomas. About then, it so happened, a young son of Caesar Cagle passed the Rome Club on his way home from a movie and observed the unruly crowd. Someone present, a Cagle family friend, according to one version, urged the boy to fetch his father. He complied, tracking down his dad at the Masonic Temple. Caesar Cagle soon was on the street. By the time he approached the crowd, which had taken on the mien of a small mob, it had swaggered a block or so to the Jefferson Hotel and numbered more than twenty well armed individuals. Spying Cagle, one in the crowd shouted, "Here he is!" With that, Cagle was engulfed. Shots pierced the night air. The anti-Klansmen quickly dispersed. Cagle was lying on the sidewalk, badly wounded. Persons watching the spectacle took Cagle to the Herrin hospital several blocks south, where the wounded John Layman had been brought earlier in the evening. Cagle died shortly after his arrival at the hospital.

Word of Cagle's death soon reached Young, in Marion at the time. In short order, Herrin was flooded by armed Klansmen at the direction of Young, who quickly got to Herrin. Klansmen patrolled the wide downtown streets of the town of more than 10,000 and even the roads leading into it. Cars were stopped and their occupants questioned. Those who didn't know a Klan password were prevented from entering Herrin.

The city was under a version of martial law. And the occupying general was Young. Even more bizarre was the next turn in the chain of events tied to Herrin's hellish February 8.

As warrants were being sworn out by Klansmen charging Galligan, Ora Thomas, Mayor C. E. Anderson of Herrin (no friend of the Klan) and others with the murder of Cagle, information reached Young that Thomas and the mayor were at the hospital with Layman. This triggered an attempted storming of the medical institution by Young and a large herd of Klansmen. When the head of the hospital, Dr. J. T. Black, refused to admit them, Young and his followers opened fire on the place, shattering windows and sending terrified patients and medical personnel to the floor. When they could, those inside the building with Layman returned the fire.

To the horror of the noncombatants in Herrin who had not fled for cover, their hospital was a fortress under a veritable siege. Of course, as Young's allies later contended, the hospital might as well had been a barracks for the "notorious Knights of the Flaming Circle." The onslaught continued until the early morning hours of the next day, February 9, when the first troops requested by Galligan arrived on the scene and ordered the attackers to scatter. Hard as it was to believe, nobody, in or out of the hospital, was hit by a bullet.

The reappearance of troops in Herrin may have stemmed further violence for the moment, but the Klan was anything but toned down. In the immediate aftermath of February 8, Herrin was under a Klan dictatorship. Young presided over the anarchy from city hall, acting as police chief, swearing in deputy policemen and ordering the arrests and jailing of certain persons. One was the mayor, who was locked up on the Klan charge that he murdered Cagle. Sheriff Galligan suffered the same fate.

On Sunday, February 10, the funeral of Caesar Cagle turned into a massive show of Klan force. Thousands crammed into and around the First Baptist Church of Herrin for the service. Before it began, a large blanket of white flowers with a KKK inscription was placed on the casket and a cross of red roses at the side. After the service, as many as 5,000 persons filed by the coffin at the front of the church, reputedly the largest turnout up to that time for a funeral in Williamson County.

On both the day Cagle was laid to rest and the following day, troops continued to arrive in Herrin. Overall, 1,700 soldiers ended up tramping through the streets or stationed with machine guns at key locales. The Illinois National Guard officer in command, Major General Milton Foreman, wasted little time putting out an order prohibiting anyone but duly authorized law enforcement officers from carrying guns. He made it clear in his directive that all appointments of special peace officers, which Young had taken it upon himself to do, were nullified. As for Young, the general declared that he had no official standing, saying that Young was not known to occupy "any position justifying him in administering law and order in the State of Illinois."

No matter what, Young played the role of Herrin police chief until February 12, when John Ford came back to take over the post. Galligan and Mayor Anderson also emerged from the jails in which they'd ended up to return to their positions.

An important factor in the freeing of the mayor and the others would be the verdict of the coroner's jury in the inquest into the death of Cagle. After questioning more than fifty witnesses, the jury concluded just a few days after the killing that Cagle "came to his death...by gunshot wounds at the hands of one Shelton described as tall and slim and one Shelton described as heavy set and sleepy eyed." Carl and Earl. Any possible anonymity still attending the brothers went down the drain.

One of the witnesses most incriminating for the Sheltons was a young Herrin mechanic named Harry Hanks. He related that he observed the confrontation between Cagle and a "bunch of men" whose "leader was Shelton." Actually, Hanks said he recognized two Shelton brothers in the front of the group, one "a tall slim fellow, and the other fellow a large man." According to Hanks, the end for Cagle started when "Shelton, the tall slim one, made a dive for him (Cagle) first and hit him over the head. Just as he fell, shots were fired, a flash from one gun and three flashes from another; and the two that I saw shoot were the Shelton brothers. I think they were the same kind of guns because there wasn't any difference between the noise of the guns." Hanks added that he then watched "Vurney" (Bernie Shelton) and his two brothers, along with another man, drive off in a Ford coupe.

The story of the killing receiving the widest circulation had a touch of ghastly humor. This account held that Earl Shelton, still smarting from his pistol-whipping by Cagle, put his gun on the Klansman by the Jefferson Hotel and snapped, "Stick 'em up, you dirty louse." When Cagle started to raise his hands, Earl was supposed to have said, "Oops, too late," put the gun in Cagle's ear and fired.[6] However, those familiar with the placement of Cagle's wound or wounds held that this account didn't hold water.

The verdict of the coroner's jury notwithstanding, Earl and Carl were not in custody. Fearing reprisal by the Klan more than the law, they left Herrin. Heading south toward Florida, using roads familiar to bootleggers, the brothers lived off the land by doing something they were comfortable with and good at—holding up roadhouses and gambling games.

According to Art Newman, who fancied himself as a kind of self-styled chronicler of the Sheltons and their times, "They told me that they went along like regular tourists, with pots and pans tied to their car, and they used to like to tell about sticking up joints in Florida towns." Fun for the boys was illustrated by their stop at one roadhouse. After robbing the clients, the brothers ordered a black band at the place to play a favorite song of the Sheltons, "That Old Gang of Mine," a big hit at the time. The band had to play it again and again while the boys ate chicken they'd ordered the cook to fry. Before departing, they ripped ignition wires from the cars in the parking lot so they didn't have to worry about being followed.[7]

Meanwhile, back in Herrin and Williamson County, the violence ebbed—for a short period at least—as persons of good will, some organizing themselves as the Citizens' Committee, sought to combat the factional hatred that had put their part of the world on the brink of mob rule. General Foreman went out of his way to encourage conciliatory efforts by leading citizens before most of the soldiers under his command were sent home from Herrin on February 15. And there was another development. Judge E. N. Bowen of the Herrin City Court called for a special grand jury to investigate the events of February 8 and the following day, stating that "far more important than any faction's desires or ambitions is the right of law-abiding people of Herrin to enjoy peace and quiet, to have in this city a decent place in which to live and bring up families...."

Ironically, as the special grand jury began deliberations in the first few days in March, the United States District Court at Danville took up the cases of more than 200 persons accused of liquor violations as a result of Young's efforts in Williamson County. Most noticeable among the defendants were Charlie Birger and Ora Thomas. With incendiary figures like these on hand, along with many other tense individuals from Williamson, deputy marshals had to be ever vigilant in watching for guns or provocative activity. An explosion did come close to occurring at one point when Young hurled an epithet at Birger as the two met in a courthouse corridor. Birger, it turned out, received the heaviest sentence handed down by Judge Walter Lindley in the trials, one year in jail in addition to fines. Thomas, to the delight of Klansmen watching the trials, was given a four-month jail sentence and fined.

Back in Herrin, the special grand jury presented its findings to Judge Bowen on March 14. Ninety-nine indictments were returned, almost all of them involving men who had participated in the attack on the hospital. Hit the hardest was Young, whom the grand jury accused of false imprisonment, kidnapping, assault with attempt to murder, falsely assuming an office, malicious mischief, parading with arms and a few other things.

As for the murder of Caesar Cagle, the grand jury echoed the coroner's jury by singling out Carl and Earl Shelton for indictment.

It was the report of the grand jurors, though, that hit the nail on the head in the opinion of many amazed at the incredible goings-on in Herrin and Williamson County. A "reign of terror" on February 8 and succeeding days had emanated from actions of "oppression and persecution by the so-called Ku Klux Klan," the jurors concluded. They contended that the attack on the hospital was "unlawful and without any justification whatever," a "most amazing display of mob violence." As for Glenn Young, the jurors found him to be an usurper plain and simple, an individual intending, along with his cohorts, to "overthrow the civil authority in Herrin and in Williamson County, seize and imprison the Sheriff and Mayor and take upon themselves the task of government without any legal authority whatever."

Naturally, the Klan didn't take the grand jury's conclusions laying down. The most visible reaction was a protest parade of thousands through Herrin March 17, an occasion that showed the KKK, in spite of the many questionable tactics of Young, commanded widespread support. Professional men, merchants, Civil War veterans in cars, musicians, women with babies and small children, Protestant ministers. All were in the march. And bringing up the rear was Young. When the parade ended, many participants proceeded to City Hall to sign bonds for the men under indictment.

The spirit of Klan followers also had to be boosted by the great success of its candidates in Williamson in the primary election April 8, 1924. Jubilant Klansmen celebrated their success with another big parade, a procession that wound up in Marion with a cross burning. The following month saw more major Klan outpourings, including a Klantauqua at Marion featuring three days of discourse and lectures in the fashion of a Chautauqua. All of this may have appeared to bode well for Young, the Klan's strong-arm man in Williamson.

Beneath the surface, though, Klan leaders in the county who had been paying Young very well for his services had become disenchanted with him because of his recklessness. Unbeknownst to many rank and file Klansmen as well as to the outside world, the leaders were moving to curtail his salary and take other steps to get rid of him. However, the more prominent Klansmen realized they needed to proceed cautiously in breaking the tie with Young because they knew, not without reason, that he'd be apt to turn his ire on them at any time. Fortunately for them, East St. Louis provided a bailout.

During the early months of 1924, the KKK had become bogged down with strife in the East St. Louis area. With the discord serious enough to prompt the revocation of the local Klan charter, the state's grand dragon turned to Young, asking him to investigate the conditions undermining the Klan's effectiveness on the East Side. Young, who had just become an actual member of the Klan in spite of his increasingly shaky relationship with the hierarchy of the organization in Williamson, readily agreed to accept the assignment, knowing it was an invitation for him to take over the Klan in East St. Louis.

Meanwhile, as Young's move from Williamson to East St. Louis was in the works, the Shelton brothers had ended their southern exodus, returning to their home state. Although aware that they'd be facing a jury trial in coming months on the Cagle murder charge, the Sheltons also sensed that the Klan crackdown on their business interests in southern Illinois, while hard on their income, was not likely to stand the test of time. One way or another, the boys knew they had a safe haven in East St. Louis. But they didn't hesitate to show their faces back in Williamson too, certainly not after voluntarily giving themselves up to Sheriff Galligan, hardly an enemy, and filing $10,000 bonds to ensure their appearance in court to answer the charge of murder.

It so happened that May 23, 1924, was one of those days when they were out and about in Williamson. It was also a day of one of Glenn Young's braggadocio performances in the county. Standing on the running board of a Lincoln sedan given to him by supporters, Young boasted to a crowd of bystanders in Herrin that he was leaving for East St. Louis to push for the same kind of cleanup there he'd accomplished in Williamson. How ironic, or perhaps not coincidental at all, his listeners included, of all people, his arch nemeses, the Shelton brothers. After his oratory, Young drove away, heading for East St. Louis, accompanied only by his pretty young wife of three years, Maude, a daughter of George B. Simcox, a one-time United States marshal. Quickly, the Sheltons, joined by two of their men, Jack Skelcher and Charlie Briggs, took off after Young in a curtained Dodge touring car. However, they didn't pull up behind Young's car for some time, not until the Lincoln was in a desolate, unpaved stretch of the Atlantic-Pacific Highway crossing what locals dubbed the Okaw bottoms. A sluggish backwater area by the Kaskaskia River (called the Okaw River by some), not far from Venedy. A fine location for a shoot-out.

To unravel the violent transgression that ensued when the Dodge overtook the Lincoln, different versions have to be compared.

Here is Young's, based on his biography: When the Dodge trailing Young's car suddenly speeded up and passed the Lincoln on the left, the author wrote, the Dodge's occupants "poured a volley of buckshot into the Klan leader and his wife. Eighteen of these lodged themselves in Mrs. Young's face and neck, while a forty-five calibre automatic bullet pierced the body of the car and struck Glenn in the leg a few inches below the knee. The missile fractured the large bone, glanced and fractured the small bone, then remained just within the skin on the calf of the leg.

"As soon as the first volley was fired, Glenn, to prevent, if possible, further danger to his wife, stopped the car and stepped to the road, (and then) dropped to the cinders beside the car. As he groveled there, aware for the first time that his limb was seriously wounded, the bullets fairly rained around him but did no further harm. After emptying their guns and pistols the gunmen sped West on the highway. Within the space of a few seconds Young had paid a terrible price for his fearless and heroic efforts against law violators in Williamson County. If half a chance had been his to reach his automatics or his submachine gun, his enemies and those of the social body who shot him down would doubtless have received swift justice. Knowing that they had no chance with him in a fair fight, they chose the way of the coward."

A *Post-Dispatch* retelling of the encounter years later ended with a little different take. With Bernie Shelton driving, the newspaper related, the Sheltons' auto pulled up alongside Young's and "opened up" on the Klan leader and his wife.

"The cars locked bumpers for a moment, then broke loose and Young's car plunged down a bank. The door fell open and Young fell out. He then displayed what the Sheltons considered an appalling lack of sportsmanship," the newspaper said.

"The dirty louse," Carl was quoted as complaining later, "crawled under the machine."[8]

The Sheltons sped away after the attack, leaving Young and his wife, both wounded, to be rescued afterward by passing motorists. Both were transported to St. Elizabeth's Hospital in Belleville, her in an ambulance summoned from nearby Mascoutah and Young in his own car, driven by one of the persons happening on the scene of the assault. Young's leg wound would not be as serious as the damage to his wife, whose eyesight was destroyed by the load of buckshot she took in her face.

Some gang followers contended there was nothing happenstance about the Sheltons' attempted assassination of Young that warm May day, that they had planned ahead of time to kill him that day. A purse for his head had reached $1,800 in East St. Louis, where the coming of Young to lead the Klan was widely opposed. Although they failed to kill Young, the Sheltons were hailed as heroes by gangsters and many politicians in East St. Louis who wanted no part of Young's Williamson County performance in their city. Many of them figured the Sheltons were entitled to at least part of the blood money on Young's head for making the effort, and the Sheltons agreed.

So the brothers were awarded $600. However, it wasn't paid without a hitch. A character named "Big Hank" was holding the reward, and when the Sheltons received their share they discovered that he had shorted them $100. That wouldn't do. Word went out the brothers were on Big Hank's trail. No doubt he heard about it because when they came to his hotel and pounded on his door he scrambled out of bed, stumbled down a fire escape in his underwear and escaped in a taxi. A few days later, he had a cab driver deliver one hundred bucks to the Sheltons.

Meanwhile, back at St. Elizabeth's Hospital in Belleville, a strange scenario discouraged anybody from trying to finish the job started by the Sheltons. Under the direction of Earl Gibson, an operative for the St. Clair County Enforcement League, an arm of the KKK, members of the Klan guarded Young's room constantly. Others hovered around the hospital. Young himself kept two cocked automatic pistols under a pillow, much to the chagrin of the Catholic nuns who managed the hospital.

The irony of the most famous Klansman in the state recuperating in a Catholic institution was not lost on observers, including the *Belleville Daily News-Democrat* and its pull-no-punches owner and publisher, Fred J. Kern. The newspaper's "Stormoguide," an editorial column chock-full of bombast, pilloried Young as a Catholic hater in that he was "the high cock-o-lorum of the Ku Klux Klan of Southern Illinois...their duly canonized patron saint." Yet, the column noted, one of the doctors treating the Youngs was a Catholic and the son of a saloon keeper.

The sharpest jab, though, was reserved for the discovery in Young's bullet-riddled Lincoln of not only an arsenal of weapons but also a five-gallon jug of wine in the car's tonneau. "Strange and inexplicable," lampooned the column. "Glenn Young begrudges even the sick and the aged their glass of wine and beer to brace them up a little when they are faint and feeble and weary, but he happened to be caught with the goods on him, hauling it along as contraband—forbidden product and forbidden fruit, in his own machine—red, sweet-smelling and foaming."

"Stormoguide" also may have been peeking into a crystal ball when it prophesied that Young and his confederates would "finally insist on blimps and airplanes equipped with bombs and hand grenades and poison gas with which to enforce the Eighteenth and the Volstead Act..."[9] Ludicrous as that appeared, the prediction wouldn't be entirely off base in regard to upcoming events in southern Illinois. At least not on the plane and bomb bit. But it'd be the Sheltons behind it, not Young and his crowd.

The scorn for Young typified by the *News-Democrat* was hardly universal, though. His attempted murder sparked outrage especially among his still large following in southern Illinois. Before the night of May 23 was out, a large group of Klansmen in the Herrin area was appointed as deputies, and, acting on a tip that Young's attackers were heading to the city, they set up roadblocks around Herrin. Sure enough, on the morning of the following day, a Saturday, a curtained Dodge touring car fitting the description of the vehicle of Young's assailants tried to run through a Klan post on the road from Carterville to Herrin. After an exchange of shots between the Klansmen and the auto's occupants, the Dodge smashed into another vehicle on the road. Two men tried to run from the wreckage, but were shot by the Klansmen. One died within an hour. He was Shelton lieutenant Jack Skelcher. The other man, not wounded badly, would be identified as Charlie Briggs, who'd been indicted in the not too distant past with Bernie Shelton on a highway robbery charge. As for the death of Skelcher, a coroner's jury would quickly return a verdict that he met death from "gunshots by parties unknown." However, that decision was contradicted several days later when four Klansmen were charged in warrants with murder for the slaying of Skelcher.

Four days after the attack on Young and his wife, warrants charging Carl and Earl Shelton with the attempted murders were issued in Clinton County, where the assault occurred. A third warrant, issued by Clinton's state's attorney, Hugh Murray, made the same allegation against Briggs. Murray said the warrants were based on information supplied by Glenn Young.

On June 9, it was learned that Carl and Earl, in hiding in East St. Louis since the assault on Young, had surrendered on the murder charge to the sheriff of Clinton County and furnished bonds of $20,000 each. On June 26, a huge crowd assembled in Carlyle, the seat of Clinton, for the preliminary hearing in the case. The place looked like an armed camp what with fifty deputies with shotguns on hand and Young arriving with an escort of thirty cars of Klansmen, many of them bearing weapons. The hearing was over in no time, though. Young identified the Sheltons and Briggs as some of his attackers on May 23, and a justice of the peace bound the trio over to a November grand jury while releasing them on bond.

However, the case never was prosecuted. Reportedly miffed at Clinton officials for releasing the Sheltons and Briggs, Young, nor his wife, showed up to appear before the grand jury late in the year. By that juncture, Young had other troubles to ponder besides the Sheltons.

Hardly surprising to many persons, Young had struck out with the Klan in East St. Louis. Facing a far less friendly local establishment than he had at the start of his crusade in Williamson, Young's KKK stewardship on the East Side was an exercise in wheel spinning. No, even worse than that. Young would run the Klan like a dictator for three months, even wearing the title of Klan kleagle in East St. Louis. But his stern control could not prevent further erosion of the Klan's impact on the East Side. With Klan membership in Young's domain declining instead of growing, Charles G. Palmer, the grand dragon for Illinois, deposed Young in the summer of 1924 in favor of the Reverend Robert (Fighting Bob) Evans, who had left the Bond Avenue Methodist Church in East St. Louis the previous year to become a national lecturer for the Klan.

The ouster of Young from his Klan position came on the heels of a protest by W. O. Potter, the United States attorney at East St. Louis and a strident anti-Klan person. He complained about methods employed by Young in his campaigns as well as about Young's diatribes against Potter and other federal officials deemed by Young to be in bed with bootleggers. Bitter feelings between Potter and Young became so intense that Klansmen urged Palmer to act as mediator. The upshot, in tandem with Young's dismissal, was a public letter from Palmer to Potter in which the grand dragon apologized for Young's behavior, saying it did not repesent the official attitude of the Klan.

By any measure, Fighting Bob Evans seemed to be a good choice for trying to resuscitate the KKK on the East Side. Active in East St. Louis civic and political affairs and an opponent of municipal corruption, the minister unsuccessfully had sought election as a city commissioner with the endorsement of the Klan in 1923. Undaunted, he declared later that year, in leaving his church for the KKK lecture position, that he still intended to fight for the "little red schoolhouse" against the East St. Louis city administration. He pledged during his farewell sermon (at which time he was presented with a gold watch by the Klan) to never relinquish the fight against his enemies, a list including parochial schools and St. Louis newspapers in addition to East St. Louis officialdom. However, Fighting Bob proved to be no more successful than Young or other predecessors in combating the East Side schisms in the Klan or the wile of the unholy but profitable alliance in East St. Louis of the liquor-running Sheltons and their wallet-greased allies sporting badges and sitting in public offices. Again, one had to remember that, in certain city circles, cold beer mugs were raised to the Sheltons as the toast of the town after they tried to knock off Young.

Down in Williamson County, as 1924 moved into summer, the Sheltons may not have been highly regarded, but they had reason to believe their chance of weathering the storm there was looking better. With the departure of Young from the Klan crusade, the pot of hostilities seemed to more simmer than boil for a spell. The Sheltons' friend, Sheriff Galligan, appeared to be making headway in regaining some degree of control over the law and order process. Nevertheless, nobody held any illusion that the Klan was moribund, Young or no Young. (Since Young still considered Williamson his home, he was in and out of the county anyway.)

The next big test for the Sheltons of where things really stood in Williamson loomed in their scheduled trial on the charge of murdering Caesar Cagle.

Not to be overlooked was the coroner's inquest testimony of Harry Hanks directly accusing Earl and Carl of the killing. With the outlook for the brothers uncertain at best, the Sheltons' lawyer, J. L. Fowler, was to be joined at the defense table by an attorney from East St. Louis, Joseph B. McGlynn. Now, prior to the trial date for the case of the *People v. Carl and Earl Shelton* a number of the other cases growing out of the riotous night of February 8 had been heard in Herrin City Court. Some cases against Klansmen were dismissed, and in other cases the defendants were acquitted. Nevertheless, the Sheltons remained uneasy.

But it turned out that they had no worry.

Saturday, August 30, 1924, ended up being the next calamitous day in Herrin's unending ordeal. Before the morning was over, the jury to hear the Cagle murder case was selected. However, the panel heard no testimony because Delos Duty, the beleaguered state's attorney of Williamson, moved abruptly that the case be dismissed. He had insufficient evidence to prosecute, Duty explained, because the primary witness linking the

Sheltons to the slaying could not be found. Too, Duty noted, Tim Cagle, the father of the dead man and a justice of the peace at Carterville, requested dismissal because he'd come to believe that the two Sheltons had not murdered his son. That was enough for Judge Bowen to hear. He granted the motion of the state's attorney. Carl and Earl were free men. The wish of Caesar Cagle's father notwithstanding, many in the Klan were incensed as word about the outcome of the case spread quickly. Herrin again was on edge.

In view of the explosive atmosphere, the timing of the next development on August 30 could not have been worse.

Within an hour of the Sheltons exit from the courtroom, Galligan headed for the Herrin garage of John Smith, a Klan leader, to seize an automobile being held at the garage, the Dodge car driven by Jack Skelcher on the day of his death—the vehicle believed used by the assailants of Glenn Young on May 23. Galligan was accompanied by a troop of Klan foes that included Ora Thomas and another special deputy, J. H. Allison, along with the Shelton brothers, Bernie, Carl and Earl. Arriving at the garage, a hangout for Klansmen, Galligan ordered that the car be turned over to him. When an attendant didn't comply fast enough, he got a poke in the ribs with a gun barrel from one of the sheriff's fellows. This prompted shoving and pushing, which attracted attention outside the garage. One car cruising by slowly, occupied by Klansmen, was halted by several of Galligan's men. The occupants were told to line up on the street.

Suddenly a shot rang out. It was followed by a fusilade inside the garage and out on the street. By the time the firing ended, six men were dead or soon to be deceased. Others, including Carl and Earl Shelton and Galligan, were wounded. Aside from a determination of the body count, trying to make heads or tails out of what happened was virtually impossible. Some would view it as Herrin's replay of the storied 1881 gunfight at the O.K. Corral in Tombstone, Arizona. To others, it was a deadly showdown, the most mortal by far, between the Klan and the Knights of the Flaming Circle. One headline simply screamed, "Sheriff and Klan at War."

"Streets of Herrin were spattered with blood again this afternoon," the *Associated Press* reported, "when the long rumbling engendered by law violations and factionalism broke out in a street fight between deputy sheriffs and citizens. Six men were killed, one a deputy sheriff."

Allison, the special deputy, was the sheriff's man killed. The other victims were three Klansmen, an innocent bystander and Chester Reid, who happened to be walking by the garage when the scuffle broke out and took it upon himself to urge everybody to put away their pistols. Carl Shelton reportedly was shot either in an arm or hand (accounts varied), while Earl, according to a later disclosure, supposedly took a bullet in a leg.

As horrified Herrinites cautiously converged on the garage to view the scene of the carnage, Galligan and the shot-up members of his band, the Sheltons included, took refuge in the Herrin hospital. Fearing the Klan would be mobilizing for another attack on the facility, the sheriff hastily phoned the state adjutant general and, once more, asked that soldiers be dispatched to Herrin. The request was granted promptly. A contingent of troops from Carbondale soon arrived and displayed machine guns around the hospital—just in time to discourage any assault by an angry crowd of Klansmen gathering a few blocks away. When more guardsmen arrived in the evening from Salem, the threat of another big shoot-out was over.

But no one doubted that Herrin remained an armed camp, divided against itself. Even many strictly law-abiding citizens carried concealed pistols when they went out, never knowing when they might be caught in the next cross fire.

The slaughter at Smith's garage, shocking though it was, epitomized what Herrin had become. A city discomposed over the Klan conflict; a community living in a continual state of agitation. Few places in America had been more torn asunder by the powerful and very emotional forces unleashed by Prohibition. It was more than the Klan versus anti-Klansmen or this faction against that faction. Families were pitted against families, even brothers against brothers. When old-line Protestants engaged Catholic upstarts, it was really a nativist versus foreigner clash. All right there, in Herrin, Illinois.

Everyday law and order, the maintenance of which most Americans took for granted, was on hiatus from Herrin. Even though each of the warring factions at Smith's garage had wildly differing versions of what happened, a number of individuals were accused of murder, including the Sheltons. Indictments against the brothers charged them, in addition to murder, with assault to murder with guns and blackjacks, conspiracy and riot. However, no proceedings were carried out on the cases, just as prosecution was never pursued on so many of the indictments handed down during the Klan war in Williamson. Many of the indictments were regarded as little more than political statements anyway, since grand juries with Klansmen were prejudiced against Galligan and many other officials while juries dominated by Klan haters automatically had it in for Young and his men. Maintaining even a semblance of neutrality, or objectivity, was not easy.

One could not have a tie to Herrin and not be affected, perhaps greatly, by the destructive discord wracking the city in the 1920s. Ray Serati spent most of his life away from his hometown of Herrin after he went over to Carbondale to study journalism at Southern Illinois University (from which he was graduated in 1959). Yet, he never hesitated during thirty-three years as the *Copley News Service* bureau chief in the Statehouse in Springfield to field questions about the volatile history of the town in which he was born and raised—a city for which he always held a strong affinity.

Serati entered life in 1937, a decade after the worst turmoil subsided, but he still grew up, in his words, "with all the talk about what happened in Herrin and the county. I knew it was an unusual situation, that it wasn't a normal way of living in the United States, the constant fighting between rival groups, people always trying to settle scores."[10]

The story of Serati's parents reflected the background of many in Herrin's Italian community. His father, Charles, an immigrant from a town north of Milan, came to Herrin in the 1920s to work in the mines. There he met Ray's mother, Caroline Pedretti, a native of St. Louis brought up in Italy. They were married at Our Lady of Mount Carmel Catholic Church in Herrin. Charles Serati never left underground mining, working until his death from a heart attack at age forty-four.

Resentment against Italians and other immigrants in the Herrin area was certainly palpable during Prohibition, a fact of life Serati remembered his parents talking about. "Prohibition itself, of course, was a catalyst for a lot of it," he said. "Many people just figured if you came from southern or eastern Europe, you made wine. Whether they did or not, everybody was lumped under the same umbrella. Italian Catholics simply weren't welcome in certain parts of Herrin."

But, ill will cut both ways, Serati pointed out, emphasizing that "the manner in which Glenn Young just went into many people's homes was really resented, too." Much heartache might have been avoided, Serati felt, "if Young just had not come into the picture." On the other hand, he added, "when Prohibition was over, much of the animosity went away. Many individuals, like my mom, just let it go. There was no sense holding grudges." By the time World War II had come and gone, Serati recalled, "even the old neighborhood distinctions in Herrin seemed to be fading away."

And what through the years lingered in Serati's mind about the prominence of the Shelton brothers in the Herrin violence? There was an impression, he answered, that "they'd freely chosen this way of life...and when you chose that path there were consequences that went with it."[11]

As 1924 rolled along, though, the Shelton boys might have been excused for believing they were immune from punishment for their actions. Let off the hook in the killing of Cagle. Never prosecuted for their role in the gunfight at the Smith garage. Escaped prosecution for the attempted assassination of Glenn Young. Walking away scot-free from all of this, the bootlegger sons of Ben and Agnes were leading a charmed life—for the time being.

That was not as true for Glenn Young as 1924 wound down. Less than a week after the battle at Smith's garage, Young and nine other Herrin residents were indicted by a federal grand jury at Danville on charges of impersonating federal officers. That was followed by his formal expulsion from the Klan. Explaining the raider's excommunication in the *Illinois Kourier*, the offical KKK newspaper, Grand Dragon Palmer underscored Young's "inordinate craving for personal publicity" along with Young's proneness to take the law into his own hands, shoot "at the drop of a hat," and give "utterance to the most incendiary thoughts." Nevertheless, the Klan proletariat in Williamson served notice that it still considered Young one of its own.

As for Galligan and his entourage, always a sharp thorn in the side of the Klan, the sheriff left no doubt of his newest main man when he appointed Ora Thomas a permanent deputy in October 1924, his chief deputy in fact. This enraged the Klan and more than a few others because Thomas had only a short time before completed serving his federal jail sentence for being caught in Young's raids. Furthermore, just before his appointment by Galligan, Thomas was under indictment for murder at

Smith's garage. With the Sheltons laying low again in East St. Louis, there could be no greater visible lightning rod for Klan hatred in Williamson than Shelton friend Thomas, a slim man, quite unpretentious for one recognized even by his enemies as fearless.

To say Herrin remained on edge was an understatement. Thomas was now walking around with a badge. Young, a man hated by Thomas, still circulated in the city with his followers, going from one scrape to another with his abusive behavior. A collision appeared inevitable, put off only it seemed by the unending presence of soldiers. The November general election in 1924 did little to defuse the situation as Klan-backed candidates swamped their opponents, with the most notable winner being Arlie O. Boswell, who was elected state's attorney of Williamson.

Nevertheless, for a year of such violent outbursts in Herrin, the final weeks of 1924 were relatively placid. The troops finally departed, and families had a chance to celebrate the Christmas season in a normal manner in Herrin and in other parts of Williamson, in contrast to the uproar dominating Christmas the previous year in the wake of Young's first huge raid. However, the peace, assuming people really did relax, was only a recess from the tumult.

With all the attention showered on Williamson in 1924 by the press far and wide, developments elsewhere during the year that would prove crucial to the Shelton story received either minimal play or went unnoticed.

For instance, it was understandable that nobody would take note when a young man named Theodore Carl Link began a lengthy career in newspapers in 1924 by going to work for the *St. Louis Star* as a cub reporter. Link would go on to become a famous investigative reporter, for the *Post-Dispatch*, and he and the Shelton gang would get acquainted, very well acquainted.

Just as anonymous in 1924 was a bright, young, ambitious attorney in Chicago named Dwight Herbert Green, who was fascinated with the raging underworld violence in his town. He'd land a job the following year in Washington with the Bureau of Internal Revenue, the first step on an odyssey taking him to the Illinois governorship—where his standing in the end would be colored greatly by the Sheltons.

And, not ignored but hardly as titillating as Williamson County events was a botched robbery September 27, 1924, of a bank at Kincaid, a small town southeast of Springfield. The heist would get much more play three years later with the indictment of Carl, Earl and Bernie for allegedly staging the holdup.

However, there'd be a flood of more headlines for the brothers before they had to face the music on Kincaid. And before touching the lives of Link and Governor Green.

6

Bullets, Bombs and Tanks— And a Pile of Corpses

Predictably, the silence of the guns in Williamson County at the close of 1924 didn't last long. Not with Ora Thomas and Glenn Young roaming at will, each waiting for the most advantageous moment to kill the other. They might have been two gladiators, warily eyeing each other, poised to strike, with Herrin as their arena. Only the timing seemed uncertain, and that question was answered when the ultimate clash, with all the dramatic tragedy of a Shakespearean scene, occurred on January 24, 1925. In a hotel cigar store, of all places.

In looking back, that episode brought the Klan war in southern Illinois to its peak. Afterward, the hostilities subsided, except for one more bloody shoot-out in Herrin in early 1926 which turned out to be, for all purposes, the last attempted show of force by a then declining Klan. However, the demise of the Klan in the open warfare business only opened the door for another reign of widespread terror in Williamson, a vicious gang war spearheaded by a fall-out between the Sheltons and Charlie Birger.

Back to Young and Thomas, the end of the road for the two mortal enemies came during the evening of that January day, a Saturday, in the Canary Cigar Store in the ground floor corner of Herrin's European Hotel. In the annals of gunfights, this one became even more celebrated than the one five months earlier at Smith's garage. Yet, as with the encounter at the garage, no narratives of the clash in the cigar store are alike, leaving historians free to pick out a favorite among the various versions of the battle. Only the outcome was undisputed. Young and Thomas lost their lives in the clash, along with two of Young's henchmen, Ed Forbes and Homer Warren.

Although the Shelton brothers were not in Herrin the night of this shoot-out, as far as anyone knew, several written accounts asserted that they were very much on the mind of Young at the time. Young had been walking the streets that day with a dozen or more of his followers, Carl Baldwin wrote, amid "reports...that the Sheltons were coming from their East St. Louis headquarters for a final showdown with the ex-Klan leader."[1] Author John Bartlow Martin contended that Young was looking for the Sheltons when he and his bodyguards were approached by Thomas in the cigar store.[2]

Most versions pointed out that the first shot of the evening mysteriously rang out after Thomas and others had left the Herrin City Court, where he'd been in charge of a jury in deliberation. The bullet struck a concrete pillar near their heads, sending Thomas and the rest scurrying for cover. Young and some of his followers then suddenly arrived at the scene and inspected the spot where the bullet hit, after which they drove off. Nothing more transpired right then. So Thomas strode to the European Hotel, where he often found a cab to take him home.

When he reached the hotel and went in, Thomas overheard heated words coming out of the cigar store. Entering the little shop, he discovered Young chewing out a coal miner for spreading an allegation that Young was a protector of scabs. Thomas was clasping the butt of a well-oiled automatic in his overcoat pocket, prompting Young, upon seeing Thomas, to sternly declare: "Don't pull that gun, Ora!" However, Thomas' pistol came out of his coat in a split second. Gunfire erupted immediately.

One witness, peering through the cigar store window from the sidewalk, later testified to the coroner's jury investigating the affray that he saw Thomas fire the first shot before the witness dropped to the walk to escape the hail of bullets and shards of flying glass. In the end, pinning down exactly just who plugged whom was nigh impossible. The verdict of the coroner's jury was that Young "came to his death from a gunshot wound at the hands of Ora Thomas" and that Thomas was killed by a shot fired by Young. Forbes and Warren were shot by "parties unknown," the verdict stated, leaving room for the conjecture in some quarters that one or more persons outside the shop also fired into the small cluster of individuals inside.

If Baldwin's account was true, the badly wounded Young crawled into a barbershop next to the cigar store before he died. As for Thomas, Baldwin wrote that those cautiously entering the hotel after the shooting was over found the deputy sheriff "had sunk to the floor...dying from a bullet which pierced his brain." Added Baldwin, "Williamson County's native-born fighting man was on his way out, as he had predicted, with an automatic in his hand. Months before he had told a *Post-Dispatch* reporter: 'I'm ready to go if those other fellows are willing to swap.' He had driven a hard bargain. He died 15 minutes after reaching the Herrin hospital."[3]

No one remembered any Herrin policemen coming to the shooting scene. If so, they'd have been treated harshly by the armed Klansmen soon covering the streets and, as in the past, halting all vehicles seeking to enter Herrin. The Klansmen were not dispersed until troops arrived in the early hours of the next day, bringing calm to the troubled town.

Three days after the shooting, Galligan was among those standing in the snow for a simple Protestant funeral service for his chief deputy in Marion. The procession to Thomas' grave site drew a large throng of marching miners and a huge number of cars. The date of his burial, January 27, 1925, took on added meaning because early that morning bandits robbed a mail messenger in Collinsville of a $15,000 money package— another stickup destined to play a role in the Sheltons' future.

Young's burial was a spectacle of high pageantry normally more associated with European monarchists. First, the body lay in state for three days, attracting as many as 75,000 viewers. Years later, many would recall with poignancy the pathetic figure of the raider's blind wife seated by the head of the casket, reaching over at times to caress the forehead of her dead husband. On the day of the funeral, January 29, only a small number of the anywhere from 25,000 to 40,000 people jammed into Herrin managed to get seats in the First Baptist Church, where the long service was conducted by a team of ministers.

With night falling, the frigid weather did not curtail a funeral procession of extraordinary length. Hundreds of Klansmen, donned in their regalia, led the cortege to the Herrin city cemetery, where Young was placed in a hastily constructed concrete mausoleum. Mrs. Young rode in the procession in the Lincoln punctured by Shelton bullets in the Okaw bottoms. As many as 500 autos trailed the hearse. A cross burned at the cemetery as the Klan burial ritual was read. Young may have been kicked out of the KKK by its Illinois leader, but his funeral was a show of the exaltation still accorded the Prohibition raider by many southern Illinois Klansmen.

In the months that followed, a chain of events took place in Herrin that relegated outright violence to a back burner for a considerable period. Governor Small and the Illinois attorney general, Oscar E. Carlstrom, played key roles in negotiating a truce or compromise between the Klan and anti-Klan factions in Williamson that provided, among other things, for Galligan to step aside as sheriff for a spell (three months as it turned out). Cooler heads in the county began asserting themselves, too. Like Hal W. Trovillion, the editor and publisher of the *Herrin News*, who was instrumental in bringing to Herrin a young evangelist, Harold S. Williams, for a series of old-fashioned revival meetings. Even some of the gamblers and bootleggers turned out to receive the word about Christ's teachings. The new state's attorney of Williamson, Boswell, moved to strike from court dockets many of the pending cases linked to the activities of Glenn Young, cases in which few county or municipal officials in Williamson were not charged with multiple law violations in addition to Young himself and Ora Thomas. Another development thought to soften the tension was the cessation in the summer of 1925 of the publication of the *Herrin Herald*, a Klan newspaper.

The tranquillity was just on the surface, though. Those in the Klan now eschewing violence, and others in Williamson also, saw the liquor interests gradually resuming business as usual with minimal interference. Roadhouses of the Shelton boys and Birger again were humming in the lower part of the state, a testament to the Sheltons' belief that the Klan-inspired enforcement of Prohibition, the strong-arm variety, would peter out.

To be honest, by the middle of the 1920s many of the adherents of Prohibition were losing faith in the likelihood of its success. The KKK was but a sympton, an off-color aberration in certain regions, of a push by conservative evangelical Christians to exercise their voice in the broader arena of public policy. To try and thrust their moral conservatism on the whole of society was a move as well-intentioned as the motives of scores of other forces seeking to impose their will on the American mind-set during this epoch or that. To have not prevailed, as the old-line Christians did not in matters such as Prohibition and the Scopes trial on the teaching of evolution in 1925, did not diminish the righteousness of the cause. It was just that society, a great mixed bag of heterogeneity, wasn't buying it. The diversity in the nation had become, well, little short of schizophrenic.

Following their defeats in the hedonistic years of the Roaring Twenties, the fundamentalists and the evangels pulled in their horns politically, not to reemerge so overtly again in national politics until a half century later in response to irritants such as court decisions on issues like abortion and school prayer. Then they came out marching in droves behind the flags of, most noticeably, the Moral Majority or the Christian Coalition, juxtaposing once more religion with political conflict. Political liberals were the adversaries, not the Sheltons of the world.

The Scopes trial was one of the noteworthy happenings replacing Williamson County and Herrin on front pages in 1925 once the excitement from the Young-Thomas shoot-out died down. John T. Scopes was a young teacher in Dayton, Tennessee, who agreed to become a test case for a challenge by the American Civil Liberties Union of a Tennessee law making it a crime to teach Darwin's biological evolution theory—a contrast to biblical scripture.

Aging orator William Jennings Bryan, a native of Salem, Illinois, unsuccessful presidential candidate and religious fundamentalist, helped prosecute Scopes. The teacher was represented by skeptical Chicago attorney Clarence Darrow, the greatest defense lawyer of his generation. Although the trial resulted in Scopes being found guilty of violating the state law (he was fined $100), Darrow's brilliant dissection of Bryan on his strict allegiance to biblical language was regarded widely as a discreditable setback for Christian fundamentalism, in turn hastening the declining influence of religious values on American life.

As mesmerized as Americans were about the Scopes trial, the ordeal of farmer Floyd Collins in 1925 was every bit as consuming. Collins was an unfortunate young man whose entrapment in a Kentucky cave received the nation's undivided attention for two weeks in February. The country was heartbroken when he couldn't be rescued and died. Southern Illinoisans had a reason even closer to home for anguish when a tornado ravaged their region on March 18, 1925, leaving death and devastation in its wake.

The tornado, crossing Missouri, the Illinois counties of Jackson, Williamson, Franklin, Hamilton and White and then Indiana, killed 689 persons in the three states (the bulk in Illinois), injured thousands of others and left property damage estimated at well above $15 million. Murphysboro was nearly demolished, and the wreckage was almost as severe in West Frankfort, Gorham and Hurst. Few school buildings in the tornado's path escaped damage. Once again, National Guard troops were called to active duty in southern Illinois, this time to assist relief efforts. And the War Department granted an appeal by Governor Small to ship immediately from Chicago's reserve depot tents and other necessities for housing the homeless.[4]

The distress caused by the storm did serve, for a time, to detour the minds of people from the long preoccupation with the Klan and the bootlegging gangsters.

With the Klan in remission in 1925, one benefit for the Sheltons was the additional time on their hands to consolidate and expand their power base in St. Clair and Madison counties. This enabled them to shore up sufficient strength to discourage attempted incursions into the East Side by the gangs in St. Louis, no small doing. Not only had the Sheltons helped greatly to undermine S. Glenn Young's intended takeover in East St. Louis, the brothers also provided a first line of defense for the East Side underworld in preserving its hegemony.

St. Louis had not exactly been dullsville, gangland-speaking.

The city was the home of Egan's Rats, the Hogans, the Cuckoos, the Russo outfit and some very vicious Italian mobsters. All of them naturally desired a piece of the lucrative action on the East Side during Prohibition, but there was another deterrent besides the coming of age of the Shelton gang in Illinois. It was the mutually destructive warfare the St. Louisans waged against each other in their city and St. Louis County.

The Kefauver committee summed up the St. Louis situation by noting in its report that in "the early 1920s St. Louis' most important mobs—the Egan Rats and the Hoganites—engaged in a war of attrition for the control of the rackets. These gangs operated largely in north St. Louis, and the citizenry of St. Louis finally became so appalled at the open shootings and murders that the president of the police board, together with the chief of police of St. Louis, called the respective leaders of the gangs into a conference and asked them to sign a truce. The Egan gang had steadily been gaining an advantage over the Hogans and this truce was arranged with the leaders signing an agreement."

While the Shelton boys were battling the Klan, the report pointed out, another bad fight was raging in St. Louis. "A gang of hoodlums called the Green Dagoes, reputedly Mafia members from Sicily, began attempting to take over the bootleg operations from a group of American-born Italians," the report said. "Thirty-six gangsters were killed in this bloody exchange, and during the peak of the war in 1927 an average of one Italian a day was murdered for one month. This string of murders killed or dispersed most of the active Mafia and left the American-born Italians in control of most of the bootleg area in certain St. Louis areas."

Then there was the bunch with the silly name, Cuckoo gang. About it, the Kefauver panel reported the following: "South St. Louis was the area controlled by a group of American-born hoodlums and hoodlums of Syrian descent who operated under the name of the Cuckoo gang and worked as hired killers and 'musclemen' for other gang organizations. There were several factions of this gang, and they assisted the American-born Italians in the extermination of the Sicilian mob.

"Another portion of the Cuckoo gang worked with the Shelton gang as guards for stills, (and) guards for trucks hauling bootleg liquor, and performed other duties incident to large-scale crime operations."[5]

Everybody understood, though, that the presence of Cuckoo mobsters on the East Side occurred with the blessing of the Sheltons, and only to assist or provide backup for the Sheltons at the specific direction of the brothers. (Eventually, some Cuckoo gangsters would find themselves sharply at odds with the Sheltons.) With the Klan seemingly subdued, the Sheltons' need for help in protecting their backside in the East St. Louis area did not take on great importance until well into 1926, the year that the Shelton-Birger relationship deteriorated into an all-out shooting war. However, even through the early months of that year, the Sheltons, having shared common ground with Birger in the fight against the Klan, maintained a workable if tepid coexistence with the Saline County gangster.

The most noticeable falling out for the Sheltons prior to 1926 involved Art Newman. It was interesting in that his relationship with the brothers followed a course repeated later on by some other formidable figures in the Shelton story. Ally or accomplice to begin with, then a cooling off of the friendship followed by pure enmity.

Newman never forgot that he was enjoying prosperity when he first acted as a friend to the Sheltons. Coming to East St. Louis after selling a lunchroom he ran in the Madison County village of Maryville, Newman had put his know-how to use in bootlegging and gambling, and had amassed a tidy pool of as much as $100,000, a small fortune at the time. As he liked to boast, "I always was a good hand at the dice, just like any of the boys will tell you. I learned most about shooting them in the army, and I can bean any old game. I think. Leastways, I don't remember ever losing a gamble at dice."

It was at these games that Newman became a fast pal with Fred (Freddie) Wooten, a Newman sidekick from then on, but no admirer of the Sheltons. Sitting in big crap games with crowds of supposedly "amateur shooters," Newman and Wooten each quickly recognized the other as a true expert with the tumbling ivories and, as a result, each refrained from wagering while the other was shooting.

Newman's cordial tie to the Sheltons began to slide after he and his wife kicked the brothers out of Newman's Arlington Hotel, forcing them to move to the Savoy Hotel right across Missouri Avenue. Although Newman continued to fraternize with the brothers, several incidents led him to suspect that the Sheltons had decided to do him in. First, in May 1925, Newman's home at 177 North Park Drive in East St. Louis was wrecked by the explosion of a dynamite bomb. Like many in their trade, the Sheltons were keen on explosives, and knew how to use them. Then, a month later, one of the Sheltons summoned Newman to the Shelton saloon in East St. Louis on a pretext that a man from Harrisburg was there selling good whiskey at rock-bottom prices.

"The man was Charlie Gordon," Newman related later. "As I talked to him he pulled his automatic and put it on me. I saw the frame right away, grabbed the gun and killed him."[6] A coroner's jury acquitted Newman of the killing on grounds of self defense. However, Newman, now absolutely convinced the Sheltons had him marked for death, ended his operation of the Arlington in the summer of 1925, packed up his belongings and took Bess and their children to Memphis, Tennessee.

For a year that would turn into an Armageddon for the gangs in southern Illinois, 1926 started off peaceably. Furthermore, when the first major violence of the year did erupt, the Sheltons and Birger were on the same side—albeit for the last time.

The time of the initial outburst in 1926 was April 13, primary election day in Illinois, and the fact that the flare-up took place in Herrin should not have been a great surprise. As a prelusion to that day, several local elections had shown the Klan was still more than just breathing. KKK members or supporters had done very well in the voting. Thus, by the day of the state primary, high anxiety was in the air again with Klansmen reinvigorated and the bootleggers suddenly back on the defensive.

The initial sparks on April 13 flew when Klansman and garage owner John Smith, a poll watcher, challenged some Catholic voters, prompting a fist fight and a retreat by Smith to his garage, the scene of the awful gunfight on August 30, 1924. Soon enough, cars filled with anti-Klansmen and gangsters were proceeding ominously through Herrin streets. The guns sticking out some of the windows were hard to miss. When one of the autos passed Smith's garage, he happened to be coming out of the place. A rider in the car, Monroe (Blackie) Armes, a Shelton gunman, took a shot at Smith, grazing him in the neck. With that, Herrin instantly turned into a shooting gallery, an uninterrupted cacophony of bullets from men in cars and on foot. Some of the bullets were aimed at the garage and its armed Klan defenders while others just zinged wildly through downtown Herrin. The utter chaos of the scene, with bullets flying every which way, would have been perfect for one of those spaghetti westerns so popular on the silver screen decades later.

Seemingly directing the attack on the garage like a general was Carl Shelton, who was seated in an auto by the European Hotel, not far from the garage. Witnesses said Bernie Shelton was among the shooters. The assault lasted fifteen minutes and left the garage ravaged, but, incredibly, nobody was hit. After the attackers drew back, twenty guardsmen arrived in Herrin from Carbondale and were immediately stationed by the garage. When the Shelton-led force started another advance on foot toward the garage, the gangsters came upon the soldiers, hastily ran back to their cars and drove away. But, they only went as far as the Masonic Temple, a polling place that day.

As the gangsters' cars screeched to a halt by the Temple, the occupants, brandishing their weapons, charged up to a group mainly comprised of Klansmen on the Temple lawn. Singling out KKKer John Ford, a special constable that day watching the polls, one of the gangsters fired point-blank at Ford, but missed him. This right away triggered a new wave of gunfire that lasted only a few moments, but, unlike the first burst in the day, produced deadly results. Four men died from wounds sustained on the lawn: an anti-Klansman from West Frankfort named Noble Weaver and three Klansmen, brothers Ben and Mack Sizemore and Harland Ford, a brother of John Ford. On the street, two more were shot to death in a Buick coupe, a car reportedly belonging to Birger. The pair were Orb Treadway, a close friend of Birger (who was present during the shooting), and Charlie Briggs, the Sheltonite who took part in the attack on Glenn Young in the Okaw bottoms and who was with Jack Skelcher when he was killed.

The election day riot, as many came to call it, marked the end of the Klan war in southern Illinois. Indicative of the windup was the rapid departure from Herrin after the last battle by John Smith, who'd obviously become a hated target of the bootleggers. Leaving for Florida, Smith admitted that he no longer had the stomach to "start a raid if they put a saloon next door to me." A grand jury investigating the election day tumult adjourned without returning an indictment. Not one witness would, if they could, name a living participant in either the attack on the garage or the shoot-out at the Masonic Temple. On July 15, 1926, the troops called to quell the latest violence finally departed.

However, any hopes for a recommencement of law and order in the area after the events of April 13 were short-lived.

Without the KKK to worry about, the bootleggers, gamblers and rest of the scofflaws had carte blanche to expand their enterprises in a wide belt through southern Illinois. The always tenuous alliance of the region's underworld ringleaders, to wit Carl Shelton and Birger, could not help but be strained as each was now free to cast greedy eyes on new territory. For Birger that meant, among other things, pursuits in parts of Williamson long staked out by the Sheltons. At the same time, the Sheltons felt that some of Birger's haunts were no longer off limits to them.

Both the Shelton and Birger camps were emboldened by the ever present gunmen that each had enlisted to aid in the war against the Klan. Going back to, or trying to enter, a normal life-style was difficult for many of these men who found staying available for murderous duty far preferable to holding a regular job. Some of these fellows had gotten their first taste of blood fighting the Klan. It was intoxicating. Even seen as glamorous in certain circles. For them to next turn on each other was really only a natural progression.

The legion of tough guys running around southern Illinois in those days left an indelible impression on anyone crossing their paths. One of those who never forgot them was the Duchess, a pioneeer woman reporter in Chicago who became a legend covering the Windy City's great people, bad guys and just about everybody in between. She was Virginia Marmaduke, a beautiful lady dubbed the Duchess shortly after her first appearance in the city room of the old *Chicago Sun* in 1943. Her journalistic coups included an ample number of good crime stories, and her reputation hardly suffered either when she was escorted around Chicago by matinee idol George Raft, himself often cast as a mobster.

Encounters with gangsters were nothing new for the Duchess. Prior to her days in Chicago, Carbondale-born Marmaduke, a railroad executive's daughter, worked thirteen years at the *Herrin Daily Journal*, an operation of the family of her then husband. Before her marriage failed and she left Herrin, her duties at the newspaper brought firsthand contact with many of the thugs still hanging around Herrin in the 1930s. Her reports of gambling activities especially ticked off Blackie Armes, one of the most dangerous of the punks, putting her on his enemies' list.

Later, in reporting crime in Chicago, the Duchess posed as a lonely lady seeking excitement during an investigation into illegal gambling near Fort Sheridan. Conning her way into a secret craps parlor, she'd no sooner got her foot in the door than she discovered, of all ironies, that the operator of the game was none other than Blackie Armes.

"I cased the joint with a quick sweep and then backed out and told the doorman I'd forgotten my betting money," Marmaduke explained afterward.[7]

Blackie Armes was a perfect example of the reckless gunmen still spoiling for action in southern Illinois after the Klan conflict. Most had hooked up with either the Sheltons or Birger during or after the KKK encounters. For a few, of course, there was no trouble switching back and forth between the Sheltons and Birger since the two gangs were supposed to be working hand in hand, even to the sharing of some profits. As numbers went, Birger always seemed to have a bigger crew than the Sheltons, although the Sheltons could count on East St. Louis gunmen to augment the brothers' local followers in southern Illinois, like Blackie Armes and the ever loyal Ray Walker and his brother, Harry.

Just what exactly did prompt the split between the Sheltons and Birger was difficult to sort out. Explanations were plentiful, and more than one were quite plausible. The easiest answer was that each began to covet the domain of the other. Or that fall outs among gangsters were simply commonplace.

Besides rum running, the Sheltons and Birger were in the slot machine business. Between them, they controlled almost every slot in southern Illinois. Some felt it was this enterprise that caused their split. Birger handled the money collected from the machines; he kept books and figured how much each should receive. In the summer of 1926, somebody told Carl that Birger was keeping two sets of books. Carl suspicioned Birger was holding out on him.

Birger had a different version. The final straw, he contended, came in August 1926 when Blackie Armes and several other Shelton gangsters robbed a Harrisburg businessman and Birger friend of a valuable diamond ring. This was a slap in the face of Birger, he supposedly felt, since he had sworn to protect the folks in Harrisburg, his hometown, from gang depredations.

Another widely circulated story blamed the Shelton-Birger split on a woman named Helen Holbrook, a buxom babe with money who resided in a mansion in Shawneetown and apparently lived for sexual liaisons with gangsters. Gary DeNeal, an astute biographer of Birger, related that an unconfirmed tale had it that Holbrook, while involved with Birger, had a "whing-ding" with Carl Shelton in St. Louis when Birger was in Florida buying liquor. "Jealous as usual," DeNeal wrote, "Birger learned of their frolic and saw red—Carl's blood, preferably." DeNeal added, "Helen probably had flings with both men, as well as with several others. Of the two, the soft-spoken Carl seems to have been her favorite, as indicated by the number of times their names are linked in print. Old timers in Gallatin County's High Knob region talk of their retreat there, now an abandoned farm."[8]

Just as the real reason for the Shelton-Birger feud remained anybody's guess, so was the time of its start. For sure, bodies started turning up with disturbing regularity in southern Illinois as the hot weather of 1926 was setting in. An infamous character known as Oklahoma Curly was bumped off in a roadhouse on the edge of Herrin. A Herrin teenager was shot as he took part in a roadhouse robbery. More significant, in late August Harry Walker and an ex-convict named Smith shot each other to death in a roadhouse in what may or may not have been a personal argument. Hard to escape notice was the inordinate interest in the coronor's inquest by the Sheltons and Blackie Armes. Walker's father had been chief of police in Herrin and Walker himself had been a cop in the town.

Local newspapers tried to play down these killings, holding out hope that they were isolated incidents. Urging readers to remain calm, one averred that roadhouse murders were expected because "where there is wine, women and pistols, there is liable to be a little friendly argument any time." However, the killings continued and any mystery about the cause soon went out the window.

Nobody harbored any remaining doubt about the onslaught of a gang war after the killing September 12, 1926, of William (Wild Bill) Holland, a Shelton adherent and reportedly even a bodyguard of Carl. Holland, along with another Shelton friend and that man's wife, were ambushed by Birger gunmen after they had left a Herrin roadhouse and entered their car. Later, speculation held that the Birger men cut loose because they believed Carl Shelton may have been with his friends.

The Sheltons didn't take the murder of Holland lightly. To them, Earl lamented, Holland was "a dear little chap," a young miner who was "the main support of his widowed mother and sister."

Besides adding men to their ranks, the brothers showed their ingenuity with a contrivance that may have had little or no precedence in American gang warfare. They sheared the top off a gasoline tank truck to come up with a vehicle providing excellent protection for their henchmen to shoot from. At the rear of the monstrosity they mounted a machine gun. Lumbering along the narrow roads of southern Illinois, it became known in gang parlance as "the tank," giving rise to a widespread rumor that the Shelton boys had gotten their hands on an army tank and were shooting up the countryside out of it. When the Birger gang discovered what the Sheltons had done, it converted a Reo truck owned by Charlie into an armor-clad vehicle by sheathing the sides with sheet metal. The Birgerites then undertook their own road patrols. If the two ponderous vehicles ever met in a clash like the Monitor and the Merrimack, there was no record of it.

However, the Sheltons certainly got in licks with their war wagon. The most remembered may have occurred October 4, when Art Newman came perilously close to becoming a corpse. Newman had returned to Illinois from Memphis, realizing he was just as vulnerable to the Sheltons down there as in East St. Louis. Back in Illinois, Newman aligned himself with Birger, a union that infuriated the Sheltons when they found out about it.

Thus, Newman was a marked man on October 4 when, after visiting Birger in Harrisburg, Newman and his wife met the Shelton "tank" on the road. The men in the truck blasted away. They missed Newman, but slightly wounded his wife. Newman quickly sped off, leaving the clumsy truck far behind.

Retribution for the attack was swift. As Newman recounted it, "One night we were just sitting around wishing we could get a shot at Carl, when someone came...and told us the Shelton boys were at this roadhouse. So we piled into the armored car and a sedan and paid the place a visit. We opened fire on the joint and shot hell out of it with four machine guns, plenty of rifles and shotguns." Then they kicked in the front door, only to find it deserted. "So," Newman added, "we carried out fifteen gallons of whiskey and wrecked the bar."[9]

Tit for tat being the rule, the Sheltons were thought to have evened the score late in October. Or so it appeared. The bullet-riddled body of Birger follower William (High Pockets) McQuay was found on a lonely road between Herrin and Johnston City, and then, in another grisly find, the body of a murder victim laying in a stream near Equality turned out to be Ward (Casey) Jones, a bartender at Birger's headquarters, a rustic retreat named Shady Rest. Jones' corpse was discovered by a boy who saw a hand protruding from the water. Subsequently, in 1927, two of Birger's own men, Ural Gowan and Rado Millich, were found guilty of the murder of Jones, which evidently took place at Shady Rest. Gowan went to prison, and Millich was hanged for the crime. While the killing of McQuay was not solved, information surfacing later indicated that he, too, had been bumped off by several of his fellow Birger gang members. Shelton hands turned out to be clean on McQuay and Jones.

The next killings of note came on the night of November 6, a Saturday, adding two more to the skyrocketing body count. Although blame for the deaths was never fixed, one of the deceased, Mayor Jeff Stone of Colp, was known to be in disfavor with the Sheltons. Stone was gunned down, and James Keith, a policeman in Colp, a small coal mining burg near Herrin, was wounded when the pair responded to a report of a fracas at the Pete Salmo roadhouse by Colp. Upon arriving, the two were greeted by a number of gunmen, who quickly disarmed Keith. Then, the law officer later related, he heard "a terrific roar.

"Everybody seemed to be shooting. I heard Stone moan once and fall. Then I turned and ran for the hard road. They fired several times after me. One bullet hit my hand and knocked me sprawling, but I got up and kept on going."

What Keith didn't know, at the time, was that either just before or right after the fatal shooting of Stone the gunmen had machine-gunned to death by the roadhouse a dubious gambler named John Milroy. The reason for his elimination remained unclear, but it was pointed out that earlier in the year, at about the same spot, Stone had shot and killed John Freeman, a former police chief of Colp and ally of the Shelton gang.

Four days after Stone's murder, a homemade bomb was thrown from a car at the barbecue stand along the road at Shady Rest. It exploded but missed its target. Two days later, November 12, was one for the books. First, several homes in West City linked to the Sheltons were ventilated by machine gun bullets fired by Birger men. Later in the day, an unheard-of twist in gang feuding unfolded. Dreamed up by the Shelton side, it was probably another first in the history of crime in the United States. More on it coming up.

Murder and terrorism were like runaway freight trains in the bottom region of Illinois in the days before Thanksgiving of 1926. Law and order, where the feuding gangsters were concerned, had taken another hiatus. The

Shelton and Birger gangs were the law in Williamson County and the surrounding area, and either outfit, if it so pleased, could take control of any number of communities—subject only to interference by the other gang.

Headlines said it all. "Law of the Gun Only One Known in Williamson," blared the *Post-Dispatch*. Who could take issue? The gangsters virtually ignored officers of the law. In the manner of Capone and his compatriots in Chicago, the Sheltons and Birger did not feel bound by the rules governing ordinary folks. When the Sheltons or Birger or their men drove into towns, police disappeared or stood by silently, afraid to make any move that might touch off the gangsters. The small-town cops usually were outnumbered by the mobsters anyway, and they also came up short against the firepower and high-octane autos of the gangs.

No wonder that Mayor Marshall D. McCormack of Herrin, in despair, recommended in an open letter to Governor Small the imposition of martial law in Williamson County as the only means of coping with the gang war.

McCormack was a man in a precarious position, not just because Herrin was often at the center of the hostilities but also as a result of his own background. McCormack had been a Klan raider under Young, but repudiated the KKK and rode into office on a wave of anti-Klan sentiment. This won him the temporary friendship of the Sheltons, which ended when he bucked their plan to take control of all Herrin saloons and roadhouses. Consequently, as an enemy of both the Sheltons and the old KKK crowd, McCormack could only expect protection from Birger, whose base was more than twenty miles away.

"I have seen," McCormack wrote the governor, "the most prosperous counties in the State of Illinois—Williamson, Franklin, Saline and Jackson—infested with gangs, armed with every means of warfare that human ingenuity can devise, including machine guns, hand grenades, armored trucks, tear gas...."

The gangs, said the mayor, "have beaten up hundreds of people and have killed a great number, for which no arrests have been made, and are now going about these counties and as far north as East St. Louis boasting of the number they have killed and of those that are yet to be 'bumped off.' Not only that, but they have denied the people of these counties the right to travel the public highways of the great State of Illinois unmolested."

Stating that no sheriff, however well-meaning, could "relieve the condition," McCormack added that prosecution also was impossible "as no citizen will produce evidence while these gangs are at large for fear of their own lives being taken, and no prosecuting attorney could live who attempted it." Thus, since nobody believed that civil authorities "can ever meet the existing conditions," McCormack concluded that the setting up of a military court, where "evidence may be submitted without witnesses being intimidated," was the only recourse for administering justice.[10]

The governor nixed McCormack's idea. The National Guard's duties did not include the maintenance of law and order unless civil agencies had collapsed, and Small said he had not seen that occur in southern Illinois. Pointing out that the state already had spent in the last few years a large amount of "the people's money" trying to maintain law and order in the region, the governor had the following to say. "The murders that happen there would have happened whether the State Militia was present or not, and would be just the same as having militia in Chicago to stop murders which happen there."[11]

In all honesty, not many local officials in southern Illinois would have dared to speak out as McCormack did, fearing that something said in public or to the press about the lawlessness only might have offended the gangsters. Sometimes reporters' best sources in covering the goings-on were the gangsters themselves, especially Birger, who could be quite loquacious. Actually, part of the Shelton-Birger battle was carried out in words, over the telephone as well as in newspapers.

Talking big, whether in earnest or to just bluff or intimidate, was part of the way both Birger and Carl Shelton operated. Each spoke openly during the feud of the dire consequences facing the other and his followers. Now and then, one of the leaders or gang members would phone one of his counterparts on the other side, trade invectives and challenge the other to show up for a fight to the finish.

"I'm ready to argue the question out with them at any time," Birger commented to a scribe from the *Post-Dispatch*. "My boys would be tickled pink to have it out on the open road."

Replied Earl Shelton, "We aren't given to boasting about what great warriors we are, like Birger, who is not a warrior but a coward. He's got himself all hemmed in with armor and machine guns, and whenever you see a man hiding behind a fortress (Shady Rest), that means he is afraid to come out in the open. He talks with his big mouth about wanting to meet us on the highway. If we didn't know he was only blowing, we might get excited and go up there and see what it's all about."[12]

The Sheltons—at least during that particularly frenzied juncture in their lives—did not court reporters and were coy about being quoted unless cornered by writers trying to track the brothers' escapades. Birger, on the other hand, saw the value of public relations, and was a good practitioner. Right down to inviting a photographer out to Shady Rest to take pictures of him and his gang. Sitting atop a car, decked out in riding breeches, puttees and bulletproof vest, Birger with his boys, weapons in hand, posed proudly. In the background was the prominent cabin known as Shady Rest.

Birger also took the unusual step for a mobster of having published in a newspaper, Harrisburg's *Daily Register*, a page-one article seeking to assure residents of Harrisburg that the minds of people "not members of the two factions may rest at ease...." No one "will be harmed in Harrisburg," proclaimed Birger, because the gangster would not tolerate crime in the city that was his home "and where he is educating his children."

Back to Shady Rest. Birger had one on the Sheltons there. Permanent headquarters for the brothers remained East St. Louis, where Carl also moved into a home, but they never showcased their base of operations. Functioning like nomads, they were continually in and out of the city anyway. But Shady Rest was famous, the best known gangster hangout in the state outside of Chicago. For a while, after Birger built it in 1925, Shady Rest had many of the amenities of a backwoods resort. Located in a clearing in a grove of trees on the north side of Route 13 between Harrisburg and Marion, east of Crab Orchard, the cabin sat well back from the road. The barbecue stand along the highway at the entrance to the property catered to passersby; motorists could eat, gas up and drink either soda or harder stuff at the eatery. The cabin was the lair of Birger and his men, and he was justifiably proud of it. The log structure had stone fireplaces, deer heads and antlers reminiscent of a state park lodge, as well as the lastest conveniences (including electric lights supplied by a small power plant on the property). Back of the cabin was a building for cockfights and dogfights.

Before the gang war intervened, Shady Rest attracted a wide variety of visitors, including gamblers from near and far and bootleggers, the Sheltons included. In running liquor from Florida to East St. Louis, they'd lay over at Shady Rest in order to make the final leg of the journey after sunset. Once the feud with the Sheltons erupted, the cabin was easily converted into a fortress, a veritable arsenal with a basement in which to take safe refuge.

As the gang war intensified, and Shady Rest was closed to most outsiders, the climate inside Birger's headquarters became increasingly paranoid as Birger and Newman, who'd become his right-hand man, plotted ways to eliminate the Sheltons, especially Carl. The effort was so highly concentrated, according to the *Post-Dispatch*, that "the Sheltons were numbered when murder plots were discussed over the telephone." Said the paper, "Carl, as brains of the gang, was known as Number One. Earl was Number Two, and Bernie was Number Three."[13]

None of the schemes worked. Employing an old girlfriend of Carl as bait, Newman and other Birger men attempted to lure Carl to the Wies Hotel in East St. Louis. There, they lay in wait with machine guns. But Carl was a no-show. The woman told her mother of the scheme, and the mother, who was fond of Carl, warned him of the plot.

Another attempt to kill a Shelton, also in East St. Louis, might have been a comedy if not for its dire purpose. The setting was St. Mary's Hospital and the target was Earl, ill in the hospital with malaria. Learning that Earl was bedridden, the unfailingly imaginative Newman schemed to slip into the hospital and, in his words, "cut that fathead's throat before he could get out of bed."

To pull off the deed, Newman and his shadow, Freddie Wooten, put on women's clothes, reasoning that would make them less conspicuous as they explored the hospital in search of Earl's room. Newman, always one to put on the dog, draped himself in a pricey Russian mink fur cape. Wooten, in a Hudson seal coat and silk dress, was even more dolled up. Hidden under Newman's wrap was one very sharp hunting knife.

Finding Earl's room, they were about to enter it when Earl's wife and another woman walked out. Thinking that the pair might be going to meet Carl, a bigger prize than Earl, Newman and Wooten did a quick about-face and trailed the two real women. However, the tracking led the gangsters only to a dead end.

Newman and his buddy intended to again dress in drag the following day and return to St. Mary's, but they got tied up in questioning by police. By the time another opportunity arose for them to get back to the hospital, Earl was out of the place.

7

High Noon at Quincy

His name was Elmer Kane, but that didn't come out until later. On November 12, 1926, he was known only as the unidentified flyer who entered aviation history on the dark side by piloting the plane from which bombs were dropped on Birger's Shady Rest. Not just a likely first in gang warfare, Kane's sortie may have been the initial civilian bombing raid in the United States.

Nobody was hurt, and damage was nil. Still, the very fact that the bombing even happened symbolized the extraordinary lengths of the Shelton-Birger battle. It also was another illustration of the quick manner in which folks were sucked into the fray—some against their will and others quite willingly, eager to be part of the excitement of it all.

The improbable tale of Kane's involvement in the fight began when the young Iowan and another aviator, Henry Mundale, were barnstorming through Illinois in two planes, a not uncommon pursuit for daring young men in flying machines in the Roaring Twenties. In landing at Benton November 11 after a flight from Sparta, Kane's plane—described as a two-seat Curtiss training model of World War I vintage—was slightly damaged. While he was repairing the craft, according to Kane's later confession, three men who turned out to be Shelton gang members approached him and Mundale, drove them into Benton for gasoline and then took them to the West City home of Joe Adams, the rotund mayor of the village on the west side of Benton and a close ally of the Sheltons. There, Kane and Mundale were greeted by a group of men that included, not only Adams, but also Carl and Bernie Shelton. In no time at all, the aviators were asked to fly over Shady Rest and bomb it.

The flyers agreed to do it, they later explained, out of fear for their lives if they refused. Under the watchful eye of the gangsters, Kane and Mundale spent the night in the house of Gus Adams, located next to the home of his brother, Mayor Joe. It was an eventful night. First off, the aviators observed the making of the bombs, crude concoctions put together by wrapping copper wire around sticks of dynamite and then attaching bottles assumably filled with nitroglycerin. Next, to further their initiation into the Shelton-Birger feud, the airmen were awakened in the early morning hours by machine gun bullets smashing through Gus Adams' house, a gift from Birger gunmen cruising by the front of the place. Kane and Mundale needed no prodding from their gangster hosts to hit the floor and kiss it hard. Before leaving the neighborhood, Birger's boys also strafed the home of Mrs. Mary Loughran, an elderly widow whose house was being utilized by Shelton men. Carl and Bernie said afterward they were elsewhere when the bullets started flying around the Adams enclave.

Later in the day, although the hour was more civil, the aviators must have thought they were under siege again. Only this time, no bullets filled the air. And the visitors were not Birger thugs but postal inspectors and other federal and Franklin County authorities. Surrounding the homes of the Adams brothers, the officials demanded the surrender of both Carl and Bernie, who now were present, on charges of complicity in the January 27, 1925, robbery of a postal messenger at Collinsville. Not around but also charged with the crime in federal indictments was Earl Shelton, who'd be taken into custody shortly at a home maintained at Fairmont City by Bernie.

Carl was in Joe Adams' house when the arresting officers appeared. Unarmed, he came out on the front porch and demanded to see credentials, explaining that he wasn't going to fall for any trick by Birger. After satisfying himself that the officers were legit, Carl was heard by the aviators to say, "I'm willing to go with you, but if you're going to take me to Saline County, you might as well shoot me, as that's all I'll get down there." Bernie was in the home of Gus Adams, and armed. But he did not resist arrest. Kane himself almost got arrested when the feds mistook him at first for a fugitive gangster.

Later, Kane said that Joe Adams and the Sheltons had agreed to give the two aviators $1,000 and a car for bombing Shady Rest. After Carl and Bernie were carted off by the arresting officers, Kane was handed the $1,000 in cash by Joe Adams, the flyer said. The automobile was delivered to Mundale.

Following the receipt of the $1,000, Kane and Mundale were driven to the field where Kane's plane, popularly known as a "Jenny," was sitting. They found it fueled and guarded by Shelton men. As it happened, Mundale did not participate in the raid, since the plane could not hold more than Kane, the bombs and a Shelton "bomber." By most indications, the Sheltonite who went up in the plane was Ray Walker (although some versions had Blackie Armes claiming to have made the flight).

Taking off, the plane soon was circling low over Shady Rest. The first of three bombs tossed out of the aircraft landed near the roadhouse, but failed to explode. Seven or eight Birger gangsters, having emerged out of the cabin, fired at the plane with rifles and machine guns. The plane circled around again, and the Shelton agent dropped the other two bombs. One was another dud. The second did explode, but accounts differed as to where it hit. One version had it blowing up in woods near Shady Rest, setting off a small fire. Another story contended that the bomb landed and went off by the cockfighting structure, killing an eagle and a bulldog. The plane itself never was hit by the gunfire coming up from the ground.

After encircling the Birger camp one more time, Kane piloted his plane to DuQuoin, where he dropped off the Shelton bombardier. Kane then flew to join Mundale at another small airfield, where Mundale was waiting with the barnstormers' other plane and their newly acquired auto. The pair perhaps felt they were finished with the matter at that point, but no such luck.

In line with the way things were going for them, the car they received for the air raid was hot. Although the aviators denied knowing it, the auto was the property of Louis Castiglioni, a former Herrin resident living in St. Louis. The vehicle had been stolen from in front of a movie theater in Herrin nine days before the bombing. When the car was recovered by authorities in February 1927 in Cedar Falls, Iowa, the arrests of Kane and

Mundale followed. Kane contended that Joe Adams had given him a bill of sale with the car, but that the flyers lost it. Kane tried to get an Iowa license plate for the auto, but struck out because he couldn't prove the car was his. Kane did later admit to forging a bill of sale purporting to show he had purchased the vehicle from a garage in Morrison, Illinois.

Later in 1927, the aviators found themselves in a place familiar to many touched by the Shelton saga, federal court at Danville. There, a jury found Kane and Mundale guilty of interstate transportation of a stolen auto. Each was sentenced by United States District Judge Lindley to sixty days in jail and fined $100.

After the eventful day of November 12, 1926, the Sheltons appeared to be making good on their publicly stated intention to untangle themselves from the war with Birger in southern Illinois. True, Carl, Bernie and Earl were suddenly behind bars, facing a trial in early 1927 for allegedly pulling off the Collinsville mail robbery—a charge they stubbornly denied. Beyond that, though, the gang battle was taking a heavy toll, physically as well as financially, on both the Shelton and Birger factions. The fighting could not help but interrupt the liquor running. And with each side shooting up and wrecking the roadhouses belonging to the other, business was hardly good. Scared to death patrons no longer were coming through the doors.

"There is too much shooting around there," Earl told a reporter, "and we invariably get the blame for all of it. Birger can have the war all to himself." Earl went even further in this particular conversation, contending to the reporter that neither he nor his brothers had killed any Birger men and that, in truth, he and his brothers did not even have a "gang."

"We have friends in Williamson County, who are commonly referred to as our gang," said Earl. "We are not robbers or gunmen, but we have never run away from trouble. We don't know if any of our friends are in the fight against Birger, but if they are they will take care of themselves. We are out of it."[1] Whether Earl related this to the reporter with a straight face the writer did not reveal.

Earl and his brothers were hardly exaggerating, though, when they quickly placed the blame for their indictment on the mail robbery charge at the feet of Birger and Newman. Birger had declared openly to anyone within earshot that the brothers had committed the heist, and it took the

Sheltons no time at all to learn that Newman had appeared before a federal grand jury at Springfield just before the indictment of the Sheltons was voted. Newman made no bones about it, saying that "if anyone wants to know, tell them that I presented the evidence that caused the indictment (of the Sheltons) and that I will be the star witness for the government at the trial." Nevertheless, ratting to the feds, and lying on top of it, was unforgivable in the Sheltons' eyes, a violation of gang warfare ethics under even the most vicious circumstances.

Not that the Sheltons themselves were above this approach. Earl convinced federal agents to take seriously his insistence that Birger ran narcotics. He made sure authorities also got word that Birger had "two hot Lincolns" in his possession. And so it went, back and forth. Only the Collinsville mail robbery charge stuck.

The jailing of Carl, Bernie and Earl on the federal indictment took the brothers out of circulation for a while, at least Bernie and Earl. A little under a month after his arrest, Carl was released from the Peoria jail where he was being held after six sureties scheduled property worth more than $120,000 to secure their signatures on his $60,000 bond. With Carl at liberty, fear of renewed bloodshed spread rapidly through southern Illinois. The apprehension was well founded, but Carl wasn't around for it. If he had been, the life of one of his most staunch followers, Joe Adams, might have been saved.

While Carl was cooling his heels in the clink, Birger moved to make good on his threat to eliminate the mayor who'd let his town, West City, become a Shelton refuge. A week after the arrest of Carl, a dynamite bomb was tossed from a passing car toward Adams' home. Its explosion did considerable damage to the structure, but neither Adams, his wife Beulah or brother, all in the house at the time, was injured.

Some three weeks later, Birger's next thrust at Adams was carried out, with a deadly result. On December 12, a Sunday, one month to the day after the air raid on Shady Rest, two young men came to the front door of Adams' home and told Beulah Adams, who answered their knock, that they had a note for her husband from Carl Shelton. Summoned by his wife, the mayor came to the door and was handed the message.

"Friend Joe," the note said, "If you can use these boys please do it. They are broke and need work. I know their father." It was signed "C.S."

As Adams read the message, the young visitors drew pistols, pumped bullets into the mayor's corpulent body and ran off to a car parked nearby. Before dying less than an hour later, Adams whispered to Beulah that he didn't recognize either of his assailants. But his wife harbored no doubt of the person behind the murder. She placed the blame at the coroner's inquest on Birger, claiming he made threatening calls to the Adams house repeatedly in previous days, once even urging her to get more insurance on her husband's life because she was going to "need it."

It was hard to find anybody who didn't think Birger orchestrated the murder, even though he denied it. "I don't know who killed Adams," Birger told Hearst's *International News Service*, "but I'm certainly glad he was killed. Everyone comes to me to ask who did this and that. What am I—a detective force for southern Illinois? What the hell does anyone care who killed Adams?" Nevertheless, as events were to prove, the shooting of the mayor finally would be Birger's undoing.

To the surprise of more than a few, the killing of Adams and even his wake failed to draw Carl Shelton back to southern Illinois. But then, he and his brothers suddenly seemed to be on the ropes in the war with Birger. Troubles beyond the mail robbery charge were mounting for Carl, he soon discovered after getting out of jail.

Seeking to lay low after his release from the pokey, Carl decided St. Louis would be a safe haven, a place for him to escape the limelight until the mail robbery trial. He figured wrong. After only a few days in the city, he was arrested at the north side home of a relative, scolded by police and "shown up" to detectives during the day in the "shadow box" at police headquarters. Then the cops turned him over to Department of Justice officers after Carl on a charge of transporting a stolen automobile. When he was released from their custody on $5,000 bond, he was immediately arrested again for questioning by the United States Secret Service in a counterfeiting investigation, a detention that landed him in a police cell for the night. All of this in one day.

Carl's intended respite in St. Louis became a hot item in the press. "A crowded day," the *Post-Dispatch* took note, "even for a man who has been in the thick of the Williamson County fighting of the past three years. But if it discouraged the dark-eyed Shelton, he failed to show it. Even when he was arrested unexpectedly...he took the new reverse cheerfully and was led to his cell at headquarters, still smiling quietly."[2]

The feds didn't retain Shelton long. In the auto episode, he was charged with transporting over a state line a Cadillac sedan stolen in July 1924 from St. Louisan John Muckerman, president of the Polar Wave Ice and Fuel Co. The car, found abandoned near the Madison County village of Worden a month after it was taken, supposedly was to be used in a stickup. The case, thought to be based on a tip to federal officers from Birger and Newman, fizzled out.

So did the counterfeit case as far as Carl's alleged role was concerned. What it came down to was that Stephen A. Connell, agent in charge of the Secret Service office in St. Louis, wanted to talk to Shelton about the operation of a counterfeiting ring putting out worthless $20 bills. Connell's agents had learned that one of the notes had been passed on a merchant in the town of Madison by a man who drove away in a car. A girl chanced to remember the license number of the auto, which turned out to have been issued to Carl. But, further inquiry showed that on the day the man passed the phony bill, Shelton still was in jail in Peoria. So, Carl got off the hook in the counterfeit scheme, but Connell still tried to press him for information of possible value to the investigation. What the gangster may or may not have known, and what Connell might have squeezed out of Carl, was not disclosed at the time. The arrest of a Shelton "cousin" the following month in Detroit on a counterfeiting charge would add fuel to speculation that Carl may not have been an innocent in the bogus bill scam. The individual erroneously dubbed a Shelton "cousin" by the press was in reality Charles Bryan (Black Charlie) Harris, then a Shelton gang member from Wayne County.

All in all, Carl found St. Louis no more hospitable than in the previous decade when the city's cops chastened him, Earl and Bernie as unwanted troublemakers. This time, the St. Louis police chief himself, Joseph Gerk, saw to Carl's departure.

"Carl," Gerk said when Shelton was hauled before him, "I don't know what the trouble is between you fellows. I do know this. St. Louis isn't big enough for you and the police force."

"I guess I'll have to go, Chief, that's all," replied Shelton.

"I know you will," Gerk shot back. "I'm telling my men to lock you up every time they find you. We have nothing against you personally, you understand, but we don't want your gang scrap brought over here. We've got troubles enough of our own."

Carl still attempted to explain to Gerk that one reason for him staying in St. Louis was to have "a sure-fire alibi" in view of a tip he'd received that "the Birger gang is going to try to frame me on some kind of an East Side job." Added Carl, "I feel so safe here."

"Maybe you do," Gerk rejoined. "But you can't stay."

"All right, Chief." With that Shelton rose and picked up his hat. "All right, I'll go." As he passed through the door, witnesses swore, big bad Carl wiped his eyes with a bandanna handkerchief.[3] Tears also were said to have welled in his eyes when he was paraded before detectives on the force wanting to see what the now famous gangster looked like in person. When word of these incidents leaked out to the street, some in the underworld tried to tag Carl as a crybaby. Many refused to believe it. There'd be more tear shedding by Carl in the near future, though, and with good reason.

The dawn of 1927 arrived with no sunshine in the forecast for the Shelton boys. The unrequited murder of Joe Adams was only one of the things taken by observers to mean that the Shelton boys had indeed ceded the southern Illinois battlefield to the Birger gang. The brothers, after all, had to be preoccupied with the mail robbery trial, set to begin January 31 in a federal courtroom in Springfield. They certainly could find no solace in the fact they were to be tried before United States District Judge Louis FitzHenry, a tough jurist with no sympathy for gangsters, even to the point of sending convicted hoodlums to prison without allowing them appeal bonds.

Back on Birger, the Sheltons—while certainly not openly waving a white flag in his direction—were of an opinion that their enemy had gone over the edge, was no longer capable of submerging paranoiac killer tendencies even in his own world. For a man who seemed to be riding high, the domain of Birger truly was being beset by strange happenings. In the final weeks of 1926, violence in the form of home dynamiting and gun battles erupted in Harrisburg, which supposedly was under the benevolent protectorate of its best known resident, Birger. Blame for the disorder was quickly laid at the feet of Shelton adherents, but the brothers denied any involvement.

Then, early on the cold morning of January 9, 1927, Shady Rest was mysteriously destroyed by explosions and fire. The bodies of four Birger associates were found in the conflagration, which was widely attributed at first to the Shelton gang, a reasonable guess since the brothers had tried to destroy the place from the air. Birger declared loudly that he'd make the Sheltons pay for the destruction of his headquarters. No surprise there either.

Yet, in the days to follow, a different picture gradually emerged. Not because the Sheltons denied responsibility for the destruction of Shady Rest, which was anticipated. More important, it became known that Birger and his playmates had removed their valuable possessions and huge store of weapons from Shady Rest several days before it was burned. And it was Birger and his cronies and not Shelton men who were spotted around Shady Rest before the fire. Too, any dime store detective could surmise that it was Birger, not the Sheltons, who had the most to fear from the individuals whose charred bodies were found in the remains of Shady Rest. During the Christmas holidays, Birger had been charged with the murder of Joe Adams. And although he was not in custody, he had to be eyeing with suspicion persons capable of linking him to the killing in event the charge against him was pressed.

It was also more than interesting that one of the dead at Shady Rest turned out to be Elmo Thomasson, who'd be fingered as one of the two young murderers (the other was his brother Harry) of Adams. And another corpse would be that of Steve George, the gold-toothed, murderous caretaker at Shady Rest who was all too aware of Birger's misdeeds and dumb enough to be tricked into talking. And the other two victims, George's wife, Lena, and Bert Owens, a Birger hanger-on, had either heard or seen enough to pose a threat to Birger.

After all was said and done, little doubt remained that Birger, along with Newman and one or two others, torched Shady Rest. But, the placement of blame was still pretty much a matter of conjecture in the days leading up to the Sheltons' trial. The same was true for the details surrounding the disappearance of state policeman Lory Price and his wife a week and a half after the destruction of Shady Rest. Considering that he was a highway patrolman, Price had maintained an unusually close relationship to Birger, and had been privy to many of Birger's nastier doings. Just like those found dead at Shady Rest.

Nevertheless, the fate of Price and his wife remained a question mark as the day approached for the opening of the Shelton trial. On January 25, a few days before the start of the trial, FitzHenry signed an order shifting the site of the proceeding from the federal courtroom at Springfield to the United States Courthouse in the western Illinois city of Quincy. The location change was made, according to the order, "upon agreement of counsel and in furtherance of public justice." In reality, the Quincy facility was more conducive to the extra safety precautions necessitated by the trial, especially since Birger and Newman were lined up as key witnesses against the Sheltons.

The potential for violence was underscored by Carl Shelton himself in a pretrial affidavit filed in support of a motion for a bill of particulars. Pointing out that Birger and Newman "have repeatedly and publicly expressed and described themselves as willing to do anything to 'get the Sheltons' in this case," Carl noted that Birger had "publicly announced in the press" his intention to kill him.

Cited by Shelton was an *International News Service* story that ran December 31, 1926, and reported that Sheriff Leigh Turner of Saline County had refused to say when he would serve a Franklin County warrant charging Birger with complicity in the murder of Mayor Adams. The story went on to quote Birger as saying that he was "not thinking of surrendering" on the warrant because he was "busy looking for Carl Shelton, rival gangster, whom, he (Birger) said, he was going to kill by midnight tonight and collect a $500 bet."[4] With preliminaries of this nature, it was understandable that the attention of an always-hungry-for-gangster-news public was focused so squarely on Quincy and a long-awaited direct showdown between the Sheltons and Birger, even if it was only in a courtroom.

The crime involved in the case had been labeled the "great Collinsville mail robbery" by Karl Monroe of the *Collinsville Herald*, and was a little more than two years old when the trial started. Accounts made it clear that the January 27, 1925, heist was the excitement of the day in Collinsville. At about eight o'clock in the morning, in keeping with his routine, James Mathias, a mail messenger in his mid-sixties, had picked up pouches from the Pennsylvania depot at the foot of Reed Avenue and headed for the Post Office in a Ford mail truck.[5] After turning off Church Street onto Chestnut, Mathias was forced to the curb by a blue Buick with side curtains. Two armed men leaped onto the Ford's running board and ordered Mathias to "put his hands up and his head down." The bandits rooted among the pouches, grabbed several and hustled back to their waiting car. The vehicle headed toward Main Street half a block away, tore down Main at a high rate of speed and then took the Caseyville Road in the direction of East St. Louis.

One of the bags snatched by the robbers contained $15,000 in currency being shipped from the Federal Reserve Bank of St. Louis to the State Bank of Collinsville to cover the payroll of the Lumaghi Mine at Collinsville.

In the course of the trial, Mathias and several other persons, including an assistant bank cashier near the mail truck when it was robbed and a baker who observed the Buick, said they could not identify the Shelton brothers as the bandits. However, the impact of their words was to be lessened by the dramatic testimony of Birger and Newman and by the contention of another witness, a Birger adherent named Harvey Dungey.

Besides giving great play to the testimony of Birger and Newman, reporters covering the trial sought to track every movement of the pair at Quincy, alert to the possibility of an outbreak of violence at any moment. It looked like they had a good story right at the start, not long after Birger and Newman slipped into Quincy amid utmost secrecy, intending to sleep the night before testifying at a small hotel under an elaborate guard. Birger rode to Quincy on a train from St. Louis. Newman came by automobile.

So great was the tension that, shortly after Newman's arrival, the loud backfiring of a car as Newman was being escorted down the street by postal inspectors led to a story that an attempt had been made to assassinate him. According to an *International News Service* flash, "two shots...were fired (at Newman) from a building across the street. The attempt to get rid of the star witness failed only because of the poor marksmanship of the would-be assassin."

Even Birger's first public sighting on the morning after his arrival was given big play by reporters. After Birger was "observed entering a small restaurant a block from the Federal Building," related one writer, "he had coffee and doughnuts at the counter, while two St. Louis detectives guarded the door." After breakfast, it was duly noted, Birger and his party "hurried to the Federal Building, pushed through the crowd at the door, and disappeared in the upper regions of the building."

Elaborate precautions were taken against attacks on any of the principals in the case, as demonstrated by the twenty-five deputy marshals scattered throughout the Federal Building. The only stairway was guarded by deputies who searched every person seeking to reach the courtroom. Only a handful of the many individuals wishing to view the proceedings made it into the courtroom. Most of the would-be spectators were turned away.

The trial reached its theatrical peak on February 1, the day of the greatest angst for the Sheltons. The government climaxed its case against the brotherly trio that day with three hours of testimony by Newman and a twenty-minute visit to the witness stand by Birger. Of the government's thirty or so witnesses, Newman and Birger gave the only direct testimony against the Sheltons, with Newman's recitation judged the most injurious to the defendants. By holding off on the appearance of Newman and Birger, United States Attorney Walter M. Provine displayed a penchant for dramatic effect.

When the time arrived for Newman to take the stand, postal inspectors and deputy marshals rose and hurriedly left the courtroom. They headed up to the third floor where Newman and Birger, under heavy guard, were sitting in an office. Within moments, the escorts surrounded Newman as he descended the stairway, passed through various outer rooms behind the courtroom in order to avoid the main corridor and came to a special door to the courtroom that had been cut behind the witness chair. Entering the hushed courtroom alone, holding a partially burned cigar, Newman took his seat. The press observed that the hoodlum's slight figure was meticulously clothed in a neat blue serge suit, white shirt, black and white tie and light tan oxfords, and that his black hair was parted precisely in the middle and slicked down.

Crossing his legs and clasping his hands over a knee, the cocky gangster turned from the jury and gazed at the Sheltons, who answered his stare as their lawyers conversed with Judge FitzHenry. After questioning started, Newman was asked to face the jury. However, during his testimony, he often turned toward the Sheltons and sent a smile of self-gratification in their direction when, in his mind, he had made a strong point against them. Each time, they grinned defiantly back at him.

In summary, Newman testified that Carl Shelton and his brothers had discussed with him their intent to rob a mail messenger at Collinsville;

that Carl had tried unsuccessfully to borrow Newman's Lincoln sedan to use in the robbery; and that, after the holdup, Newman helped the Sheltons in their attempt to establish an alibi in event the brothers were charged with the crime. At that juncture, Newman was still on friendly terms with the Sheltons.

Initially, Newman testified, Carl Shelton "came to me and asked if I wanted to get in on a good thing. I told him 'sure.' But when he told me it was a mail robbery, I backed out. I reminded him what happened to the Egan (gang) boys, who all got tucked away for quite a while for just that kind of a job. He said there was nothing to worry about—that everything was 'fixed.'" After he repeatedly rebuffed the brothers' attempts to enlist him for the heist, Newman said, talk about it died down.

Newman continued, "I heard nothing more about it until that morning—the morning of January 27, 1925. Carl called me up on the phone—I think it was about nine o'clock. He asked me if I would drive him and his brothers to Herrin for Ora Thomas' funeral. He said he and his brothers were downtown and would wait for me—that was in East St. Louis, where I live. I told him I was tired and that he would get into trouble anyway going to Herrin. Then he said, 'Well, we pulled that Collinsville job this morning, and we got to have an alibi. It's up to you to give us one.'"

Newman went on to relate that he did, in fact, drive to southern Illinois with Carl and Earl Shelton to try to make the Thomas funeral, but he stated that they arrived too late for it. After returning later in the day with the Sheltons to East St. Louis, Newman said he paid an unexpected late night visit to their saloon and stumbled on the brothers and their associate Charlie Briggs counting money in four or five bundles on a card table. "When I came in," related Newman, "Carl said, 'I'll see you later, Art.' I figured I wasn't wanted and left." (Briggs, alleged to have aided the Sheltons in the mail robbery, was among those later shot to death in the election day gunfight April 13, 1926, in Herrin.)

With each contention in his testimony, intended to build an airtight case against the Sheltons, Newman's voice exuded sarcasm when he mentioned their names. And there were few aspects of the case about which Newman didn't claim to have details, even including the auto used in the robbery. After he said no to the borrowing of his Lincoln for the holdup, Newman contended Carl Shelton told him he had "picked up" a stolen Buick touring car for $50. Other testimony in the trial revealed that the Buick used in the robbery, and abandoned in East St. Louis two days after the crime, had been stolen from St. Louis architect Frank Cann December 12, 1924.

The most anticipated moment of the trial was the meeting of Birger and the Sheltons in the courtroom. When Birger, the next to last government witness, was called, he'd already been escorted from the third floor office where he had been secluded to the district clerk's office closer to the courtroom. Stepping into the courtroom through the specially built door, Birger found himself just a few feet away from his arch enemies. He smiled at others in the room, and then looked straight at Carl Shelton.

"How are you, Mr. Carl Shelton?" Birger asked in a voice heard only by those close at hand.

With that, Birger took his seat. Not the Birger frequently observed back home in a soldierly outfit of khaki trousers, leather puttees and holster-held revolver. Quite the opposite, the Birger on this occasion was dressed smartly in a dark gray suit and light blue shirt with brown cravat. As he talked, his dark eyes flashed against his "sallow brown skin."

Birger wasted little time zeroing in on Carl Shelton when he was asked if he'd had any conversation with the defendants about the Collinsville robbery.

"Yes, sir, I did," Birger answered. "It was in January 1925 at Nineteenth and Market streets in East St. Louis (site of the Shelton tavern). Carl said he had been thinking about starting to haul whiskey up from Florida. He had a payroll job in Collinsville, he said, and when he got through with that he was going to start hauling whiskey."

"And the next time?" Birger was asked.

"That was at my house five or six days after Ora Thomas' funeral," Birger replied. "Carl, Earl and Bernie and Charlie Briggs split $3,600 in my dining room. When I looked in, Carl said, 'This is some of Uncle Sam's money, but we won't need you for an alibi because we were at Ora Thomas' funeral.'

"I asked Carl how much they got and he said about $21,000. He told me Bernie drove the car up to Collinsville, and that he and Earl and Briggs went up with him. Briggs got out and grabbed the sack, and fell down getting back into the car. That was about all they ever said about the job."

Edmund Burke, a Springfield attorney representing the Sheltons, did his best to discredit the testimony of Birger in cross-examination.

"You didn't like Carl Shelton very well, did you?" Burke asked Birger.

"About as well as he likes me," a glaring Birger snapped back.

"You never told anybody anything about this Collinsville robbery, did you?"

"I did not. I was not interested."

Taking another tack, Burke asked Birger if he knew whether Harvey Dungey, who'd taken the witness stand earlier against the Sheltons, was a user of morphine. Birger said he didn't know. Then Burke asked Birger if he himself was a morphine addict, a subject of wide rumor at the time.

The court upheld an objection, but Birger ignored it and with a smile answered, "No sir, I am not."

"I'll ask you," Burke pressed on, "whether or not you are under the influence of morphine right now?" An objection again was sustained, and Birger again ignored it. Laughingly, he replied, "Not any more than you are."

The last government witness was Marie Dawson, a black maid employed in Birger's home in February 1925. She testified that she did see Carl, Earl and Bernie at the Birger residence six or seven days after the funeral of Ora Thomas.

The corroborative witness, though, that some thought put the last nail in the Sheltons' coffin was Birger associate Dungey, a cab driver in his mid-twenties from Marion living in East St. Louis at the time of the robbery. He was driving some fares from East St. Louis to Collinsville on the day of the holdup, he said, when he saw a Buick stalled on the road near Collinsville. Carl was standing by the car, looking at the engine under a raised hood; Bernie Shelton was seated at the wheel, Dungey went on. He said he couldn't see if anyone else was in the car. It was "real early in the morning," Dungey contended. However, his particular testimony would be sharply contradicted by a defense witness. Dungey also maintained that, back in the previous December, he and his wife, while driving through the Okaw bottoms, were fired upon by Carl Shelton and several other men parked in a car along the road. Dungey said his auto went off the road and turned over, but that no one was hurt. Under cross-examination, Dungey conceded that he had discussed these matters with Birger and Newman before talking to postal inspectors.

Another government witness, a black soldier named Theodore Barkley, who had been a porter at the Sheltons' saloon in East St. Louis, testified that the brothers left the tavern on January 27 about 7 a.m., an hour before the holdup, driving toward Collinsville.

Bringing Barkley to the stand was one more move by the prosecution to counter the primary defense of the Sheltons—their insistence that at 8 a.m. on the day of the heist they were in East St. Louis or on their way to Marion to attend the funeral there that day of Thomas, the chief deputy sheriff of Williamson County and Shelton friend shot to death in the cigar store shoot-out with Glenn Young. Newman of course had testified that he and the Sheltons had left East St. Louis for the funeral after 9 a.m., suggesting that the brothers had time to drive to Collinsville and back to East St. Louis. In addition, Newman's Shelton-despising wife, Bessie, taking the witness stand in a black dress, her blonde hair bobbed, testified nonchalantly that her husband left their East St. Louis home at about 9:30 a.m. on January 27, 1925, intending to go to the Thomas funeral.

When the Shelton side got its turn on February 2, after sitting for two days while the prosecution presented its case, the first witness took issue with Dungey's testimony. The man on the stand was William Overbee, manager of the Brown Cab Co. of East St. Louis. Dungey was supposed to have been driving a Brown taxi when he said he spotted Carl and Bernie on the road near Collinsville the morning of the robbery. Overbee contended that nothing of the sort happened because Dungey did not go to work for Brown until eight months after the robbery. Furthermore, Overbee testified, the cab firm's records did not show a Collinsville trip on January 27, 1925.

An intended boost for the Shelton defense also was supplied by East St. Louisans Leo Dougherty and George Dowling. Dougherty, an automobile dealer, and Dowling, a car salesman, testified they had planned to accompany the Sheltons and Newman to the Thomas funeral, but decided against going at the last minute because the roads were slippery. They said that they still went to Newman's Arlington Hotel at about 8 a.m. on January 27, roughly the time of the holdup, before declining to go. The Shelton brothers, Newman and Joseph McGlynn, the East St. Louis attorney friend of the Sheltons, along with several other men, all were waiting at the hotel when Dowling and Dougherty showed up, the latter two swore.

Too, the defense argued that driving conditions alone on January 27 exonerated the Sheltons. The roads were too treacherous for the Sheltons to have been able to pull off the robbery in Collinsville and then drive to Marion in time to attend the funeral, the defense insisted. As it was, the Sheltons didn't make it to Marion in time for the funeral anyway—or, if they did arrive in time, they did not attend the funeral. Newman also injected his two cents worth into this matter, saying that it was true "the city streets were pretty slick...but the snow and ice was pretty well whipped off the roads."

Taking the stand in their own defense, Carl, Earl and Bernie each denied any connection with the robbery. Carl, noticeably reticent, eschewed the invectiveness of Newman and some other government witnesses the day before.

"No, sir," Carl replied in a suave voice when his attorney asked if the gangster was guilty of the Collinsville robbery.

"No, sir," Carl answered without emotion to another question, whether he'd discussed any robbery with Newman.

"No, sir," Carl said again when his attorney specifically wanted to know if Carl had ever talked about the Collinsville robbery in the Harrisburg home of Birger and had participated in the splitting of the take from the crime in Birger's house.

"No, sir." The jury heard those words from Carl again when his attorney wanted to know if he was friendly with Birger.

Light moments in the trial were rare, but one unfolded when District Attorney Provine on cross-examination asked Carl to describe his current business.

"Collection agency," Carl replied, triggering a boisterous burst of laughter in the courtroom.

Any expectation of fireworks in the Shelton rebuttal testimony was quickly doused. If anything, there was a touch of stage management about the actions of the Sheltons on their day in court. Gray-haired Agnes Shelton showed up for the day's proceedings, joined by the brothers' two younger sisters, Hazel and Lula. Although Carl had talked with his mother at the Hotel Quincy a few minutes before court convened, he arose at the start of the session, went over to his mother with conspicuous ardor and kissed her mouth in the presence of the jury. He greeted his sisters with an air of surprise that they had journeyed all the way from Wayne County to provide silent support.

Carl's testimony was backed up to one extent or another by other defense witnesses, such as McGlynn, who did ride along with the brothers and Newman to Marion. Delos Duty, former Williamson state's attorney, testified that the brothers called at his office in Marion before noon on January 27. And then there were the Pulliams, Shelton allies from Benton. Pulliam, known to some as Max and to others as Mack or Pat, contended as did his wife that they heard Birger and Newman openly declare that they intended to frame the Sheltons for the Collinsville job—testimony intended to buttress the emphasis by defense attorneys on the hatred for the Sheltons held by Birger and Newman.

The Sheltons' chief counsel, Harold J. Bandy of Granite City, endeavored to inject into the trial record as much testimony as possible about the anti-Shelton prejudices of government witnesses. He spared no effort in trying to show that Birger and Newman would stop at nothing to kill the Sheltons or, failing that, to get them behind bars.

For example, heavy play was accorded the contention by Ruth Bogan, the old flame of Carl who said she'd been forced the previous October by Birger and Newman to telephone Carl and ask him to meet her at the Wies Hotel in East St. Louis. There, Birger or his henchmen would be waiting to kill Carl, she held. Carl didn't show up, of course, after the girl's mother warned him of the trap. When asked about this, Birger denied any knowledge of the scheme.

In one feisty exchange after another with Newman, Bandy sought to bring out the vengeance motive of Newman in accusing the Sheltons of the Collinsville robbery.

"Mr. Newman, what are you doing at present?" questioned Bandy.

"I'm not doing anything now," Newman replied.

"How long has that been?"

"Since the Shelton boys have been trying to kill me."

At another point, after Carl Shelton leaned over and whispered in Bandy's ear, the attorney asked Newman: "Isn't it true the reason you are testifying is you want to get the Shelton boys out of the way?"

"No, sir."

Bandy also broached with Newman an attention-getting sidelight to the trial. "Haven't you," the lawyer asked, "branched out in the work of a journalist lately?" Newman, caught off guard, stuttered that he had not. But Bandy persisted. "Haven't you been doing journalistic work for the *St. Louis Post-Dispatch*?"

"Well, yes. But I have been just telling the truth."

"Aren't you writing a series of articles on the Shelton brothers?"

"Yes, but I'm including myself and other people."

As if coverage of the trial itself was not enough to captivate the reading public, the *Post-Dispatch* was running simultaneously a series, "Inside Stories of the Gang War in Southern Illinois." It was promoted by the paper as a string of "narratives" by Art Newman, whom the paper labeled "chief lieutenant of Charlie Birger." While the series, written by *Post-Dispatch* reporter Roy Alexander, did not paint Birger, Newman and others in their crowd as angels, the devious Shelton brothers came across as the really bad guys.

The genesis of the articles laid with a phone call by Newman to *Post-Dispatch* writer Sam O'Neal, prompting a meeting at which Newman, Freddie Wooten and another Birger man, Connie Ritter, offered to sell their version of the gang fracas to the newspaper. The *Post-Dispatch* agreed to the arrangement, and O'Neal, Alexander and another *Post-Dispatch* reporter, John Rogers, spent several days talking with the three gangsters at Carlinville. The series provided an added dimension to the already significant role of the *Post-Dispatch* as a purveyor of often exclusive information on the southern Illinois hostilities. Yet, if anybody assumed because of the series that the newspaper was openly sympathetic to the Birger side, events in the immediate future would certainly prove otherwise.

In spite of the defense's efforts to show that Birger and Newman would do anything to get the Sheltons, and despite the fact that Birger and Newman gave the only testimony directly implicating the Sheltons in the mail robbery, the trial did not end well for the brothers. On February 4, the twelve-person jury, after five hours of deliberation, found Carl, Earl and Bernie guilty as charged. The brothers listened to the verdict with faces of stone.

The following day, Judge FitzHenry sentenced each of the three defendants to twenty-five years in the federal penitentiary at Leavenworth, Kansas. Furthermore, FitzHenry ordered his court clerk to issue a "writ of commitment" directing the U.S. marshal to take the trio to the prison "forthwith."[6]

"That's a long time," Carl said with a smile when the sentence was imposed. Added Bernie, "I hope Birger is still alive when we get out. We want to interview him."

The sentencing of the Sheltons had a rival development for top billing on February 5. The other was a true bombshell, the discovery about noon that day of the badly decomposed body of missing state policeman Lory Price. The bullet-riddled corpse, an arm and hand of which had been gnawed cleanly by dogs or other animals, was found by a farmer in a field near the tiny Washington County village of DuBois. The discovery dimmed hopes that the trooper's wife, Ethel, missing with her husband since mid-January, would be found alive. An intensive search was started in the vicinity of DuBois for any trace of her.

At that point, the finding of Price's body was viewed as another possible blow to the Sheltons. Their gang had been routinely blamed by some for the disappearance of Price and his wife. This was attributable in part to an assertion by Floyd Moore, an army corporal on recruiting duty at Herrin, that he witnessed an encounter between Price and Carl Shelton a few days before Price's disappearance. According to Moore, he was riding with Price when the car of the patrolman known for his chumminess with Birger was crowded to the side of a Williamson County road by Shelton. After Price talked with Carl for several minutes, Moore said, Price appeared to be scared. Consequently, more than a few surmised, Price had heeded a warning by Shelton and simply left southern Illinois.

Moore testified at Quincy about the encounter he allegedly witnessed January 14, and he repeated the testimony at the inquest into the death of Price. Shelton lawyers angrily objected at the trial to the questioning of Carl about his whereabouts on January 14 as immaterial. They argued that Moore was lying because he didn't even know what Carl looked like.

In an affidavit in support of an unsuccesful motion for a new trial, Bernie Shelton said that Moore had approached him after testifying, extended his hand to Bernie and said, "Carl, I am sorry I had to do it." Bernie swore that Moore then carried on a conversation with Bernie before discovering that Bernie was not Carl, who was said in the affidavit to have "no great similarity in appearance" to Bernie.

Such matters had to appear pretty extraneous to the Sheltons, though, when they awoke the morning of February 7 in cells at Leavenworth. No longer Carl, Earl and Bernie, they were suddenly inmates numbered 27,024 and 27,025 and 27,026.

The brothers had been taken from Quincy to Leavenworth during an all-night trip. Earl and Bernie were handcuffed to each other, while Carl's hands were shackled. During the journey, they stayed awake, talking with their guards and hashing over the trial. Later, after the trip, Deputy Marshal Walter Moody of Springfield opined that the Sheltons "were the best behaved prisoners I have ever had in my twenty years' experience."

Approaching Leavenworth after a breakfast stop at St. Joseph, Missouri, the brothers seemed in good spirits. However, when they viewed the gray towering walls of the prison, Carl turned to a *Post-Dispatch* reporter accompanying them and said, "Say something hopeful to Bernie; I'm afraid he might break down." Carl had noticed tears in Bernie's eyes, and he had to stiffen his own jaw to control himself. Pretty soon, huddled together on a bench near the prison entrance, all three of the brothers broke down and cried.

"It was the first show of emotion by these men of which there is any record since embarking upon the stormy gang career that brought their downfall," the *Post-Dispatch* writer noted. The reporter apparently was not aware of the tears in Carl's eyes not that many weeks before in the presence of St. Louis police.

The next to last words of Carl to the reporter—after again claiming the innocence of himself and his brothers and stating that they still hoped to prove that claim—simply were: "But, we are here, and Newman and Birger have had their revenge."

On the other hand, concluded Carl, "there is some consolation in the fact that we are leaving more trouble behind than we will find here."[7]

In place of the trouble left outside the prison walls, the Sheltons found a simpler pursuit at the pen. They were assigned to Leavenworth's stone yard, where the brothers tasted manual labor for the first time since their days in coal mining a decade ago. Cutting stone for additions to the prison structure was no more fun than extracting coal. They got a few breaks, though. They were permitted to work near each other. And, they were even allowed to converse during recreation periods.

8

A Crackerjack Reporter Weighs In

None was better than John T. Rogers, and there were plenty of great reporters in those days. The Prohibition era was a field day for investigative journalists, and few if any newspapers had a more productive stable of sleuths than the *St. Louis Post-Dispatch*. For Rogers and the other probers of the *P-D*, Illinois was a fertile hunting ground, a natural target because of the endless extravagances in political corruption, criminal activity and the like.

Rogers was extremely well versed on the southern Illinois gang war by the time he was part of the *Post-Dispatch* team covering the proceedings at Quincy. Shortly before the trial, he was one of the three *Post-Dispatch* reporters to whom Newman, Wooten and Ritter had revealed the "true" story of the warfare. Before that, he'd become quite familiar with the terrain and main characters involved in the conflict. He'd also established a strong investigative track record in Illinois in other situations.

Consequently, eyebrows were hardly raised when Roy C. Martin, the state's attorney of Franklin County, contacted the *Post-Dispatch* after the trial to request the loan of Rogers' services. In trying to cope with the murder of Mayor Joe Adams and all its offshoots, Martin felt that events in his county were spinning out of control. The editors at the newspaper said it was Rogers' call. Without hesitation, Rogers agreed to help Martin.

Shortly after his arrival in the county, Rogers accompanied Franklin County Sheriff James Pritchard on an outing to investigate a reported attempt on the life of Charlie Birger. Pritchard suspected Harvey Dungey of the alleged assault, having heard that Dungey and Birger had fallen out. When the sheriff and Rogers found Dungey, the complexion of things began to change quickly.

Dungey denied firing at Birger, but he told Rogers and Pritchard, after cursing Birger, that "if I ever do see him, I'll kill him." Surprised at hearing this, Rogers reminded Dungey that, a few weeks before as a witness at the mail robbery trial, Dungey had acted like a strong supporter of Birger.

"Yeah," replied Dungey, "and that was all phony. Birger and Art Newman put pistols on me and made me do it. I testified that I saw the Sheltons in Collinsville on the morning of the mail robbery, and I hadn't been in Collinsville in four years." He went on to bitch that Birger had failed to pay him a promised sum of money for testifying.

Putting two and two together, Rogers thought back to what Carl Shelton had told him and other reporters before entering Leavenworth. "We aren't right for (guilty of) this," Carl insisted. "We were framed by Charlie Birger. And we didn't kill Lory Price either. Birger's gang did that."[1]

Realizing that Dungey's admission to false testimony blew the government's case against the Sheltons to smithereens, Rogers notified his office of Dungey's statement and then told the Shelton lawyers about it. They obtained an affidavit from Dungey acknowledging the perjury and used it as the basis for a motion filed with Judge FitzHenry to set aside the Sheltons' conviction. He responded May 4, a little under three months after the Sheltons entered prison, by ordering the release of Carl, Earl and Bernie from Leavenworth and directing their return to Springfield for a new trial. The case, however, was never retried.

When the three Sheltons arrived at Springfield, two weeks after FitzHenry's order for their release, District Attorney Provine was hard up for witnesses. Dungey's earlier testimony was kaput. Birger was sitting in the Franklin County jail in Benton, finally incarcerated for real on a murder charge tied to the killing of Adams. And Newman was a fugitive from justice in the Adams murder case, having departed from Illinois in the wake of the trial at Quincy. Although never retried, the mail robbery case remained on the docket until 1931, when FitzHenry in a housecleaning struck it and seventy-five other old criminal cases from the books. The Collinsville heist remained unsolved. Years down the line, one individual usually in the know would say enigmatically, "Collinsville got so big nobody ever (again) bothered it. It got into big-time politics."

After their departure from Leavenworth, the Sheltons expressed their gratitude to Rogers. Some took that wrong. They jumped on it as a sign of Rogers forsaking his impartiality as a reporter to side with the brothers. But FitzHenry did not think so, and he made it clear in a complimentary letter to Rogers after Dungey's recanting of his testimony.

Recapping what had transpired, the federal jurist wrote in part that "as I now recall, it developed that Dungy (sic) had admitted his perfidy to you, and you had communicated that fact to the attorneys for the Sheltons, which probably accounts for my personally thanking you for the part you had taken in the interests of justice.

"In my observance of you and your work through a number of years, I have never seen anything that would tend to indicate that you are or were in league with the underworld, or to make me suspicious that you were not upon the side of the law."[2]

FitzHenry undoubtedly had a close-to-home reason for appreciating the work of Rogers. The reporter did the lion's share of the digging in a *Post-Dispatch* investigation that led to the impeachment and resignation in 1926 of United States District Judge George W. English of East St. Louis. The inquiry revealed that English had abused his powers in disbarring attorneys without cause, in showing gross favoritism in his appointments to bankruptcy cases and in letting his son profit greatly from the deposit of court funds in favored banks. Rogers won the Pulitzer Prize in 1927 for "the best example of a reporter's work" as a result of his distinctive reporting in the inquiry.

Before probing into Judge English, Rogers had made a bit of a name for himself in Illinois by obtaining a confession in a lurid crime case in 1924. Mrs. Elsie Sweeten, a resident of Ina, a town near Mount Vernon, admitted to Rogers that, as a result of a love affair with her pastor, the Reverend Lawrence Hight, she gave her husband arsenic, causing his death. The minister's wife too was poisoned to death, by her husband. Mrs. Sweeten and Hight both were convicted of murder and sentenced to prison. However, she won a second trial on legal grounds and was acquitted and released. Her confession to Rogers was not used directly in the second trial.[3]

The incredible talent of Rogers for obtaining improbable confessions from criminals and others surfaced often during his twenty years as a *Post-Dispatch* reporter. When Rogers died suddenly in 1937, at the age of fifty-five, his obituary in the *Post-Dispatch* cited his "remarkable facility for gaining and holding the confidence of persons of all conditions." His photographic memory for details and accurate remembrance of conversations made Rogers a big asset for public officials as well as for his newspaper, the obit pointed out. State's Attorney Martin of Franklin County was just one of those in public offices—places often with very limited resources— not hesitant to seek aid or advice from Rogers.

Dungey's turnabout was only the start of the slide for Newman and Birger in the aftermath of the Quincy trial. In early March, a month after the windup of the trial, Harry Thomasson and several other Birger followers were convicted of robbery and sentenced to ten years of imprisonment. Because he was only nineteen, Thomasson was ordered to serve the first two years of his term in the Pontiac reformatory instead of a penitentiary. While Thomasson had been under lock and key awaiting trial on the robbery charge, Roy Martin skillfully figured out that he and his brother Elmo, not seen since the destruction of Shady Rest, most likely were the two young men who had murdered Adams. Martin arranged for the late mayor's widow to view Thomasson in jail, and she identified him as one of the killers of her husband. She named Elmo Thomasson as the other one from photos.

Martin played a further hunch by visiting Thomasson at Pontiac and taking with him the best interrogator of criminals that Martin knew of, John Rogers. By the time Martin and Rogers arrived, Thomasson was ripe for questioning because he had come to believe that his brother Elmo had to be one of the four persons whose bodies were discovered in the ruins of Shady Rest. Consequently, Martin and Rogers convinced him that they knew he and his brother had killed Adams and that he should come clean with it all. Thomasson, now sure in his mind that it was Birger who had destroyed Shady Rest and caused the death of Elmo, caved in. After spilling out the truth to his two visitors, Thomasson agreed to plead guilty to the Adams murder and confess everything about it in open court. And he did just that, not only pleading guilty to the killing but also relating in detail how Birger, Newman, Connie Ritter and Ray Hyland, another Birger lieutenant, had put the Thomassons up to the killing and orchestrated it. The confession immediately earned him a sentence of life in prison.

As for Birger, he was already cooling his heels in the Franklin County jail when Thomasson fessed up in court, having been arrested the previous day in connection with the Adams killing in view of Thomasson's upcoming public confession. Newman, on the other hand, was at large and would not be arrested on a charge of complicity in the Adams murder until being tracked down in California in late May of 1927.

When Newman was apprehended, Roy Martin again asked Rogers for assistance. Now he wanted the reporter, who knew Newman, to accompany Sheriff Pritchard on a trip to California to pick up the gangster and return him to Illinois. Martin did not have to ask Rogers twice. He jumped at the invitation. Furthermore, Rogers remarked to Martin before leaving with Pritchard that "when we come back with Newman, I will bring you back a solution of the Price murder." To put it mildly, Rogers would deliver. And, in doing so, he would mesh, to an amazing extent, the role of a journalist with the flow of events and individuals that had left an entire region of Illinois in stark terror. (Such deep involvement by a *Post-Dispatch* reporter with the story being covered would occur again two decades later; the Sheltons would be the primary focus of the story; and the reporter would be Ted Link. However, in 1927, Link was only one of a myriad of young reporters in St. Louis in awe of John Rogers and his scoops.)

In many ways, reporters like Rogers from the big city dailies had an easier task in covering the hostilities in southern Illinois than the editors and writers at the smaller newspapers in the region. The local papers seldom had sufficient staff or the financial wherewithal to cover the KKK and gang wars to the degree of the big city boys. Beyond that, newspersons in Herrin, Marion, Harrisburg and other towns in the center of the action may have had face-to-face dealings with the gangsters and other troublemakers on a daily basis, making them much more vulnerable to threats of violent repercussions than, say, reporters in St. Louis a hundred miles away. Slamming in print an acquaintance, or a friend or fellow one may have grown up with, hoodlum or not, was hardly easy.

Yet, the record showed that a number of the papers in the backyards of the gangsters brought incisive and fair coverage of the goings-on to their readers. In numerous places, the strongest, most respected voices of reason throughout the chaotic happenings belonged to the local editors and publishers, persons such as Hal Trovillion of the *Herrin News*. And few more respected newspapermen came out of southern Illinois in the twentieth century than Oldham Paisley of the *Marion Daily Republican*. As a reporter, editor and eventually publisher of the *Daily Republican*, Paisley was a standard-setter for his profession.

In a telling biography of Paisley, Margaret N. O'Shea detailed the challenges faced by Paisley in providing home-front coverage of the KKK strife and the subsequent gang battle in his paper's circulation area. Since Paisley usually knew individuals in each of the warring camps, doing his job required the constant traipsing of a reportorial tightrope. The inherent danger at every corner never could be pushed to the background. This came through clearly in the work of O'Shea, sometimes with a touch of humor. After the aerial raid on Shady Rest, Paisley went over to Birger's cabin to obtain a firsthand account. Greeted in a friendly manner by Birger, as were many newspaper types, Paisley was entrusted by the gangster with one of the bombs that failed to explode. Transporting the device back to Marion to take a picture of it, Paisley first noticed the parcel's nitroglycerin. Frightened, he slowed his car until he came to a creek, where he threw the bomb into the water.

O'Shea also made note of a fried rabbit dinner that Paisley and John Rogers shared with Birger at Shady Rest as they questioned the gang leader about his fight with the Sheltons. Both journalists were restless during the visit, most notably when Birger suggested they move from the secure basement to an upstairs room quite susceptible to an attack.

Not long afterward, Rogers received word that his pursuit of the Shelton-Birger story had alienated Birger and that the gangster intended to "spit in Rogers' face." Rogers immediately hailed a cab and directed the driver to take him to Birger's Harrisburg house. The cabbie refused to convey Rogers any further than a block away from the home. Entering the residence, guarded by several armed men, Rogers confronted a surprised Birger with what he'd heard. Birger said little or nothing, and Rogers departed, soon to tell other reporters that "it was just a false alarm."[4]

When Rogers died, editorialists made much of his image as a reporter "of the old school," taken to mean that he was fired by an ambition to serve his paper and the betterment of society, a high calling that customarily relegated concern for one's own physical or financial well-being to second place. The *Post-Dispatch* was a hotbed of old school reporting in Rogers' years and for some time afterward. Its practitioners included many besides Rogers, who was a telegraph operator in Louisville when he broke into reporting with that city's *Courier-Journal*. Among the other old schoolers was Roy Alexander, no slouch himself in delving into the southern Illinois turmoil and later an editor of *Time* magazine and executive assistant to Henry R. Luce, cofounder of the publication.

Reporters like Rogers, Alexander and another ace bloodhound, Paul Y. Anderson, blossomed because of the crusading tone of the liberal *Post-Dispatch* under the helm of the second Joseph Pulitzer, the paper's commander from 1912 until his death in 1955. During many of those years the man who cracked the whip for Pulitzer was another famous American journalist, Oliver K. Bovard, the *Post-Dispatch* managing editor for thirty years until his retirement in 1938. A printer's son born in Jacksonville, Illinois, Bovard was a man of sarcastic, even cruel wit, who oversaw the paper's news gathering with a tyrannical style. Nevertheless, in the words of Anderson, Bovard was without dispute "the best friend of every competent man who ever worked for him."[5]

Because the *Post-Dispatch*, and other St. Louis newspapers, found muckraking in Illinois so rewarding, criticism did arise that the St. Louis press often seemed to find little in the state to cover besides the shenanigans. There were some in the St. Louis newspaper world itself acutely aware of this school of thought, such as Irving Dilliard, the scholarly editor of the editorial page of the *Post-Dispatch* in the 1950s, a resident of Collinsville and onetime president of the Illinois State Historical Society.

Reminiscing on the *Post-Dispatch* at his home on a warm summer day in 1998, Dilliard allowed as to how "it was true that there were editors in St. Louis who could never see anything of interest in Illinois outside of the crooks and the thieving politicians. Yes, there was a touch of snobbishness in looking over at Illinois, and I would have to remind people about the culture and many fine things that made Illinois a great state."

But, explained Dilliard, who began his career with the *Post-Dispatch* as a reporter in 1927, "there was a mandate from the top to expose wrong-doing, which the staff was imbued with, and Illinois had these wild things happening." While not casting any aspersions on newspapers in Illinois, Dilliard noted that "people in Illinois who wanted the bad stuff disclosed often came to *Post* reporters." Staff members like Rogers "were specialists on those subjects who got to be very well known for what they did," Dilliard said, and added that "even a lot of the gangsters wanted their stories out in those days, and when they did they often talked to our people for, I guess, a lot of reasons."[6]

Not many conversations between a gangster and a *Post-Dispatch* scribe had more impact than the revelations of Art Newman to Rogers as Newman was brought back to Illinois from California.

When arrested in California May 22, 1927, Newman was said by one wire service to have been living in Long Beach and working in the oil fields. Information received by the Illinois State Police, though, indicated Newman was operating a detective agency under the name, unlikely as it may have been, John Rogers. Newman, in resisting extradition to Illinois, said that the fugitive warrant for his arrest was part of a frame-up designed to get him back to Illinois to be "bumped off" before he could again testify against the Sheltons in any second trial in the mail robbery case. In fact, after his arrest Newman was heavily guarded by deputy sheriffs in Los Angeles because of a report that nine members of the Shelton gang had been sent to the West Coast to "get" Newman, a rumor apparently without basis. Finally, after days of legal wrangling, a Los Angeles court ordered the handing of Newman over to Pritchard for the gangster's return to Illinois, a journey that ended with his imprisonment in the Franklin County jail June 5.

It was on the train between Los Angeles and Kansas City that Rogers persuaded Newman to make a clean breast of it, just as Rogers had succeeded in getting Harry Thomasson to do at the Pontiac reformatory. Newman confessed to Rogers that he, Birger, Ritter and others abducted Price and his wife, and that Birger murdered Price while one or more of the others killed Mrs. Price and threw her body into an abandoned mine shaft. Reaching Benton, Rogers handed Newman's confession to Martin. He in turn gave it to officials of Washington County, where the trooper's body had been found.

A few days later, on June 11, a special grand jury sitting at Nashville, the seat of Washington County, heard Newman insist that his confession to Rogers on the train was accurate down to the last comma. As a result, Newman, Birger, Ritter and three others, Ernest Blue, Riley Simmons and Leslie Simpson, were indicted for the murder of Lory Price.

The killing of Adams would earn Birger a date with a hangman's noose, but the gruesome details of the murders of Price and his wife, drawn out by Rogers from Newman, ended any possibly remaining public feeling that Birger and his gang were anything but cold-blooded killers. After getting the trooper and his wife out of their house late on the cold, rainy night of January 17, Birger ordered some of his men with him at the time to do away with Ethel Price while Birger himself dealt with her husband.

As related by Newman, Price was taken for a ride and scolded severely by Birger for asking too many questions about the Adams killing and for talking too much to other law enforcement officials. Finally, after stopping at the recently burned Shady Rest, Birger—enraged at Price's denials of double-crossing him—pumped three bullets into Price. About that time, according to Newman, the car in which Ethel Price had been taken away pulled up to Shady Rest and its occupants reported that they'd killed the woman, dumped her body into the shaft and covered it with timbers, tin and debris. After that, Birger put Price, still alive, in the backseat of Newman's car, and Birger, gun in hand, sat on the policeman. Near Carbondale, with Price continuing to groan, Birger ordered the car to stop. Jumping out, the gang leader vomited.

Then, Newman said Birger was heard to say: "I can kill a man, but I can't sit on him. I don't know what in the hell is the matter with me. It isn't my nerves. Every time I kill a man it makes me sick. Must be my stomach."

Birger directed Connie Ritter to next sit on Price, who was choking and spitting blood and pleading for mercy. Ritter soon had all he could take, and another one of the gangsters parked himself on top of Price. The party intended to dispose of Price at an old mine, but found a watchman on duty. The two cars moved on to a schoolhouse, which Birger proposed to burn with Price in it. But, it was raining too hard for that to work. Moving on, the party eventually stopped at a field near DuBois.

Hauling Price out of the car, Newman said that Price "laid a bloody hand on my shoulder" and gasped, "Art, I thought you were my friend." Newman said he replied, "By God, I am Lory, but I can't help this." Newman said that Birger and others dragged Price away, laid him down and finished him off with a round of bullets. On the drive back south, Newman said one of the abductors of Ethel Price told him of the mine shaft where she'd been shot and her body disposed of.

Newman's confession to Rogers, which appeared in the *Post-Dispatch* on the day of Newman's appearance before the grand jury at Nashville, cleared up many of the ambiguities surrounding the gangster atrocities in southern Illinois near the end of 1926 and in the early days of 1927. Up to the time of the confession, some people still were prone to blame the Sheltons for the destruction of Shady Rest, as well as for the murder of Lory Price and the assumed killing of his wife.

One test of the veracity of Newman's account would be the accuracy of his disclosure of the location of Mrs. Price's body. Would her remains be found where Newman said? Searchers had looked in vain for her since the discovery of her husband's corpse four months earlier. The answer came June 13. Newman was shown to have told the truth when her body was uncovered in the abandoned shaft he'd pinpointed, not far from Whiteash between Marion and Johnston City, by miners working in relays with what seemed like the whole world watching.

Rogers harbored no doubt that he'd gotten the straight goods from Newman on the train, unlike some months back when Newman hardly had leveled in relating his version of the southern Illinois gang fracas to the *Post-Dispatch*. Besides relying on his extraordinary sixth sense to feel confident about his latest dealing with Newman, Rogers was quick to recognize the importance of seemingly insignificant details. For instance, Newman had related to Rogers that, in throwing a sheet of corrugated iron into the shaft to cover Ethel Price's body, Ritter had cut his lip with the metal. This rang a bell with Rogers since he'd noticed, in talking with Ritter after the disappearance of the Prices, that his lip was not only cut, but infected. (By the time the truth about the Price killings came out, Ritter was no longer around. Ritter, who came from a merchant family in the small Franklin County town of Orient and was one of the more dapper and sociable of Birger's men, would not be located and arrested until October 1929, in Gulfport, Mississippi.)

There was another thing about Newman that Rogers picked up on that, in the reporter's eyes, lent credibility to Newman's confession. Rogers surmised on the train that Newman now hated Birger about as much as the Sheltons; that he blamed Birger as much as the Sheltons for the disrepair of his life. No way was the talkative Newman tailoring his story of events any longer to protect Birger, Rogers was convinced.

The confession of Newman and the subsequent uncovering of Mrs. Price's body ensured that the downfall of Birger was without question only a matter of time. As it happened, his fate was sealed in virtually no time at all.

Before the summer of 1927 was out, the tying up of loose ends and wrapping up of unfinished business from the gang war were under way in earnest. The only questions seemed to revolve around which gangsters would be tried for which of the murders since Birger and Newman—and not just those two among the Birgerites—faced charges in connection with the killing of Adams in addition to the murders of Price and his wife.

Birger, Newman and Ray Hyland went on trial in July of that year at Benton for the murder of Adams. The jury found each of the three guilty. Birger was sentenced to be hanged, while Newman and Hyland were condemned to life in prison. When informed by the court of the day he was to go to the gallows, Birger was granted a request to be heard. He lashed out at Newman and his wife as the real culprits in much of what had happened and added some choice words for John Rogers, a reporter who, in the estimation of Birger, "has conspired and condemned me to the public."

In January 1929, Newman went on trial at Marion, along with Leslie Simpson, Riley Simmons and Freddie Wooten, for the murder of Lory Price. All of the defendants pled guilty, leading to sentences of life in prison for each (as if the sentencing of Newman for the Adams murder apparently was not sufficient). Following his arrest in Gulfport late in 1929, Ritter entered a plea of guilty to the Adams murder in court at Benton (after maneuvering to face that charge instead of standing trial for the murders of Lory and Ethel Price) and was sentenced to life behind bars. Ernest Blue, another charged in the Lory Price murder, was never apprehended.

In looking back at 1927, any list of the year's winners and losers would have had Rogers coming out smelling like a rose, irregardless of

Birger's opinion of him. In what was hardly an everyday occurrence, State's Attorney Martin wrote a letter to the *Post-Dispatch* declaring that the newspaper deserved "full credit" for the solution of the Price case. The communication praised in particular the work of Rogers, especially in getting Newman to talk.

Those in the public swept up by the Shelton-Birger feud lapped up every word of the writing by Rogers of Newman's confession. It gave some folks something to talk about besides the unbridled reaction in St. Louis and the rest of the country to the first solo transatlantic flight by Charles A. Lindbergh, a heroic undertaking in late May 1927, about three weeks before Newman's revelation hit the press. Interestingly, when the Lindbergh baby was kidnapped and found dead in 1932, it was a measure of Rogers' reputation that, when President Hoover arranged for the Intelligence Unit of the Internal Revenue Department to take charge of the hunt for the culprits, Rogers was invited to assist in the investigation. In pursuing leads in trying to solve the crime, Rogers was in conferences at the Lindbergh home, a role leading to a "gratifying" relationship between the reporter and famous aviator.[7]

In contrast to the way it was for Rogers, 1927 was a bummer in the lives of many ensnared in the clashing of the gangs—those who weren't already six feet under before the year started. For those not going to prison, life would be a hard and lonely road with few exceptions. Getting away didn't seem to help.

Remember Helen Holbrook? The well-heeled woman from Shawneetown, who reportedly slept with both Birger and Carl Shelton, was found dead February 7, 1927, at St. Petersburg, Florida, killed by poison. A coroner's jury ruled she committed suicide, but not many back up in her home area believed it. Gossip held that she was just one more victim of southern Illinois gang vengeance. But, if true, which faction bumped her off and why?

One acquaintance of the Sheltons, thirty-six-year-old Arthur McDonald of Daytona Beach, Florida, was arrested February 10 in St. Louis by detectives for questioning on Holbrook's death. He said he did not know the woman and only knew the Shelton brothers through his courting of their sister, Hazel Katherine. He was released. On February 18, McDonald and Hazel, who was twenty-two, were married in East St. Louis by a police magistrate.

For a while, it appeared that Carl, Earl and Bernie might have emerged from 1927 in pretty good shape, at least in comparison to the doomed Birger and his defunct gang. After their release from Leavenworth, the brothers seemed to be facing an unobstructed path to the resurrection of their bootlegging network and attendant command of the downstate Illinois underworld. But the sun didn't stay out long for them.

The Kincaid bank robbery in 1924, a shoot-'em-up affair, had remained an unsolved crime, one that had left law enforcement officials baffled. However, in August 1927, they contended the mystery was over. Carl, Earl and Bernie were charged with pulling off the job. The brothers were headed back to court.

9

Behind the Eight Ball in Taylorville

A flashback. To the morning of September 27, 1924, in Kincaid, a village of 1,500 souls in Christian County, smack dab in the heart of coal fields. A mining burg in every sense of the word, Kincaid was a town laid out by Peabody Coal Company and developed under the supervision of the Kincaid Land Association, a subsidiary of the coal firm.[1] It was a tough town, where a lot of the folks kept guns handy, where the love of beer and bocci ball never waned, and where prosperity seemed apparent at the Kincaid Trust and Savings Bank.

It was the bank that they were after, those occupants of the large green Cadillac touring car that glided slowly into Kincaid on that fall morning in 1924. They had to know that the bank's safe was holding $60,000 to cover a Peabody mining payroll.

Inside the two-story structure fronted by white bricks in the middle of town, Bruce Shaw, the institution's president; Ira Aull, the assistant cashier; and employees Lyndall Wells and Maude Quinn were going about their morning business when three men who had just exited the auto entered around ten o'clock. Shaw was walking into the vault and Aull sitting at a back desk when one of the trio, standing at the teller's window, ordered all present to "put 'em up." Shaw's immediate reaction was either an act of bravery or foolhardy, depending on how one looked at it. Producing a gun, he opened fire in the direction of the robbers, while also pushing the burglar alarm. The man at the window fired back, knicking Shaw between two fingers. The bank president, apparently out of bullets, retreated into the vault.

The man who'd returned Shaw's fire moved rapidly back to Aull and directed him to stand with his hands up and face the wall. Putting his gun against Aull's back, the robber ordered the cashier to get into the vault and open the safe containing the payroll—a tricky feat for Aull since one of the other robbers was taking potshots at the vault. Nevertheless, Aull and his companion soon joined Shaw in the vault. The situation quickly turned ugly when Aull informed the robber that the safe couldn't be opened because of a time lock. Furious, the bandit turned on Shaw, directed the banker to stop looking at him and, for good measure, hammered his revolver into Shaw's head, dazing him and leaving him with deep gashes. The robber then wheeled or spun Aull around, pushed him out of the vault and ordered him to stuff a satchel sitting on a counter with money. Aull complied, dumping $7,785 into the bag. At the same time, shooting erupted on the street close to the bank, and one of the robbers inside the place began to fire sporadically at unseen targets outside.

Within seconds, gunfire filled the air in Kincaid. The town suddenly had turned into another Herrin. Or, better yet, Coffeyville, Kansas, where in 1892 the bank-robbing Dalton boys got their comeuppance in a hail of citizens' bullets. Or maybe Northfield, Minnesota, where Jesse James and his brigands ran into a murderous cross fire from the guns of home folks in 1876 when they knocked off the First National Bank. People were killed in Coffeyville and Northfield, but, miraculously, nobody was wounded fatally in Kincaid.

As the bandits prepared to exit the bank, they ordered Aull to go with them. His hands raised high, Aull and the gunmen rushed to the waiting Cadillac parked about 100 feet away. As they neared the car, Aull saw that one man had emerged from the auto and was firing away with a sawed-off shotgun, answering shots coming from different places up and down the street. The men escorting Aull also were putting their guns to use.

Harry Vancil, the Kincaid village marshal, was one exchanging shots with the robbers, primarily with the individual who'd been shooting from inside the bank. Another was Henry Clerick, a night watchman who upon hearing the shots quickly got a gun at John Lucas' shoe store and, from

200 feet away, began shooting at the bandits coming out of the bank. Vancil and Clerick didn't hit anybody, but not all the townspeople were bad shots. Grocer Albert Matozzo wasn't.

Matozzo was in his store a half block south of the bank when he was informed that a ruckus had broken out up the street. Grabbing a pistol, he scurried toward the bank. Just as he reached it, a fellow came out of the bank, pointed a gun at Matozzo and told him to "get out of there, you son of a bitch." Matozzo ran and sought refuge in a nearby hardware store doorway. He turned in time to see another man who'd left the bank fire shots in his direction. Albert jumped out from the doorway, fired back at the man and then retreated from the line of fire. Matozzo repeated this shooting and ducking back bit several more times, not hitting the robber, or for that matter, anyone else.

However, that changed as the men escorting Aull pushed him into the Cadillac and attempted to get in. Taking aim, Matozzo fired at the one holding the satchel, hitting him in the lower part of his right leg. The man, in nearly keeling over, stumbled against the running board and dropped the loot to the street. While the guy with the shotgun remained outside the car shooting, those in the Cadillac pulled their wounded comrade back onto the running board as the auto slowly moved off. After going only a short distance, the man on the running board made a move to retrieve the satchel. However, the men in the car resisted that effort, with one yelling, "Come on, goddamn it to hell with the money!" The wounded fellow was pulled into the car.

By this time, the bandit with the shotgun was running in an attempt to jump into the vehicle. Matozzo too was now running, along the street in the direction of the Cadillac. He fired off one more shot toward the man with the shotgun. The grocer was sure he hit him. The targeted gunman dropped the shotgun, but kept on running as one fellow in the car was heard to scream, "Come on, Bill! Come on, Bill!" Making it to the car, Bill was hauled in, and the auto picked up speed to head out of town.

As for Ira Aull, when he was shoved into the back seat of the Cadillac, he was ordered to hold his head down on his knees. As the car began to move south through the village, several of the robbers fired random shots through the auto's windows. Aull thought there were five or six men in the car when he was pushed in. Before going very far, the auto stopped and picked up another chap. The only occupant of the Cadillac doing any talking was a small man in the rear. The others said little or nothing. Aull remembered that one person in the car did have a leg wound and that he, Aull, gave him a handkerchief to put on it. After going about a mile south of Kincaid, the car turned west. Not long afterward, the Cadillac stopped. Aull was told to get out, cross a fence along a field and lay down. He did.

That was the high drama of September 27, 1924.[2]

Nearly three years later, on August 29, 1927, a grand jury in Christian County Circuit Court returned an indictment charging seven persons with the robbery of the Kincaid bank. Four of them were William O'Hara, William Diedicker, Paul Blackburn and Edward Mitchell, alias Eddie Nicholson. However, it was the names of the remaining three that made the indictment hot stuff. Carl, Earl and Bernie Shelton. They were the ones arousing tremendous interest.

When the case went to trial the following January, the three Sheltons were the only defendants seated before the jury in the Christian County Courthouse in the heart of Taylorville. Eddie Nicholson, of Joliet, was granted a motion for a separate trial, effectively arguing that he never was a member of the Shelton gang and that putting him on trial with the Sheltons would prejudice his right to a fair trial. Hard to ignore, Nicholson contended in his petition, was "the desire of law-abiding citizens of this State to see that the alleged Shelton gang is exterminated for the good of this commonwealth." As for O'Hara, Diedicker and Blackburn, news accounts indicated they were fugitives when the Sheltons went on trial.

Although the Sheltons remained free on bail following their arrest on the indictment, the brothers had to be gnashing their teeth at the gloomy prospect of facing another trial with some of the same repugnant earmarks of the Collinsville mail robbery one. Just as in the Collinsville case, Art Newman was slated to be a star witness for the prosecution. Newman would be telling the jury that he was privy to planning by the Sheltons for the Kincaid heist and then also discussed details of the holdup with Carl after it occurred. Newman also would testify that the shotgun dropped by one of the fleeing Kincaid bandits had been loaned or given to Carl Shelton by Newman prior to the robbery. Even though Newman was tied to the disgraced testimony of Harvey Dungey at the trial in Quincy of the Collinsville case, he'd be plaguing the Sheltons again at Taylorville. For the brothers, there simply was no shaking of Newman and his hatred for them, even though Newman had begun serving a life sentence at the state prison at Chester for complicity in the murder of Joe Adams.

And there'd be another damaging witness at Taylorville in the vein of Dungey at Quincy. His name this time was Hobart Summers, and he happened to be a fellow con with Newman at the Chester pen.

Just as at Quincy, the Sheltons faced a vigorous prosecutor at Taylorville. Christian County State's Attorney Carl H. Preihs knew going in that the opportunity to send the Shelton boys up the river (or down as might be the case) was his shot at immortality. To beef up his effort, Preihs had assistance from three able attorneys, John Hogan, William Greer and Harry B. Hershey. Hershey was a Taylorville lawyer who had been state's attorney of Christian County and, years after the Taylorville trial, would be an unsuccessful Democratic candidate for governor and later chief justice of the Illinois Supreme Court. Preihs also had a good feeling that the circuit court judge presiding at the trial, William B. Wright of Effingham, would not be giving the Sheltons and their lawyers any breaks.

On the other hand, the Sheltons were hardly defenseless, not with the twosome that had represented them at Quincy, Bandy and Burke, again in place for the brothers at Taylorville. Harold James Bandy was a tough cookie from the railroad town of Roodhouse in Greene County, where his father was, appropriately, a rail worker before becoming a lawyer. Seeking the same profession as his dad, Harold did prelegal studies at the University of Illinois and then entered law school at Washington University at St. Louis. Before graduating, though, he passed the Illinois bar examination and joined his father's law practice in Granite City. Edmund Burke was an attorney of considerable reputation in Springfield, having served before the Taylorville trial as state's attorney of Sangamon County, a neighbor of Christian. Burke was a personal attorney for John L. Lewis, the legendary president of the United Mine Workers of America, during Lewis' years in Springfield.

Bandy was an outstanding trial lawyer—he successfully argued a case before the United States Supreme Court in the early 1930s—and his services often were sought by individuals in trouble with the law. Many were recognizable names, but none as widely known as the Sheltons. Bandy's son, James H. Bandy, himself an attorney, remembered his father striving through the years of his association with the Sheltons to "remain as objective as possible about them because they were clients." However, avoidance of some personal feelings for the brothers was too much to expect of Harold Bandy, who was about the same age as Carl and Earl.

"Carl was the dapper one," James Bandy recalled. "He always looked like he'd just stepped out of a Brooks Brothers store. And Bernie? Well, he was just different. But Earl, he was the one who became a friend, a good friend, with dad, and with me, too. Earl was just very affable, usually in fine humor. Earl was tall, like Carl, and heavyset, and he always had a good story to tell. In later life, Earl got completely away from what he'd done earlier in his life."[3]

From the start at Taylorville, Bandy and Burke realized they again had their hands full in defending the Sheltons. With the brothers pleading not guilty to the robbery charge, steadfastly insisting that they were in East St. Louis at the time of the holdup, the same alibi they'd advanced at the Collinsville mail robbery trial, Burke and Bandy moved to quash the indictment. The motion was denied. The defendants also moved for a continuance or delay in the conduct of the trial, if only for a few days, to permit the testimony of three East St. Louisans, Leo Dougherty, Roy Baker and Howard Lee, whom the Sheltons contended would confirm their presence in the St. Clair County city the day of the heist. The argument here by the Sheltons was that they and their lawyers weren't formally notified of the early January starting date for the trial until several days ahead of time, precluding them from contacting Dougherty, Baker and Lee before they left East St. Louis for the Christmas and New Year holidays. The continuance motion also was denied, even though Carl Shelton made a strong plea for its approval in an affidavit.

Shelton held, in part, that "the public press has been filled with stories concerning affiant (Carl) and his two brothers," articles so "lurid" that "the public mind has become greatly prejudiced" against the Sheltons, making it essential that their witnesses be in court "where the jury may hear, see and observe them."

Newspaper coverage leading into the trial gave credence to Carl's fear. Citing "slow progress in selection of a jury," the *Post-Dispatch* opined: "The trouble seems to be that most of the citizens in this part of the State have a decided complex against gangsters and such fixed opinions that it is most difficult to qualify a juror with an open mind."[4]

Finally, after a day and a half, during which more than fifty veniremen were examined, a jury loaded with farmers was selected. All on the panel admitted to being familiar with the case, meaning that the parade of prosecution witnesses, beginning January 5, 1928, might not provide a lot of information the jurors and everybody else it seemed had not already heard through the grapevine. Still, interest in the case couldn't have been higher. Based on one account, the thought of seeing the famous Shelton brothers on public display in Taylorville attracted more than 700 persons to each of the sessions in the anything but large courtroom. Those who couldn't find seats, not even the temporary ones put in place, blocked every aisle, standing six to eight deep. The old regulars in the gray stone courthouse, built in 1902 and topped by an Italianate tower suggestive of Florence or Siena, were hardly used to such a spectacle.

The first witness for the state, Thomas Nave, was a bothersome one for the defense in that he was a surprise witness, meaning the defense had been given no chance to prepare for what he would say.[5] Nave testified that, while at his farm southwest of Kincaid during the hour after the robbery, he saw a large Cadillac touring car, green with a white stripe on the body, pass by his property. Saying the auto had at least five men in it, Nave was asked if he could identify any of them. "If I ain't mistaken," Nave replied, "I saw that man over there at the wheel." The man he was pointing out was Bernie Shelton.

Testimony by law enforcement officers after Nave departed the witness stand noted that a 1923 Cadillac phaeton (touring car) fitting the description of the auto used in the robbery was found abandoned in a field road near Mascoutah, seventy-five miles south of Kincaid, the day after the holdup. The auto had bullet holes in it and blood on the rear seat. The vehicle also had the initials "S. S." on each door, which was logical since the car had been stolen before the robbery from a gentleman in St. Louis County named Sam Stiles.

After a procession to the stand of individuals in Kincaid at the time of the robbery who identified this Shelton or that Shelton as among the persons possibly—maybe but not for sure—involved in the stickup,

Preihs put his clutch witness on the stand, Newman. If the delicate-looking gangster was telling the truth, there could be little doubt the Sheltons were guilty.

According to Newman, Earl told him in August 1924 that he and his brothers were going to hit the Kincaid bank. Newman even quoted Earl as saying that, after the heist, the Sheltons would follow dirt roads from Kincaid to Mascoutah, where they intended to stash the stolen money at a "brewery" operated by Eddie Nicholson. Later on, Newman recounted, all three of the brothers discussed the intended holdup with him at his Arlington Hotel. Charlie Briggs, still alive at the time, was in on it too, Newman said. Carl finally asked Newman, he maintained, to drive the Sheltons and Briggs to Kincaid for the robbery, but Newman said no. However, Newman testified that he did drive the four men to Taylorville, a few miles from Kincaid, early on the morning of the robbery. There, at the square, Newman said, his passengers got out of his Lincoln sedan and piled into a waiting car, a greenish Cadillac or Lincoln occupied by a couple of men.

Several days after the robbery, Newman went on, he got an earful from Carl in East St. Louis about the rough going at Kincaid.

"He (Carl) said, 'We run into a pretty hot spot out there; it was pretty warm.' He said Earl got shot in the leg, and he said, 'What little money we did pick up from the teller's window, we had to drop.'"

To this, Newman added that he later saw Earl limping and using a cane at the Sheltons' saloon. Newman also quoted Carl as saying that, in addition to the wounding of Earl, Carl himself "got shot in the privates with shotgun shot."

Preihs intended the clincher in his questioning of Newman to be the gangster's testimony about the shotgun he allegedly loaned or gave to Carl. Newman said the weapon had a long barrel when he obtained it in 1924 from a fellow named Slim Farmer as security for a $10 loan. When Farmer never returned to reclaim the gun, Newman said he sawed off the barrel with a hacksaw. But he did a crooked job of cutting, he said, which made the weapon readily identifiable. He said he gave the gun to Carl Shelton to use when Carl expressed a need for additional firepower in his fight with the KKK in Williamson County. When the state introduced into evidence the sawed-off shotgun dropped by the fleeing robber at Kincaid, Newman said the gun was definitely the one he'd given Carl.

In event the testimony of Newman did not doom the Sheltons, the last two witnesses for the prosecution, Hobart Summers and Fred Reiske, were geared to do so.

Summers, incarcerated in the Chester prison at the time for robbery, painted himself as an intimate of the Sheltons, contending he'd known Carl, Bernie and Earl since their early days in East St. Louis and had joined them in the "whiskey business and robbery part of the time." As Summers said this, the three brothers, who'd already insisted to their lawyers that they'd never seen or heard of Summers, stared at the witness with incredulity. Then they just broke out in laughter.

Nevertheless, Summers went on to state that Carl had asked him, just as he had Newman, to "drive the machine" in the Kincaid robbery. At first he balked, Summers related, but finally consented to be the wheelman for the job and, consequently, accompanied the three Sheltons on a visit to Kincaid in July 1924 to look over the roads and case the village. At that juncture, Summers said, the bank was to be robbed August 27 insead of a month later. Ironically, Summers wouldn't have been available on either day because he was imprisoned at Chester on August 17, 1924, for violating his parole from an earlier sentence at Chester. After he was released in December 1926 from that stint in prison, Summers testified, he saw Carl Shelton, mentioned the Kincaid robbery and quoted Shelton as lamenting that "them hoosiers up there opened up on us with everything from a pistol to a shotgun."

If glares from the Sheltons could kill, Reiske also would have withered on the witness stand.

Reiske, another surprise witness, identified himself as a fisherman and boat builder living in a house along Horseshoe Lake, not far from Granite City. In reply to questioning by Hershey, Reiske related a somewhat murky account of one man bringing a wounded man to Reiske's home late in September 1924. The wound-free individual left, leaving the other man at Reiske's place for what he guessed was close to six hours. Finally, a third man appeared at Reiske's house. He had a small satchel in his hand and told Reiske he was a doctor. After examining the wounded man in a room in which Reiske was not present, Reiske said the doctor told him that the man was "hurt" and would be leaving with the doctor. The two departed.

Reiske told Hershey that none of those coming to his house that day gave him a name and that Reiske "didn't say anything" to his wounded visitor, who just "stayed there." However, when Hershey asked Reiske if he'd ever seen the wounded man before he was dropped off at Reiske's place, the witness said he had.

Proceeding, Hershey said: "I wish you would look over the three Sheltons, the defendants, that sit here, and tell the jury if anyone of the three was the (wounded) man that came there."

"I think," Reiske answered, "the center one (indicating Earl Shelton) is the man."

The defense sought to counterattack with a bang. Of all things, Carl Shelton petitioned the court to have none other than Charlie Birger brought to the stand. But this time, unlike his appearance at the Collinsville mail heist trial, he was to be a witness on the side of the Sheltons. It seemed that Birger, no longer enamored of his former running mate, Art Newman, had alerted the Sheltons after the start of the trial that he was willing to testify that he'd heard Newman declare an intent to frame the Sheltons for the Kincaid job. The unexpected message was conveyed through a phone call to Bandy from Charles Karch, an East St. Louis attorney representing Birger. However, getting Birger to Taylorville presented a challenge since he was behind bars in the Franklin County jail at Benton awaiting execution for his role in the Adams killing. Consequently, Carl Shelton requested the issuance of a writ of habeas corpus commanding the sheriff of Franklin County to transport Birger to Taylorville so he could testify. However, Judge Wright denied the petition, ruling that its filing—late on the day of January 5—was too late for serious consideration.

The defense's next thrust, which was played out in court, spurred every bit the uproar an appearance by Birger would have triggered. Moving to show that the Sheltons, or at least Bernie and Earl, had a surefire alibi for getting them off the hook on the bank holdup charge, Bandy and Burke marched a contingent of East St. Louis police officers into the courtroom. Three of them testified that Bernie and Earl were under arrest and confined at the East St. Louis police station at the time of the robbery. As proof of this, the defense introduced a page from the East St. Louis police blotter or arrest registration book purporting to show Earl and

Bernie to have been taken into custody a little more than seven hours before the crime occurred.

The appearance at the trial of cops from East St. Louis, which the good denizens of Taylorville considered a frightfully wicked city, was more than a little unsettling in itself. Not that it should have been all that unexpected in view of the Sheltons long-established working relationship with the law enforcement crowd in their stronghold city. The prosecutors hit the ceiling, though, in charging that the entries of the names of Earl and Bernie on the blotter were eleventh-hour forgeries, and done by none other than Mr. Carl Shelton himself. Admittedly, the blotter entries looked fishy.

M. J. O'Rourke, a detective sergeant in charge of East St. Louis police records that included the blotter, explained that the blotter page in question, marked September 26, 1924, was a record of arrests from 8 a.m. on September 26 to 8 a.m. on September 27, the day of the robbery. The last five entries on the page, all in the same handwriting, included the names of Earl Shelton and Bernie and indicated both were arrested at 2:40 a.m. on September 27. O'Rourke added, in reply to questions from Bandy, that the book with the page in question had been in his particular care since May 1, 1927.

"And during that time has there been any change in it?" Bandy asked.

"Not that I know of," O'Rourke replied.

On cross-examination, though, O'Rourke acknowledged to Hogan that the blotter books were open to inspection by any member of the public as long as "there is a police officer around." This was important to note, Hogan asserted, because the page at issue appeared to "be entirely torn out and pasted back in" its blotter book. O'Rourke said he didn't know how that might have happened.

Trailing O'Rourke to the witness chair were Ray Cashel, a detective in the East St. Louis department; Floyd (Buster) Combs, a detective sergeant, and a lieutenant on the force, Thomas F. O'Brien. Each testified to seeing Bernie and Earl at the police station at various times during the fourteen hours the brothers supposedly were held (according to the blotter) on September 27. Cashel said that he observed the two Sheltons at about 9 a.m. after roll call. Combs, saying he was working nights in 1924, explained that he was at the station at about 3 a.m. on September 27 when another member of the department informed him that two of the Shelton brothers had been pinched for bootlegging.

Stating he knew Carl Shelton, Combs said he "went back and looked at the blotter and saw it was Bernie and Earl." Then, the witness added, "I went back in the cell room and saw the two of them."

O'Brien said under oath that he was at the station switchboard when Earl and Bernie were "brought in," as he recollected, by officers named Hobbs and Grimes. He noted that both of those officers had died in the months before the Taylorville trial. O'Brien testified that he did not know who Earl and Bernie were when they entered the station, but soon "heard who they were." O'Brien went on to say he did become more familiar with the two brothers later on in East St. Louis when he "put pistols on them and shook them down and looked over their car for whiskey and stuff."

Preihs was, to put it mildly, enraged at the testimony of O'Brien, Cashel and Combs. He branded them liars and associates of gangsters, scoundrels unfit to hold office as guardians of the law.

"I am deeply concerned for the residents of East St. Louis if they must depend upon such officers as these for protection," the state's attorney declared. "If the high officers of their police department are of the character of the men we see here, what must we think of the patrolmen who have not attained such ranks as sergeant or lieutenant?"

Hogan bluntly charged Carl Shelton with "doctoring" the blotter page when he, Earl and a friend, Jack Fisher, had made a hurried visit to East St. Louis a few days before to seek defense witnesses. A handwriting expert brought to Taylorville, John Stockton, a penmanship teacher in Springfield, said Shelton's signature—handed to Stockton in court—and the questionable entries in the blotter either were made by the same person or by an individual who had Shelton's signature before him when he made the blotter entries.

Since the information on the blotter, if true, precluded the possibility of Earl and Bernie being in Kincaid during the holdup, reporters at the trial closely scrutinized the blotter after it was produced in court. Following up on the point raised by Hogan in his questioning of O'Rourke, the scribes saw that the page at issue had been obviously torn out of the blotter and pasted back again. It was the only page in that volume so mutilated. The last three names on the page were Jim Brown, Will Smith and Tom Jones. The blotter showed that they also had been arrested by patrolmen Grimes and Hobbs, and the blotter further revealed that Brown,

Smith and Jones had been dismissed by order of then East St. Louis Police Chief John J. Barry. Directly above the names of those three were the names of Bernie and Earl, and the record indicated that after fourteen hours in custody they too were released by order of the chief. The handwriting recording the names of the Sheltons and Brown, Smith and Jones was unquestionably that of the same individual, whomever he was, but strikingly different from the handwriting for the twenty or so other names ahead of the last five on the sheet. In addition, the ink used for the last five names, beginning with the Sheltons, seemed to be fresh, while for the preceding names, it was faded with age.

Carl's alibi to avoid conviction for the bank stickup was that he was in East St. Louis the entire day of the crime, and that one or more persons would vouch for it.

Bandy got right to the point in his direct examination of Carl, the only Shelton to go on the witness stand at the trial.

"State whether or not you went to Kincaid, Illinois, on the 27th day of September 1924 and participated in the robbery of the Kincaid Trust and Savings Bank there," directed Bandy.

"No, sir, I did not," Carl replied.

"Did you at any other time go to Kincaid and participate in the robbery of a bank?"

"No, sir. I don't know where it is at."

After Carl insisted he never left East St. Louis on September 27, 1924, Bandy asked him where Earl and Bernie were that day.

"I know," answered Carl, "they were in East St. Louis."

"Do you know anything about their having been in jail in East St. Louis?"

"I know they were in jail."

Carl denied any discussion with Hobart Summers about the Kincaid bank, stating for the record that Summers was completely unknown to him before the trial. Shelton certainly acknowledged knowing Newman, but pooh-poohed Newman's testimony about the Sheltons seeking his collaboration in the robbing of the Kincaid bank.

"Has Art Newman ever accused you of any other crime?" Bandy questioned his client.

"Yes, sir," responded Carl, adding that Newman "accused me of killing Lory Price and his wife." Carl did not mention Newman's attempt to pin the Collinsville mail robbery on the three Shelton brothers.

John Hogan's cross-examining of Carl was lively and informative for those trying to keep up with the latest about the leader of the Shelton gang. Questioned about his business interests in East St. Louis, Carl said he'd been running "a battery and radiator station" for about a month and, before that, operated a gasoline station. Asked whether he had a "whiskey running business," Shelton said no.

"Did you run a saloon?"

"No, sir. I run a soft drink parlor."

Carl also testified that he still had an East St. Louis collection agency, the mention of which at the earlier mail robbery trial had brought a guffaw from those on hand. Actually, Shelton said he'd been engaged in that business since July 1924. Furthermore, under prodding by Hogan, Carl admitted there'd been a partner in the business, identified by Shelton as "Judge Bowen of Herrin, Illinois." That revelation was not pursued in the questioning, but some present could not help but be curious as to whether this Shelton business associate was the Klan-hating Judge E. N. Bowen of Herrin City Court who on August 30, 1924, granted a motion to dismiss a murder charge against Carl and Earl Shelton in the killing of Herrin constable and Klansman Caesar Cagle. Strange bedfellows? Maybe; maybe not.

Pressed by Hogan for details about his whereabouts on the day of the Kincaid job, Carl testified that he started off the morning in East St. Louis trying to find a bondsman to get his brothers out of jail. During the crucial hour between 10 a.m. and 11 a.m., he said he was at the Century Cigar Store on Collinsville Avenue, an East St. Louis main drag. Jack Fisher was with him, Carl added. After 11 a.m., Shelton related, he went to the police station to "get them boys out of jail." Fisher was still with him, he said. However, Shelton didn't secure the release of Earl and Bernie at that time.

In regard to that trip to the station, Hogan wanted to know whom Carl saw.

"The chief of detectives," Carl replied.

"Who was he?"

"That big fat fellow. I believe his name is Leahy."

As for other people that Shelton saw that day in East St. Louis, he specified the aforementioned Dougherty, Baker and Lee and added, "I tried to get them to be here for witnesses, and if I had got a continuance, I would have got them here."

Another part of Carl's testimony drawing special interest was his calling attention to his wound from a gunshot late in August 1924 in Herrin. In so doing, he sought to preclude speculation by those who suspected he was one of the two robbers thought to be wounded in the Kincaid heist since his arm was in a sling after the robbery.

In case some at the trial had forgotten, Carl wanted to refresh the memories of all present about the bullets both he and Earl reportedly had taken in the bloody shoot-out at John Smith's garage in Herrin on August 30, 1924, that produced six deaths. After Carl brought up the subject, Hogan picked up on it in his interrogation.

"Did Dr. Ryan of East St. Louis attend you?" Hogan inquired of Carl.

"Dr. Black of Herrin," answered Shelton.

"Didn't Dr. Ryan attend you one time, after a shot, at East St. Louis?"

"I don't think he did. Dr. Black took care of my arm. I had my arm shot on August 30th (1924) in Herrin."

"Were you ever shot in the leg?"

"No."

"Which arm were you shot in?"

"Left arm."

"Was it a revolver shot?"

"It was a bullet, but I don't know whether it was shot out of a revolver or not. I couldn't say. I know my arm was in a sling that day...."

"Your arm was in a sling on the 27th day of September (1924)?"

"Yes, sir...it was in a sling for five or six weeks."

"How long did it continue in a sling after the 27th day of September?"

"I guess ten days or more. It was in that shape at the time they (Earl and Bernie) were in jail."

Dr. Black was of course the same Dr. J. T. Black who was the operator of the Herrin hospital during the infamous siege of the institution by an angry mob of Klansmen early in 1924. Later on, a number of those wounded in the outburst of fire at Smith's garage, in which the Sheltons and others battled Klansmen, were tended to at Dr. Black's hospital. The physician and surgeon may not have been a close friend of the Sheltons, but he certainly had shared their antipathy for Glenn Young and the KKK.

In a later sworn statement, Dr. Black struck a blow for Earl Shelton's denial of the prosecution's charge that he was the Kincaid bank robber shot in the lower right leg by Albert Matozzo. According to Dr. Black, he treated Earl at the Herrin hospital for a bullet wound in his right leg after the gunfight at Smith's garage. A bullet, said the doctor, "entered the leg of...Earl Shelton below the knee, in the front of the leg, and came out at the back of the leg, splintering the bone of the...leg." Subsequently, Dr. Black added, he treated Earl three more times for the wound.

Carl Shelton's friend Jack Fisher was the only witness making it to the stand who personally vouched for the presence of Carl on the day of the bank robbery. Fisher, a colorful individual claiming in his testimony to be the professional wrestling lightweight champion of the world at the time, echoed Carl's testimony in relating that he, Fisher, was with Carl in East St. Louis a good part of the morning of September 27, 1924.

The only other defense witnesses of note were two inmates at the Chester prison, Floyd Armes and Paul Chapman. Armes, imprisoned for rape, was believed to be a member of the Shelton-aligned Armes clan of Herrin (one of Blackie Armes' brothers was named Floyd). Armes, who said he was in the same work gang as Newman at Chester, sought to refute Newman's testimony against the Sheltons by replying in the affirmative to one key question by Bandy:

"Did you...have a conversation with Art Newman, in the penitentiary, in which he said this, or this in substance to you, that he was going to frame up on the Shelton boys—that he was not going to let them stay out, riding around in fine cars, while he was inside?"

Bandy also asked whether Hobart Summers had told Armes in the prison that "Newman was trying to get him (Summers) to testify against the Sheltons in connection with the Kincaid bank robbery, but that he did not know the Sheltons?" To this question Armes also replied, "Yes, sir."

Chapman, sent to prison from Macoupin County for murder, contended that Newman had secretly passed notes to him at the pen in which Newman said that he could have Chapman's sentence commuted if he'd testify against the Sheltons on the Kincaid heist. Chapman said he communicated back to Newman that he couldn't do that because he did not know anything about it.

The odds for an acquittal of the Sheltons may well have been bolstered by the often vague testimony of persons in Kincaid during the holdup who were asked to finger one or more of the brothers as the robbers. Henry Clerick, the night watchman who'd fired at the bandits as they exited the bank, testified that he thought one of them was Carl Shelton but admitted that "it is pretty hard to identify a man" from a tumultuous event more than three years before. S. S. Stone, a barber whose shop was across the street from the bank, said he observed several of the robbers, including the one carrying the money bag who was shot in the leg as he reached the Cadillac. However, when Preihs pushed Stone to identify that robber as Earl Shelton, Stone did no better than surmise that the wounded bandit "looked like one of these men (the defendants) back there, but I can't say that he was the man."

Strangely, the prosecution pressed Ira Aull for descriptions of one or more of the bandits, but failed to ask the assistant cashier if he recognized any of the Sheltons as among the robbers. If any one person's identification of the Sheltons had carried weight, it would have been that of Aull since he was accosted in the bank and then taken hostage by the robbers in their getaway. Yet, William Greer went no further on this matter in direct examination of Aull than to ask him to describe the bandit with the leg wound to whom Aull gave his handkerchief in the Cadillac. "I can't do it," Aull replied. "I was sitting with my face downward." Likewise, bank president Shaw was not asked if any of the Sheltons were among the holdup men shooting inside the bank or if a Shelton was the bandit who slammed his gun into Shaw's head because Shaw was looking at him. Shaw's testimony so clearly failed to implicate any of the defendants that the Shelton lawyers waived cross-examination.

Albert Matozzo's appearance on the witness stand was hardly convincing for the prosecution. It was Bandy, not the prosecutors, who asked Matozzo to identify the satchel-carrying robber shot in the leg by Matozzo. Bandy began the questioning:

"Do you know who the man was you shot in the leg?" Bandy asked.

"I can't recognize him because I was not so close to him, about 75 or 80 feet," Matozzo replied.

"Can you see in this courtroom the man you shot?"

"I can't say it was the man exactly, but the description is of that man in the front there." (Matozzo designated Carl Shelton.)

"...is that the man you shot in the leg?"

"I could not say for sure."

"What is your judgment?"

"The man looked just like him."

With that, Bandy moved immediately to "let the record show that the defendant, Carl Shelton, is the man that was pointed out." In so doing, Bandy intended to show that Matozzo's recollection was just as confusing as that of other firsthand witnesses in that testimony before and after Matozzo's indicated that Earl Shelton, not Carl, was allegedly shot in the leg by the grocer.

After the windup of the testimony of Matozzo and others at the crime scene, the *Post-Dispatch* concluded that "the State has failed on one important point." Said the newspaper, "No witness could positively identify either Carl, Earl or Bernie Shelton as one of the robbers."[6]

Preihs entertained no doubt that he'd made the case against the Sheltons, though, in his blistering closing argument to the jury, a moment in the sun for the prosecutor. Rotten individuals to the core, Preihs argued, the Sheltons invaded Kincaid "not alone to take the money, but to take the life, if necessary, of our citizens...to do anything in order to take away their money and rob our honest working people."

The police blotter alibi again drew the ire of the state's attorney, who said to the jurors, "God pity those poor people in East St. Louis when the police record of that city is kept in the handwriting of a robber." Preihs still couldn't restrain his contempt for the city's police officers brought to the trial as defense witnesses, saying that East St. Louis was a "beautiful spot" and "wonderful place" where "they have monkey lieutenants, where they have liars as officers, and when I say liars I mean liars."

Preihs also attacked the Sheltons' attempt to refute the testimony of Art Newman, seeming to expect the jury to be outraged at the defense's depiction of Newman as "a criminal." Preihs did allow that he didn't think Newman "was a Sunday school fellow" because "if he was, he would not have been running around with these three fellows." Still, Newman turned in the Sheltons on the Kincaid robbery, contended Preihs, because "he has to live to himself and do the things he should do" in order to "clear" his conscience and "get right with God Almighty."

In conclusion, the state's attorney appealed emotionally to the jurors to return a verdict of guilty, saying it was their "duty under this evidence."

"It is the thing you should do...to preserve the name and decency and respect of the county which bears the name of Christian," he added. Otherwise, Christian well could be lumped in the public mind with "other counties in this State which have the picture of blood hung below them, such as bloody Williamson."

The final words of Preihs were not discounted by the jury. But the verdict wasn't rendered right away. The panel deliberated seventeen hours. Its first ballot was eight to four for conviction. Then the vote to convict changed to nine to three, and stayed that way until the fifth ballot when it stood ten to two. A unanimous vote for conviction was not attained until the seventeenth ballot on the afternoon of January 7.

One juror who consistently voted for an acquittal up until the end said he simply became worn down by others who said they just could not let the Sheltons go free. "I'd be ashamed to face my friends if I didn't return with a verdict of guilty," one juror was quoted as saying when the panel was deadlocked. Another held, "I can't go back home and face friends there if I turn these fellows loose."[7]

When the guilty verdict was read, the *St. Louis Globe-Democrat* reported that the three Sheltons were at first "unmoved," but that "their wives silently broke into tears." If any of the brothers gave a hint of being shaken as the verdict started to sink in, Bernie came closest. The newspaper reported that Bernie did begin to "appear nervous while his older brothers, Earl and Carl, although calm, lost a bit of the air of confidence that they have worn since this trial started."[8]

Less than a year after the start of their three-month confinement in Leavenworth, Carl, Earl and Bernie were facing a return to the clink. The sentence for each, imposed on the heels of the jury's finding, was from one year to life in the prison at Chester, already the domicile of a number of their gangland acquaintances. Burke promptly filed a motion for a new trial, a hearing on which was set by Judge Wright for the following January 21, two weeks away. In the meantime, the brothers were to remain free on their original bonds of $15,000 each, which they furnished back upon their arraignment on the robbery indictment.

Convinced the prosecution's case leaked like a sieve, Bandy and Burke pursued the quest for a new trial with the zeal of eager beavers. They moved, in particular, to undercut the testimony of some of the more damaging witnesses against their clients—particularly the witnesses that Bandy and Burke said they'd been given no chance before the trial to prepare for. Consequently, the new trial motion was accompanied by affidavits flatly countering what some of those witnesses had said on the witness stand.

Take Thomas Nave for example. He testified he saw the robbers' Cadillac, with Bernie at the wheel, pass his farm outside Kincaid not long after the heist. However, the Shelton attorneys came up with affidavits from two men, Carl Nichols and Robert Warrington, who swore that Nave was at their auto garage in Kincaid's neighboring village of Bulpitt during the time after the robbery as they worked on Nave's Ford coupe. Then there was the testimony of elderly Kincaid restaurant operator Sadona Bender, one more surprise witness at the trial, who said she ran out of her diner to the street during the holdup and got a good enough look at the bandits as she dodged their bullets to identify Earl and Bernie Shelton as two of the robbers. However, Bandy and Burke produced an affidavit from one Arley Rogers of Christopher, who said that he was in the restaurant of Bender, a friend of his, during the robbery. She never left her place of business during the heist, Rogers stated. Furthermore, he contended, Bender was suffering at the time from eye trouble so impairing her vision that "she would frequently stumble over chairs and other objects in the daytime...."

Some of the affidavits backing the new trial motion were predictable, such as Charlie Birger's. Denied an opportunity to appear at the trial, Birger attested in a sworn statement that he repeatedly had heard Newman say at Shady Rest and in Harrisburg that he intended to send Carl, Earl and Bernie to prison for the Kincaid robbery—as a way of getting rid of them—even though Newman "was satisfied the Sheltons did not have anything to do with such robbery." An affidavit not expected came from Harry Vancil, the Kincaid marshal in 1924 who traded shots with the bandits. He said that none of the Sheltons were the robbers he fired at.

The most surprising affidavit, though, was obtained from Fred Reiske. In a recantation of his testimony, Reiske said that he'd "made a terrible mistake and had done a great wrong" in testifying at Taylorville that a wounded Earl Shelton had been dropped off at Reiske's cabin by Horseshoe Lake to be examined by a doctor late in September 1924. Reiske said somewhat mysteriously that he was persuaded to give this untrue testimony by Hobart Summers, a frequent visitor to Reiske's residence during the periods when Summers was not behind bars. In his new sworn statement, Reiske said he had never seen any of the Sheltons before he took the witness stand at their trial.

However, neither the recanting by Reiske nor any of the other new information submitted in support of a second trial convinced Judge Wright to change his mind. After a day of heated argument, in which the opposing attorneys lashed out at each other, Wright denied the new trial motion. Exasperated, Burke without delay filed a motion for a stay of execution of the prison sentence for each of the Sheltons pending an appeal to the Supreme Court of Illinois. Wright did go along with that, ruling that the bonds upon which the brothers were at liberty remained in effect.

The hearing on the new trial motion, like the trial itself, was conducted before a packed courtroom at Taylorville. And the audience got its money's worth, most noticeably when Burke and Preihs almost came to blows. Over each impugning the other's county. Burke, rankled by Preihs' depiction of Christian County as a bastion of virtue, got under the state's attorney's skin by calling on Christian "to sweep before its own door before attempting to go as a preacher of purity to other counties."

Preihs shot back that in the years that Burke served as state's attorney of Sangamon the county "created a stench that permeated the entire country." He declared that "bootleggers controlled Burke's office, and he comes here defending them and their ilk so piously one would think he was defending ministers." To keep the hearing from getting out of hand, Wright called the two lawyers down several times, sternly reminding them he was holding court to consider a plea for a new trial and not to hear attorneys wrangle.

Even Carl Shelton chipped in to the day's circus-like atmosphere. After he and his brothers left the court, Carl summoned newspaper reporters on hand to witness an encounter that he said would show the extent of the frame-up against the Sheltons. "Watch me," Carl told the writers. The gang leader then stepped over to Fred Reiske, who was questioned at the hearing because on that day he was holding that part of his affidavit recanting his trial testimony contained inaccuracies.

"Good evening, Mr. Reiske," Carl said. Reiske gave him back a blank look.

"You don't know me, I see," Shelton continued. "My name is Johnson. I'm running for office in the next election. I want your vote."

"I'm pleased to know you, Mr. Johnson," Reiske replied before moving on.

Turning to the reporters with an all-knowing expression on his face, Carl said: "There goes a witness who testified against us. And his was the kind of evidence on which we were convicted."[9]

The next round in the Shelton boys' fight against their conviction was a doozy. In early March 1928, word got out that Hobart Summers admitted, in an affidavit made at the Chester prison several weeks before, that he lied at the Taylorville trial in order to help Newman frame the Sheltons for the Kincaid robbery. Summers, a lowlife from the small city of Ashley in Washington County, now said that he knew nothing of any alleged plans by the Sheltons to rob the Kincaid bank. In fact, Summers acknowleged, he'd never seen any of the Shelton brothers before taking the witness stand against them. Summers also stated that, in conspiring with Newman to set up the Sheltons, he did recruit Reiske to testify falsely at the trial that a doctor had looked at a wounded Earl Shelton at Reiske's cabin in the wake of the robbery. Reiske did what Summers wanted, said Hobart, because Reiske "is under various obligations to me."

"I know it to be a positive fact that the Shelton brothers did not rob the Kincaid bank, as Art Newman told me that they did not," Summers declared in his sworn statement. He added that Newman "was sure that he (Newman) knew who did, but he was putting the Shelton brothers in their place."

In a transcribed conversation with Burke at the prison in conjunction with the affidavit, a discussion witnessed by the warden, Summers contended that he played along with Newman's fabrication because prosecutors indicated to Summers that they would help him with his legal problems if he was telling them the truth about his alleged knowledge of the Sheltons and Kincaid. However, when Burke asked Summers whether any of the involved officials knew from day one that Summers was lying, Summers replied, "Yes, I think Carl Preihs did."

Was history repeating itself for the Sheltons? Less than a year earlier, Federal Judge FitzHenry had set aside the Sheltons' conviction for the Collinsville mail robbery and ordered their release from Leavenworth after Harvey Dungey had revealed to John Rogers that he'd testified false-ly against the brothers at the mail holdup trial. The only different circum-stance this time around appeared to be the absence of Rogers.

Not surprisingly, Summers' changing of his story did spark a back-lash. The Illinois Bankers' Association fired off a letter to Preihs express-ing appreciation for his "good work in connection with the prosecution and conviction of the Sheltons." And Newman's wife, Bess, insinuated that Summers was funneled $1,800 in prison for recanting and, further-more, that he was the go-between in an offer of $10,000 to her husband to "lay off" the Sheltons, starting with a reversal of his testimony in the Kin-caid case. She claimed that Summers showed Newman the $1,800 in cash, which Summers had hidden in his prison cell.

Nevertheless, Burke and Bandy felt the recanting by Summers surely would be enough to finally trigger a favorable ruling by Wright. Armed with the Summers affidavit, the two attorneys asked the circuit judge to vacate or annul the verdict and sentence against the Sheltons in the Kincaid case. At the same time, the lawyers continued their effort to appeal the out-come of the Taylorville trial to the state high court. And a good thing they did. Refusing to bend, Wright held that the apparent perjury of Summers at the trial was not sufficient ground to undo the verdict. However, the jurist did extend the bond of the Sheltons so they could remain free pending a development at the Supreme Court—which was not long in coming. In line with a writ of supersedeas issued by Justice William M. Farmer of Van-dalia, which stayed the proceedings of the circuit court, the Supreme Court signified before the end of April that it would review the case for a ruling, possibly as early as October 1928. In the meantime, Carl, Earl and Bernie would remain out of prison on new bonds of $25,000 each.

An assurance that the highest tribunal in Illinois would be consider-ing the Kincaid case—leading, the Sheltons hoped, to a reversal of their failure to make headway with obstinate Circuit Judge Wright—was not the only happening in the spring of 1928 possibly auguring well for the brothers. Another was the hanging of Birger April 19, 1928, at Benton— a highly celebrated event. Birger may have retreated from his hatred of the Sheltons near the end of his life, but his enmity before that had wreaked havoc with the Shelton bootlegging enterprises in southern Illinois. With Birger gone, the Sheltons more than ever stood to have a seemingly unobstructed path to the resumption of control of the underworld in the state's lower environs. But only if the sword hanging over the Shelton heads in the Kincaid bank heist conviction did not fall.

It didn't, because the Supreme Court took the brothers off the hook.

In an opinion filed October 25, 1928, the high court set aside the judgment against the Sheltons at the circuit court trial and remanded or returned the case to the lower court for a new trial. The opinion, delivered for the high court by Justice Frank K. Dunn of Charleston, declared that an examination of the trial court proceedings showed that Wright was in error in denying the motion by the Sheltons for a new trial.

The Supreme Court made it quite clear in its 31-page opinion that it believed the Sheltons were denied a fair opportunity at the trial to adequately defend themselves. To buttress this finding, the court pointed to the testimony of Nave, Reiske and Sadona Bender, described in the opinion as "material and important." Yet, the high court emphasized, Bandy and Burke were given no notice ahead of time that these individuals would be testifying, precluding any effort by the defense to counter at the trial itself the damaging testimony of the three.

Just as significant, the high court indicated, was that the eyewitness testimony against the Sheltons did not hold enough water to support their conviction. As the opinion put it, "The only question contested on the trial was the identity of the defendants." But, the opinion continued, "the testimony of the witnesses on this question was rather vague and uncertain."

Expounding in this area because of its importance, the Supreme Court held that the "identification of the defendants by the witnesses who testified to the circumstances attending the robbery is not convincing. Not one of them directly and positively identified any one of the defendants. Each of them qualified his testimony by the statement that he thought this was the man; that he would not say for sure but there were features that had a resemblance; he looked like one of these men, but he couldn't say he was the man; or similar expressions of doubt by the witness himself of the correctness of his identification.

"The burden rested upon the People, not only to prove the commission of the crime beyond a reasonable doubt, but also to prove by the same measure of evidence that it was committed by the person accused, or some or one of them, and a conviction cannot be said to be sustained by the evidence beyond a reasonable doubt where the testimony of all the witnesses shows that their identification of the defendants is doubtful...A conviction of crime cannot rest upon probabilities alone, but the proof must be sufficient to remove all reasonable doubt that the defendants and not somebody else committed the crime, and it is not incumbent on the defendants to prove who did commit it."

The opinion proceeded to note that the other evidence "tending to support the conviction" was the testimony of Newman and Summers, convicted felons. Their testimony, it was added, "was of a character which is always regarded as subject to grave suspicion." Not only were Newman and Summers "in the class whose testimony is legally discredited because of their conviction of felony," the Supreme Court stated, "but they were self-confessed accomplices, according to their testimony, whose evidence the jury could receive and act upon only with great caution."

After the Supreme Court action, not many individuals would bet even a plugged nickel on the chance of the Sheltons ever reappearing in the courtroom at Taylorville for another trial of the case. When the high court denied the following December a request to reconsider its ruling, it was revealed that Preihs, by then no longer the state's attorney of Christian, had foretold the court that "the result of reversal and direction for a new trial practically amounts to a discharge of these defendants. This case was difficult in its inception because of the lapse of time and the methods used in the robbery. Even with the expenditure of large sums of money, it would be practically impossible at this late date to again have a hearing where all the facts could be presented and all the witnesses be present, and thus secure a conviction."[10]

The new state's attorney of Christian County, Harry B. Grundy, said only that he wanted "to examine the testimony more fully and talk to the witnesses before deciding what to do." However, the case never was retried.

The Sheltons, like cats with nine lives, had another new lease on life. They wouldn't blow it.

10

Gangland Monarch

When George Thomas Duffy resigned as editor of the *East St. Louis Journal* in 1961 to become a professor in the School of Journalism at the University of Missouri at Columbia, culture shock set in. There was a staidness to the school and its faculty that was jolted rudely by the coming of the hard-bitten newspaperman who'd gotten his education covering a rough and tough town during a thirty-year career with the *Journal*. Duffy wasted no time imparting his real-life knowledge of reporting to impressionable students. He often concentrated in his talks on the rampant background of East St. Louis, his native city, which became his beat when he went to work for the *Journal* as a reporter in 1931. It was a great time to be a reporter in East St. Louis, he reminisced, because the city of 75,000 was dominated by the Shelton gang.

G. Thomas Duffy, as he preferred to be known, did not like the Shelton brothers. It angered him that they further soiled his town's image. But he knew they were good for the newspaper game, and he never could bridle his fascination with them, even years after they were gone. One did have to remember that when Duffy cut his teeth in the business, two years after graduating from high school, the older reporters dwelled on the Sheltons.

With the trials at Taylorville and Quincy behind them, Birger dead and buried and the Klan put to rest before the elimination of those other obstacles, the Shelton brothers finally were free to make hay again in their chosen field of enterprise. A comeback was in order. Financially at least, for battling the court cases had left them severely strained for money. On the other hand, their reputations had been enhanced by the gauntlets they had survived. They appeared fearsome and extremely calculating, and suddenly, if only for a while, they had no more challengers. In no time at all, they were back on their feet, running more things and more lives than ever before.

Their bootlegging soon was going at full tilt again, with Earl taking the lead in transporting their liquor up from Florida, the Bahamas and other points down south. They became big wholesalers, middlemen acquiring a boatload of booze and reselling it a case at a time for a terrific profit. The business required a payroll of drivers and persons to guard the trucks and the secret warehouses. Old Shelton standbys, such as Blackie Armes and Ray Walker, were still on board, along with newcomers—young thugs like Frank (Buster) Wortman, a son of an East St. Louis fire captain.

The Sheltons also took a new, hard look at the long-standing gambling in East St. Louis, and encountered little resistance in moving to bring it under their management. Not just the big operators, but even the small guys paid the Sheltons weekly for protection, something the Sheltons could readily provide because of their payoffs and other ongoing ties to East Side officials.

By 1930, the Sheltons had more on their plate than they ever could have imagined in their wildest dreams during their poverty-stricken days as youths in Wayne County. In bootlegging alone, they were the undisputed kingpins of the trade in downstate Illinois—so secure in their hold on their widespread territory that the Capone crowd in Chicago kept at a respectful distance. The reinvigorated expansion into gambling by the Sheltons also spread in short order beyond the East Side, and in a most organized fashion.

In putting the history of the Shelton gang into perspective, 1930 had to be considered the year that Carl, Earl and Bernie attained their zenith in fame and fortune. The Kefauver committee reached that conclusion in looking back on the brothers and trying to pin down their take. The panel turned up some pretty hefty figures.

"A careful estimate of their income at the peak of their success in 1930," the committee reported, "was that they were collecting $2,000,000 a year from slot machines, $1,500,000 from handbooks and $1,000,000 from other gambling, such as dice...and $250,000 from vice. Estimates were that they had collected approximately $5,000,000 a year, and after paying for protection and other costs of operation, the Sheltons netted between $1,500,000 and $2,000,000 each year."[1] Two points had to be made about these findings. One was that the income listed from vice was debatable in that the brothers maintained they avoided drug dealing and prostitution. Second, the committee enumerated no money from bootlegging, even though the Sheltons were world-beaters at it.

Certainly, the brothers were in the clover for a three- or four-year stretch beginning in 1928. With ample dough to spread around, the Sheltons encountered few officials unwilling to succumb to their already finely honed skill at the fix. With East St. Louis authorities pretty much sewed up all along, Carl ventured into other parts of central and southern Illinois to bring local officials in those places into the fold. Carl's ingratiating manner was as much a part of his salesmanship as his bulging billfold. Besides supplying the brains for his gang, Carl was its ambassador, a role he played quite well. The man had acquaintances everywhere, and a large number of them, whether gamblers or politicians, regarded him as a friend. Carl maneuvered with a velvet glove whenever he could, or until a situation dictated otherwise.

With the world seemingly at their feet, for a spell at least, Carl, Earl and Bernie were on the verge of going beyond being just household names. Not that Earl particularly coveted notoriety. The farm boy was, after all, always in him. Some also saw lingering traces of diffidence. And as for Bernie, the impression was that he cared little what people thought. As one who knew him recalled, the priorities of Bernie were to have "good clothes, a big automobile and those gaudy diamonds, and to go out with a gal and have a hell of a time." The other sure thing about Bernie was the .45 caliber automatic he always stuck under his belt. It was different, though, for Carl. He was very image conscious (even though he was seldom seen without his pearl-handled, frontier model revolver).

As far as his line of endeavor went, Carl couldn't have secured a much higher standing than he was accorded at the end of the Roaring Twenties. Carl Baldwin well may have put it best. "At the beginning of the decade (of the 1930s)," declared Baldwin, "Carl Shelton, the soft-spoken leader of the gang which bore his name, was monarch of all he surveyed in downstate Illinois."[2]

However, that pertained to the gangland stuff, and Carl Shelton wanted more. He craved across-the-board respectability. He wanted the same recognition accorded any successful businessman, which he believed himself to be. Carl obviously did stand apart from many of his associates. He neither drank nor smoked, and he refused to gamble, considering it a fool's undertaking. He had a generous streak which surfaced often, numerous individuals insisted, especially when he encountered those beset by hard times. He resided in the better parts of East St. Louis. His demeanor truly was anything but loud, and he definitely was no braggadocio, a far cry from Bernie. Yet, he was shunned by the social set, including persons who gladly downed the liquor Carl provided. To him, this was the application of a double standard, and it upset him. On the other hand, the society crowd hardly could overlook the fact that the Carl Shelton palling around with officials by day was the same fellow at night running liquor trucks, many disguised as telephone line repair vehicles, to either deliver booze or hijack somebody else's.

Carl also did not help his standing in many circles by his profligate pursuit of women. Anybody wearing a skirt was fair game. When he favored a certain gal in a cathouse in the Valley, he made it known that this was the place he wanted patronized. The grapevine held that he even footed legal expenses for selected prostitutes, in spite of his adamant denial that he and his brothers pocketed any red-light district profits.

Judging by their articles, a number of newspeople couldn't make up their minds about Carl Shelton. But Thomas Duffy was not wishy-washy on the subject. Duffy wrote scathingly about Shelton and his men. After Carl's death, Duffy sought to remind readers of the *Journal* of Shelton trademarks in East St. Louis in the days when the gang domineered.

"It may seem strange...to many East St. Louisans today to read that men like the Sheltons once patrolled the streets of this city with tommy guns slung across their arms, with only a newspaper wrapping to hide them from the light of day," Duffy recalled.

"Carl Shelton," argued Duffy, "was no legend, although some romantically inclined soul might persuade himself to see around Shelton's life a sort of Robin Hood aura. Carl Shelton was a businessman, even though he used mobsters' 45s and tommy guns as his bookkeeping tools and the rum runner's car as his office. Carl was the smart one of the four Shelton brothers who turned to crime as a career; because he was smart, he was the leader of the Shelton gang. He was hard-headed enough to realize that if you're going to be a gangster, work at it and stay on your own side of the tracks. He didn't countenance the occasional forays to the other side of the tracks in which his brothers and others of the gang indulged. Carl preached that it would wind up in trouble....If the above sounds a bit too positive, blame it on Shelton lieutenants such as Jack Britt and Blackie Armes and the like. They thought Carl was too much of a disciplinarian and they talked to reporters about it frequently."[3]

Duffy, a son of a railroad clerk, took umbrage at what he deemed the unmitigated gall of Shelton followers. Wrote Duffy, "The Sheltons' trusted lieutenants lived with the brothers...and in their spare time managed to enliven the neighborhood with such little eccentricities as chasing their women out into the street in their nightgowns, threatening to shoot them; the women, or molls if you must use the term, of course would make the welkin ring with their pleas for mercy; the street lights shining through their gowns...."

To attract other women near their abodes, the fun-loving Shelton henchmen employed a lighter touch. If Duffy had it right, they tried "to strike up acquaintance with the young women in the neighborhood by such ingenious devices as chasing a dog into a yard and then reclaiming the pup, apologizing all the while for said pup's bad manners. Blackie Armes, a rather handsome devil, especially was adept at the...stunt, although he never made much actual progress. Stern fathers made even Blackie shy off.

"The point is, of course, that the Shelton gangsters—apparently secure in their contact with officials—had no scruples about trying to contaminate decent neighborhoods."[4]

As if all of this wasn't bad enough, Duffy also recollected that the gang "liked to 'take over' a small business—not for the purpose of muscling in on profits, for profits in those places were small; they just liked to have a hang-out and they also liked to see the small merchant slowly lose his mind as business fell away from contact with the underworld rats."

If the Shelton reign in East St. Louis had a bright side, it might have been a noticeable ebb in major gangster bloodshed on the East Side as the 1920s drew to a close. Anything that did occur could not have competed anyway with the St. Valentine's Day massacre in a North Clark Street garage in Chicago in 1929, a bloodbath in which Capone gang members blasted away with submachine guns and other weapons at members of a rival bootleg crowd headed by George (Bugs) Moran. Seven men died in the hail of bullets, a slaughter that shocked the nation.

Yet, not all was hunky-dory in the Shelton province, or at least Carl Shelton didn't think so. The St. Louis gang with the screwy name Cuckoo still was around on the East Side, a presence going back to its alliance with the Sheltons during the Shelton-Birger war. Carl and his brothers felt they needed the Cuckoos for protection of their back door while they engaged the Birger gang in southern Illinois. However, with Birger out of the way and the Sheltons cruising along in East St. Louis, Carl no longer needed or wanted the Cuckoos around. He ordered them to get out of Illinois. Cuckoo leader Herman Tipton ignored the directive.

Carl Shelton's next step was typical of the man at his best. It gave Tipton a brutal taste of what Baldwin perceived in suggesting once that Shelton was a mastermind who "won his battles not by bravado alone, but usually by delegating someone else to pull his chestnuts out of the fire."[5]

Employing crafty subterfuge, Carl successfully convinced Tommy Hayes, a fish-eyed killer in the Cuckoo gang dissatisfied with Tipton's leadership, to enforce his will. A violent upshot erupted early on the morning of October 2, 1930, when Hayes machine gunners fired a couple of hundred rounds into a cabin, along the Mississippi River near Valmeyer, Illinois, in which five Tipton followers were sleeping. The Tiptonites were guards for a large still operated nearby by the Cuckoo gang. Peter McTigue, a Cuckoo gorilla, and William Boody, a onetime plumbers' union business agent, awoke with death rattles in their throats. The three other guards escaped, two severely wounded.

The killing of McTigue and Boody ignited exactly what Carl Shelton desired, a feud within the Cuckoo ranks that decimated the gang. In the month after the murders near Valmeyer, the two men suspected of doing those shootings, Cuckoo extortionists Lester Barth and Dewey Goebel, were machine-gunned to death in broad daylight in the Hill neighborhood of St. Louis. After that, the factions of the Cuckoo gang went at each other with a vengeance, leading to the deaths of at least fourteen more gang members or their associates. Herman Tipton would be one of the few principals in the gang living long enough to die a natural death. Hard not to notice was that the elimination of the Cuckoos did not cost the Sheltons one member of their mob, a testament to the clever quarterbacking of Carl. It was true, as Baldwin said, that Carl was adept at getting others to do his dirty work for him.

St. Louis police were very cognizant of the Shelton role in egging on the Cuckoos' internal strife. The cops tried to get reporters not to obscure that factor in following the Cuckoo story. Thus, when a bomb went off early in 1931 above the offices of racetrack news service operators Beverly Brown and William (Gully) Owen in St. Louis' Buder Building, one headline blared: "Bombing Called Shelton Defiance of Cuckoo Gang." The targeting of Brown and Owen, bondsmen for the Cuckoos, was labeled "a gesture of contempt" by the Sheltons, and tied to Shelton-aligned Cuckoos who'd worked for Brown and Owen but "split with them because they did not believe they were being paid in proportion to their value in the racing news business."[6]

Try though he did to keep his own hands clean, especially as the years progressed, Carl Shelton could not always avoid direct action. One of those times came, many authorities believed, in what Baldwin called East St. Louis' "bloodiest shooting affray."

Finding a body here or there hardly raised eyebrows in St. Clair and Madison counties, but the discovery of three of them February 2, 1931, in a ditch near Granite City went beyond the norm. The best known of the shooting victims, who had been bumped off in an East St. Louis speakeasy run by bootlegger Ralph (Wide-Open) Smith, was Joseph P. Carroll, an ex-policeman, gambler and former partner of Bernie Shelton in operation of the Red Top Taxicab Co. of East St. Louis. The others were Theodore Kaminski, a onetime bus driver and gang hanger-on, and David Hoffman, owner of an East St. Louis pawnshop. According to a story circulating immediately in the East Side underworld, the murders were a result of a quarrel between Bernie and Carroll over Carroll's investment in the cab firm. Within a day or two, police let it be known they wanted to question Bernie and Carl in the killings. Both denied any involvement.

Bernie actually got publicity by walking into the office of the East St. Louis police chief and asking the chief if he wanted to question him about the triple slaying. Whatever may have been discussed, Bernie departed undeterred, and that was that.

Years passed before a supposedly accurate account of what transpired at Smith's place finally emerged, and it wasn't pretty. It also punctured the claim by the Sheltons that none of them actually ever murdered anybody (they certainly did try as in the shooting of S. Glenn Young and his wife, but no member of the Shelton family was ever found guilty of murder).

Based on Baldwin's writing in the *Post-Dispatch* and his personal memos, Carl and Bernie were invited to a business meeting at Smith's beer flat at 330A East Broadway with Carroll and Tommy Hayes. Carl had an inkling that Hayes, the former Cuckoo gunman, had begun to entertain thoughts of supplanting him as East Side underworld chief. His notion was right on target. As Carl and Bernie alighted from their auto near Smith's joint with Thompson submachine guns, a friendly cab driver suddenly appeared and warned them they were walking into a murderous trap. The Sheltons kept their appointment, but instead of being victims they rushed into the speakeasy with their machine guns blazing. When the stuttering roar of the weapons ceased and the smoke cleared, pseudo-tough Smith found himself with three bodies, plenty of broken plaster, bloody rugs and the beginning of a nervous breakdown. He was on the next train out of East St. Louis, aiming to get as far away as possible.

According to Baldwin's accounts, Carroll and Kaminski were gunned down intentionally. Hoffman died because he just happened to be sitting in the wrong place at the wrong time. Hayes escaped, for the time being. Although the shooting occurred on a Saturday night, Baldwin said that the bodies were not "carted away until the following Monday." This was accomplished—Baldwin contended in a memo but not in what he wrote in his newspaper—with "the connivance of East St. Louis police."

Baldwin's memo on the triple murder also shed light on the circumstances behind the nearly two-day lapse between the killings and the time they became public. After the shots were fired, the reporter noted, the East St. Louis police station, just two blocks from Smith's place, got a call from a person who said he'd heard the shots. "The desk sergeant made a notation on his scratch pad, (and) made some fancy doodles around the notation," wrote Baldwin. "He intended to turn the information over to the 'hot shot' crew, but forgot about it. The notation became lost in a maze of doodles."

It was also pointed out by Baldwin that "Charley Marsalek, East Side reporter for the *Post-Dispatch* working the night trick, heard the shots as he paid for his late supper at Hodges Chili Parlor," not far from the scene of the shooting. "He (Marsalek) made a mental note to investigate whether the noise was shots or backfire—and forgot about it," added Baldwin.

No documented follow-up action was taken by anybody, Baldwin continued, until the following Monday afternoon when "a tipster called the *St. Louis Star* with information that three men had been shot to death in a beer flat...at Collinsville and Broadway (in East St. Louis). *Star* reporters, accompanied by St. Clair County deputy sheriffs, went to the address and discovered a porter erasing the last evidence of blood stains on the stairway leading to the flat. The *Star* broke the story of the shooting...and all the newspapers then took up the scent." At about that time, Baldwin concluded, the victims were found in the ditch a few miles north of East St. Louis.[7]

When the apparently true narrative of the slaughter at Smith's place came out many years later, it put blood directly on the hands of Carl and Bernie, something not done very often in spite of their many exploits with lethal consequences. When the Kefauver committee touched on the slayings at Smith's flat in a compilation of gang murders in the St. Louis area, the panel's report stated that "the job was believed to have been executed by Bernie Shelton" (thereby implying that either Carl did not join Bernie in the shooting as Baldwin contended or, if Carl did fire his Thompson, he didn't hit anybody).

After setting the trap for the Sheltons, Hayes was a sitting duck, a marked man now sought by the Sheltons as well as by his enemies in the remnants of the Cuckoo gang. As might be expected, law enforcement folks weren't fully aware of Hayes' plight because they were still in the dark about the real reason for the carnage at "Wide-Open" Smith's den. Thus, they were in a quandary when Hayes met death at the hands of machine gunners in April 1932 near Granite City. His murder came only minutes after the killing in Madison County of two Hayes' bodyguards, East St. Louis mobsters "Pretty Boy" Lechler and Conrad (Willie G.) Wilbert. The skeleton of diminutive Homer DeHaven, one more Hayes gunman, was found later near Horseshoe Lake. It was not until long afterward that investigators, including those of the Kefauver panel, decided that Hayes and his buddies were done in by Shelton executioners. In conclusion, it appeared that Hayes certainly turned out to be a classic example of an individual used by Carl Shelton and then exterminated by him.

Examinations of the Sheltons' lucrative period on the East Side invariably focused on one key—their quite amazing rapport with so many public officials, especially the East St. Louis police. Baldwin underscored this relationship when he asserted that the bodies of the Shelton shooting victims at Smith's speakeasy were secretly moved from the crime scene with the "connivance" of the East St. Louis cops. And then there was, of course, the trial of the Sheltons at Taylorville for bank robbery, where it was charged that an East St. Louis police arrest record submitted in defense of Earl and Bernie Shelton was an obvious forgery.

Reacting to public indignation in the wake of the Taylorville trial, East St. Louis city councilmen ordered the city's board of police commissioners to investigate the apparent forgery along with the testimony for the defense of the three East St. Louis cops that was intended to give credence to the police blotter page in question. However, the inquiry was a bust. Two of the three police board members, Stephen Hynes and Henry Bischoff, voted in late February 1928 to drop the investigation. Besides citing a lack of evidence of any wrongdoing, the board said it would proceed no further because of unwarranted "coercion" of the board by two councilmen, John J. Hallihan and A. P. Lauman. Hallihan countered that he and Lauman had tried to assist the board in the inquiry, but had done nothing improper. The board found fault with the unrequested help of the two councilmen, Hallihan argued, only to establish a smoke screen to avoid a critical finding against the police officers. The abrupt end to the investigation was not a surprise to those aware of the bond between the police and the Sheltons.

Baldwin, in the background material he assembled on the Sheltons, observed that the *Post-Dispatch* had a picture taken during the trial at Taylorville of Carl standing outside the courtroom with George Dowling, a future East St. Louis police chief, and another oft-mentioned friend from East St. Louis, businessman Leo Dougherty, later a Democratic boss of St. Clair County.

Even when the East St. Louis police acquiesced to public opinion and took a stand against the Sheltons, it didn't last. In the summer of 1930, James Leahy, the police chief of East St. Louis, ordered the arrest of the brothers and some of their men in a purported drive to rid the city of undesirable characters. After their apprehension, the brothers avoided jail by agreeing to stay out of East St. Louis for six months. However, the exile was short-lived. Three weeks after its start, the Sheltons were seen moving freely around East St. Louis, driving by police headquarters and City Hall and talking in the open to law enforcement officers. This effort, and others, to clip the wings of the Sheltons rang hollow.

If there was an officer of the law willing to wage an earnest campaign against the Sheltons, he'd been hard to find. But one surfaced. When he first appeared on the scene, he was not taken very seriously, and few people expected great things from Jerome J. Munie, whose election in 1930 as the new sheriff of St. Clair County was something of a political accident.

Munie, the first Democrat to capture the St. Clair sheriff's office in more than three decades, had been what politicians dubbed a throwaway candidate, not even expected to win by leaders of his own party. However, the Depression was setting in following the stock market crash of 1929, and antsy voters were beginning to take it out on Republicans in many places, including the county of St. Clair.

Nevertheless, when the thirty-seven-year-old Munie took office December 1, 1930, the occasion was not exactly a heralded one. The *Belleville Daily News-Democrat* primarily noted that his new office in Belleville, the county seat, "resembled a flower shop."

"At least ten bouquets were lined up on the desk and tables of Munie," the paper observed, one from the Democratic County Central Committee and the others "from the admirers and friends of Mr. Munie."[8]

A bigger play was given that day to the discovery of the bullet-pierced body of a "St. Louis police character" named Irvin Lochman in the rear seat of his new car on a road near Venice in Madison County. Newspaper coverage held that Lochman was an independent operator reportedly pursuing "liquor interests in East St. Louis." Consequently, police were said to have "tentatively laid his death to the Shelton gang, which has warned St. Louis gangsters to keep to their own side of the river."[9]

On the day Munie started wearing the badge much attention also was showered on the previous day's death of centenarian Mary Harris Jones, the Irish-born American labor leader known as Mother Jones, whose firebrand tactics left her lionized by union miners in Illinois.

Yes, Munie would have better days in future newspaper columns. But, at first glance, the Sheltons probably saw little reason to sweat the new sheriff. They'd befriended many of his counterparts in the counties where they plied their trade, like George Galligan in Williamson. Others were bought off, or gave way to compromise. After all, sheriffs in Illinois simply did not have the reputation of being the hardest of the law enforcement people to get to.

Surely the Sheltons would have no problem with Jerome Munie.

The family of Benjamin and Agnes Shelton in the early 1940s. Seated (left to right): Lula, Benjamin, Agnes, Hazel. Standing (left to right): Roy, Carl, Earl, Dalta, Bernard. *Photograph courtesy of James S. Zuber.*

Fairfield, Illinois, in the 1920s.

The young family of Agnes and Benjamin in the 1890s. Left to right: Benjamin with hands partly around Earl, Roy, Carl, Nora and Agnes, who is holding Dalta. Bernard, Hazel and Lula were born after this picture was taken. *Photograph courtesy of James S. Zuber.*

Carl, left, and Earl Shelton have good reason to smile as they take a break from their successful bootlegging enterprises in the 1920s. The brothers rose rapidly to the top of their profession, leading, for a while, to the rolling in of dollars. *Photograph courtesy of James S. Zuber.*

Carl Shelton, the smooth talking leader of the Shelton gang. By the time of his early heyday period around 1930, Carl was the best known gangster in Illinois south of Chicago. *Photograph courtesy of the Bowen Archives at Southern Illinois University-Edwardsville.*

Bernard Shelton, the youngest son of Ben and Agnes and the hot-tempered muscle man of the Shelton gang. Known as Bernie, he was a heavy drinker who had a fondness for partying and beautiful women. *Photograph courtesy of the Bowen Archives at Southern Illinois University-Edwardsville.*

The modest home of Ben and Agnes Shelton at the Merriam crossroads, four miles east of Fairfield. The couple maintained a very unpretentious life-style even after their gangster sons achieved success in their chosen field. *Photograph courtesy of the Bowen Archives at Southern Illinois University-Edwardsville.*

James Shelton Zuber with his grandmother Agnes and mother Lula, the youngest daughter of Agnes and Ben Shelton. Carl Shelton was a surrogate father to James Zuber, who spent part of his boyhood living with his mother in the home of his grandparents. *Photograph courtesy of James S. Zuber.*

Carrie Stevenson, the girlfriend and later wife of Bernie Shelton in the 1930s. Blonde and vivacious, Carrie got a lot of attention from newspaper reporters following the Shelton gang. *Photograph courtesy of Mrs. Miki Cooper.*

Bernie and Carrie mounted for the good life at Happy Hollow, the dude ranch they operated near Millstadt, Illinois. Bernie often played polo at the ranch, which was frequented by paying guests as well as mobsters seeking a respite from the limelight. *Photograph courtesy of James S. Zuber.*

Bernie in summery attire in the 1930s. The picture was taken by Carrie Stevenson, one of the few persons who took no guff from the often violent Bernie. *Photograph courtesy of Mrs. Miki Cooper.*

Bernie in a familiar pastime, playing with a dog. The gangster and his brothers loved animals, none more so than horses. *Photograph courtesy of Mrs. Miki Cooper.*

Ray Walker, a chief lieutenant to Carl, Bernie and Earl Shelton, with an unidentified friend. Gangster loyalties seldom lasted, but the hard-bitten Walker remained at the side of the Sheltons through thick and thin. *Photograph courtesy of James S. Zuber.*

Carl Shelton sits at the piano in his well-appointed home in Peoria in the 1940s. His last wife, the former Pearl Vaughan of Fairfield, is seated, while the woman standing by Carl is not identified. Carl was the overlord of the rackets in Peoria during World War II, a period in which Peoria's wide openness prompted some to call it "sin city." *Photograph courtesy of James S. Zuber.*

Pallbearers carry the casket of Carl Shelton from the First Methodist Church in Fairfield after the funeral services for the slain gang leader in October 1947. The murder of Shelton triggered a wave of violence against his family that led to the killing of two of Carl's brothers and the  wounding of another brother, a sister and a nephew. *Photograph courtesy of the Bowen Archives at Southern Illinois University-Edwardsville.*

Some of the thousands of persons who crowded into Fairfield the day of Carl Shelton's funeral. The murder of Carl was the major news story in southern Illinois in 1947 after the Centralia coal mine disaster. *Photograph courtesy of the Bowen Archives at Southern Illinois University-Edwardsville.*

Bernie's automobile remains on the parking lot of his Parkway Tavern in the hours after he was fatally shot while walking to the car from the tavern office (inside the white door). Shelton was hit by a single bullet from a gunman hiding in thick brush near the bar. *Photograph courtesy of the Bowen Archives at Southern Illinois University-Edwardsville.*

The body of Bernie Shelton lies in the emergency room of St. Francis Hospital in Peoria. Shelton was shot by an unknown assassin July 26, 1948, outside a tavern that he ran near the edge of Peoria. Rushed by ambulance to St. Francis, he died shortly after his arrival. *Photograph courtesy of the Bowen Archives at Southern Illinois University-Edwardsville.*

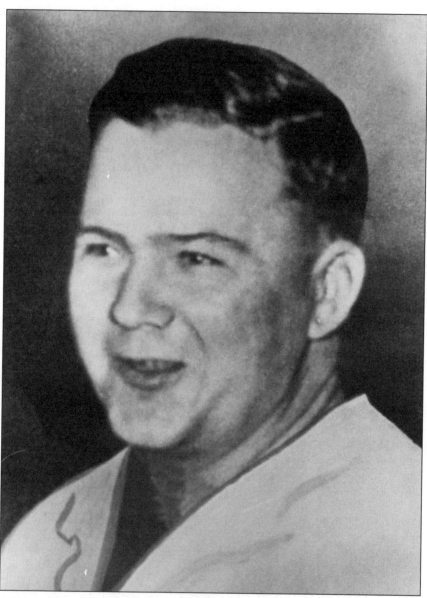

Earl Benjamin Shelton, a nephew of Carl, Earl and Bernie. Little Earl, as he was called, survived more than one attempt on his life as Shelton enemies sought to exterminate surviving members of the family of Ben and Agnes in 1949, 1950 and 1951. After serving in World War II, Little Earl worked as a bodyguard for several of his uncles. *Photograph courtesy of the Bowen Archives at Southern Illinois University-Edwardsville.*

Big Earl Shelton on the beach by Jacksonville, Florida, in the 1960s. A canny businessman, he prospered in property investments in the Jacksonville area, where he lived to the age of ninety-six after leaving Illinois in 1951. *Photograph courtesy of James S. Zuber.*

The Shelton family grave site in Maple Hill Cemetery at Fairfield. Ben, Carl and Roy are buried at the site. Others in the family are interred elsewhere. *Photograph by the author.*

11

An Honest Sheriff

ld-timers may have laid it on a little thick when they said Jerome Munie detested Carl Shelton, hated him with a passion. True, Munie had no tolerance for scofflaws, and none of them stood out like Shelton and his men when Munie became sheriff. Also true, the Shelton gang guessed wrong in assuming it could deal with Munie, and it became a new experience for gang members to encounter a sheriff who tracked them as relentlessly as a coonhound. He actually haunted them, leaving them scratching their heads at his incorruptibility. But was it accurate to say Munie despised Carl Shelton? Leland Munie, a son of the sheriff, wasn't totally convinced of that.

As Lee Munie put it years later in 1999 at his home in Belleville, "My dad and Carl Shelton certainly were not friends, even though they came to know each other well. What dad did say about Carl was that he would have been a big executive if he'd been in any other business. Dad also said that Carl told him that my father and his family would not be hurt because Carl believed my dad was a man of his word."[1]

Although only two years old when his father began his four-year term as sheriff, Lee Munie grew up immersed in tales of the engrossing interplay between his dad and Carl Shelton. When Munie launched a drive soon after taking office against gambling establishments, vice and whiskey stills in the county, Carl and his men at first tried the usual routes to get him to back off. They offered him a Cadillac, which he spurned. They offered the sheriff, whose annual salary was $4,000, as much as $100 a day to ignore their activities, but to no avail. If not these things, they asked, what did he want? The answer was nothing.

The Sheltons "tried everything to bribe dad," recalled Mrs. Shirley Truttmann, a daughter of Sheriff Munie, "but he refused them. He could have become a rich man. He told us, his children, 'I could have a lot of money to give you, but I can't do something that goes against my conscience. I have to be able to live with myself the rest of my life.'"[2]

Carl even tried to soften up Munie by currying favor with the sheriff's little daughter Jeannene. This was possible because the sheriff's family lived in the old brick county jail building at First and Washington streets in Belleville (where Munie's wife, Mary, served as jail matron for the great sum of $85 a month). Sometimes when Carl was brought to the jail for questioning by the sheriff, Lee Munie said he learned later, "Carl would give a dollar to Jeannene as she wandered in and out."[3]

When offers of money, even handing out bucks to Jeannene, didn't help, the Sheltons resorted to other tactics to turn around Munie. Carl, and Bernie too, knowing Munie was a devout Catholic, sought to score points with him by wearing scapular medals when they met him. The sheriff was not impressed. Then the brothers, or rather their followers, attempted to make fun of Munie.

Everybody seemed to hear about the time not long after Munie took office that Tommy Hayes, still in the Shelton fold, was hauled in by Munie for questioning about a murder the day before, a Sunday. "Where were you yesterday, Hayes?" Munie asked. Turning his fish eyes on the sheriff, Hayes sneered back, "In Sunday school, you dope!"

After none of the Shelton overtures worked on Munie, several Shelton adherents, perhaps not aware of Carl's supposed pledge to Munie, warned the sheriff in exasperation that he might find one of his five children missing someday. Thus, it was no wonder that panic was visible when young Shirley Munie could not be found one October evening after she and two of her brothers had walked to massive St. Peter's Cathedral in Belleville for a service. Years later, when she was Shirley Truttmann, a retired grade school teacher, she put on paper what happened that night.

Although not saying where her brothers sat in the church, she wrote that she "went up into the balcony in the first pew." Then, she continued, "I fell asleep and slid down into the pew. After the service, my brothers waited outside for me; but I didn't come out. They asked the janitor, who was closing the church, to help look for me. They didn't see me sleeping in the pew, so they went home to tell my parents. My mother was sure that I was sleeping in the church; but when they called the rectory, they were told there was no one in the church. Remembering the...threat, many deputies in sheriff cars scoured St. Clair County looking for me. Finally, my mother persuaded the priests to look one more time in the church. I was there. I had awakened and was waiting for someone to come to get me."[4]

Regardless of time or place, the interaction of Munie and Carl Shelton always had the same bottom line. It couldn't have been spelled out more clearly than in one conversation between the two, while the sheriff had Carl in custody, that Munie loved to resurrect in his later years as a warden in the Illinois penal system and as mayor of Belleville.

Shelton wanted to know, Munie related, "what he could do to get along with me. I told him there was nothing he could do." Munie said he added, "Let's get this thing straight—there's nobody I know of who wants you in St. Clair County." Carl still expressed disbelief that he could not reach an accord with the sheriff, Munie said, noting that Carl reminded him that he was a property owner and taxpayer in the county and considered himself a friend of the law officer. He continued to press Munie about what he should do. Getting no answer, Carl had another question. "How am I going to live?" Munie quoted the gangster as asking. The sheriff had a quick reply to this one.

"I told him, 'If I were you I'd take your pistols and guns and go from town to town and say here is the notorious Shelton boys in person. You could make a million.'"

For two men whose life paths were so different, Munie and Carl Shelton had a few things in common. Munie, born in the old Reeb Station neighborhood by Belleville in 1893, five years after Carl entered the world, was also a son of a farmer. After spending part of his youth helping his father work a farm near O'Fallon, a few miles north of Belleville, Munie, as did Carl, labored in a coal mine. But unlike Carl, Munie served in the army in World War I, putting in time in France as a military policeman. After coming home, Munie clerked in a hardware store in O'Fallon and then ran his own business, a confectionery that was a popular hangout in the city of 2,500.

In 1922, when Carl and his brothers were still fledglings in the beer business in East St. Louis, Munie entered public life by getting elected an alderman in O'Fallon. He also became a Democratic precinct committeeman, the start of a lifelong allegiance to the Democratic Party. Although working his way up to secretary of the St. Clair County Democratic Central Committee, Munie was anything but a seasoned politician when he ran for sheriff in 1930. Democrats were weak in St. Clair politics then, and party leaders viewed Munie as just another sacrificial candidate. But he won, not only as a result of sudden GOP unpopularity tied to the depressed economy, but also because of the strong support for his candidacy by the American Legion and other veterans' groups. Not unexpectedly, Munie moved without delay after becoming sheriff to stack the office with veterans of World War I.

More telling of Munie's first days in office was the observation of onetime East St. Louis newspaperman Robert E. Hartley. "This 'country bumpkin,' as politicians called him, gave a polite audience to the party elite that had given him lukewarm backing, and then went on his independent way," wrote Hartley.[5]

Munie suspected his intended crackdown on crime would step on the toes of many political honchos, especially in East St. Louis. And he was right. As Hartley recorded it, "Throughout his term as sheriff, Munie encountered resistance from East St. Louis municipal and law enforcement officials, all of whom were captives of the system, and none of whom wanted to battle the Sheltons."[6]

The Valley was the first major target of the new crusading sheriff. Four days after he took office, he ordered the lowering of window shades and the removal of bright lights and pianos from the houses of prostitution. Munie was credited by Hartley with striking at "an icon of sin, a sleazy fixture in the heart of the city." Munie also recognized that, in attacking the Valley, he was challenging the traditional tolerance of it by East St. Louis officialdom—the same tolerance granted the Shelton gang. As a result of Munie's order, open solicitation decreased, and some women left the Valley. But it was far from shut down. Consequently, in

February 1931, he ordered a complete closing of the Valley and demanded that its remaining women "get out of St. Clair County." Simultaneously, Munie instructed deputies to shutter gambling spots and hoodlum hangouts, as well as the hidden liquor distilleries throughout the county.

Later in 1931, Police Chief Leahy of East St. Louis, although miffed at Munie for butting in to affairs in Leahy's city, felt he had no choice but to end his inertia against organized crime by also ordering a shutdown of the Valley. Too, Leahy felt compelled to follow up on Munie's seeming fixation on gambling in East St. Louis, a zeroing in that produced a sheriff's order for the seizure of all slot machines. Leahy ordered a halt to handbook operations in the city. In so doing, though, he could not refrain from taking a potshot at the sheriff. "Every time Munie gets mad about anything, he talks to the newspapers about shutting off gambling and vice in East St. Louis," griped Leahy. "He better clear up the county outside East St. Louis, where things are running wide open."

Munie was trying to do just that. But he lacked sufficient manpower to hit all the targets. Some Shelton operations were curtailed, but others hung on during Munie's first two years in office. Prostitution certainly was not stamped out in East St. Louis, but the Valley was toned down, no longer the mecca of sin that it had been for decades. Still, Munie's main quest, for complete elimination of the Sheltons from his turf, was not likely to succeed without outside assistance—and not the kind entailed in the largely surface gestures of the East St. Louis police. Munie needed real help. Perhaps he even beseeched such in his daily prayers. In any event, Munie got some breaks. They were developments that seriously helped turn the tide against the Sheltons.

One was the removal of Carl Shelton from the scene for a while, courtesy of federal prosecutors.

Come March 1931, Shelton found himself sitting in United States District Court at Danville in two separate trials. The first was on a charge against Carl of possession of liquor and maintenance of a public nuisance in East St. Louis in violation of the Volstead Act and the other trial was on an alleged violation by Carl of the Dyer Act, a federal law prohibiting interstate transportation of stolen cars.

In the liquor violation case, Shelton and another defendant, George Martin, were arrested in August 1930 at Shelton's home on North Nineteenth

Street in East St. Louis. Prohibition agents, after tapping the phone line into the home, heard Shelton call his residence from Granite City to tell a follower at the home that he would be arriving soon with a "load of alky." When Shelton and Martin, who was accompanying Carl, arrived at Shelton's house, they were arrested by federal agents awaiting them. Although Carl's auto contained no liquor, the agents claimed to have discovered five gallons of alcohol in his garage. That was sufficient, the feds held, for the charge against Carl and Martin. The federal court jury at Danville apparently agreed since it found Carl guilty of the liquor violation (but acquitted Martin).

Following the conviction, Federal Judge Walter Lindley, an old hand at dealing with Prohibition transgressions by big-name individuals, sentenced Carl to one year in jail and fined him $500. However, Lindley directed that Shelton serve only half the sentence in the Vermilion County jail and then be admitted to a five-year probation period.

The second trial, which began right after the verdict was revealed in the first one, was a rerun of a trial conducted previously on the stolen car charge against Shelton, a proceeding in which the jury failed to reach an agreement. The allegation by the government was that Carl had been in possession at one point of a Hudson coach stolen in Detroit and driven to East St. Louis. However, once again, a jury was unable to agree as to Shelton's guilt or innocence in the case. After ninety-six hours of deliberation, the deadlocked panel was dismissed by Lindley.

While in jail, as the jury pondered the stolen auto case, Carl made a little extra news by coming to the rescue of a jailer being beaten by two robber inmates trying to escape. Carl subdued the two criminals, locked them back up and called for a doctor.

The incident may have been on Judge Lindley's mind when he addressed Carl in open court before the windup of the multitrial proceedings.

"You are a man of intelligence and ability," Lindley told Shelton. "And from your appearances in court here and your conduct while in jail, I believe that you are not without character. I am sure that the same amount of energy applied to some legitimate pursuit would be more satisfactory to you, and I know it would be much less dangerous."

The judge had a question for Carl. He wanted to know if the gangster intended to lead a better life and learn to respect the law and property of others.

"Yes," Shelton answered in a low voice.

But it was not to be. Or at least not until years later—when it was too late.

In facing Lindley, and at other moments during the trials at Danville, Carl displayed humbleness that many onlookers had not anticipated from the most famous living gangster in Illinois south of Chicago. Bernie also was present during most of the time Carl was in court, but he left his swagger back in East St. Louis. In fact, the *Danville Commercial-News* gave both of them a thumbs-up.

After saying that "Danville got a good chance...to see what real gangster chiefs looked like," an article in the newspaper stated that Carl and Bernie "seemed to make a rather favorable impression." In the opinion of "most of those who were able to get a 'close-up' of their manner, conversation and actions," continued the *Commercial-News*, Carl and Bernie appeared to be "pretty nice fellows."[7] One of the federal officers on hand even gave the paper an account of how Bernie once saved the life of an undercover Prohibition agent by disarming a drug addict moving to shoot the man after finding out he was a fed in disguise. Another federal man at the trials who claimed to know the brothers quite well was quoted as saying that Carl and Bernie "have always acted pretty nice while I was around."

Getting favorable press was not something at which the Shelton brothers had excelled. It may have thrown Carl and Bernie for a loop. But, it shouldn't have. Depiction of certain gangsters in a less than harsh light was not all that uncommon at this traumatic juncture in American history. Saying they were mollycoddled went too far. But more than a bit romanticized? Well, yes. The movies were certainly prima facie evidence of it.

Nineteen thirty-one was the year that gangster films captured the public's fancy. Stymied by the Depression, Americans desperate to escape the nation's economic plight flocked to movie houses to catch, instead of the westerns or Mickey Mouse, Donald Duck or Betty Boop, scowling Edward G. Robinson in *Little Caesar* or pugnacious James Cagney's *The Public Enemy*. Living by their own savage code, the silver screen hoodlums, often pictured sympathetically as offsprings of social inequities, appealed to many with their brutal irreverence for the system. The same system that had left millions out of work and disillusioned. Apparently, a kind of perverse comfort could be derived at theaters as Cagney and Robinson challenged the establishment. Heroes they were not, but it was hard to believe the cinema gangsters were not glorified, were not glamorized like many of the real mobsters running around.

However, not even Hollywood (with an exception here and there) had the audacity to conjure up happy endings for its gangsters. Sooner or later, they were on the run. Just as in real life. As in Illinois. Cooping up Carl Shelton in a jail in Danville for some months was not enough by itself to put his gang on the run in St. Clair County. But it was the first of the breaks coming Munie's way that gave him momentum in his Shelton chase.

Munie also was lucky in not having to contend with Earl Shelton on a day-to-day basis. The sheriff and Earl did not avoid clashing, but Earl was preoccupied much of the time Munie was in office with an ongoing battle with the federal government over his liquor running down south. During Munie's first full year in office, 1931, Earl was arrested more than once for smuggling foreign booze from the Bahamas to places along the coasts of southern Georgia and northern Florida. One of the arrests, off the coast near St. Augustine, had a comical overtone. A liquor-laden boat with Earl and two other men aboard ran aground in shallow water. But Earl didn't try to escape because he couldn't swim and mistakenly feared the water was too deep for him to jump out of the boat. This made him easy prey for Prohibition agents who had to rescue him and the other two, also nonswimmers, in addition to arresting them.

Those arrests triggered a mess of difficult legal proceedings for Earl in which he found little relief from a run of charges and subsequent convictions on Prohibition and tariff law violations. While lawyers appealed his convictions in the cases—one of which reached the United States Supreme Court, where the panel denied a review of the case—Shelton pretty much remained free on bond, and was often hard to find. Eventually, having exhausted his legal recourses, Earl would serve an eighteen-month sentence in the federal prison at Atlanta, beginning in 1935, for his conviction in the St. Augustine smuggling case.

Earl's rum-running troubles actually began before Munie entered the picture. Back in 1929, Earl was indicted at Montgomery, Alabama, on a charge of transporting liquor from the Gulf coast to East St. Louis. His trial on the allegation was scheduled in December of that year in federal court at Montgomery, but he failed to appear, thereby forfeiting a $4,000 bond. For the next two years, he was noticeably out of the public eye in the East St. Louis area. Not until 1932 would he again be seen routinely in the open on the East Side with Bernie and also Carl, who by that time had returned to East St. Louis from his jail stay in Danville.

The next reverse for the Sheltons—one that set them up for a later knockout blow by Munie and some really tough guys teaming up with the sheriff—climaxed a bitter situation going back many months before Carl and his men figured into it. Involved was one of the most troubled labor disputes ever in the St. Louis area, a confrontation between the boiler-makers' union in East St. Louis and the Phillips Petroleum Company over the building of a $15 million pipeline terminal for the firm on the south edge of the city.

Violence in the dispute, ignited in part by Phillips' use for storage tanks of steel prefabricated by an open shop Chicago contractor, broke out late in 1930 when a mob beat carpenters and drove away others working on the building of company housing at the terminal site. From then on, workers on the project toiled under guard. Barbed wire was strung around the site, and armed men patrolled the grounds. In March 1931, laborers ferried across the Mississippi River to work on the project were ambushed by a hundred armed men on Hog Haven Farm Road near the river. Many rounds were fired, and four of the laborers' guards were wounded. Days later, Phillips filling stations in East St. Louis were dynamited. Even after the Phillips plant was opened in the summer of 1931, the violence continued. In July 1932, Phillips tank trucks attempting to enter East St. Louis at Eighth Street and Piggott Avenue were turned back by hundreds of armed men, and the drivers were beaten. That particular embroilment stemmed from the reported use by Phillips of imported painters on the storage tanks. When the roughing up of the gasoline truck drivers went on, the situation reached a boiling point.

About the same time that the beating of drivers began, rumors surfaced that Carl and Bernie and a number of their gang members had been employed by Phillips as guards. Lawmen thought they sighted some of the hoodlums when patrolling in the vicinity of the plant.

Shelton people were not guarding the tank trucks, but, sure enough, they soon were observed inside the company gates. One who saw them was Carl Baldwin, who in 1931 at the age of twenty-three had left the *East St. Louis Journal* to go to work for the *Post-Dispatch* as its East Side correspondent.

Shortly after the start of the slugging of the drivers, Baldwin, while accompanying a deputy sheriff, was peering at the Phillips complex through field glasses. Familiar faces were spied right off. "Here were members of the Shelton gang walking around wearing special emblems showing they were guards and carrying all kinds of guns," related Baldwin. "They had been hired by Phillips to protect its property."[8]

The addition of the Sheltons to the Phillips saga made an already exciting story for young Baldwin more explosive. Getting just the opportunity to observe this kind of drama close up made Baldwin never regret going into newspapering, much to the disappointment of his father, Ben Baldwin, who in 1918 had moved his family (including ten-year-old Carl) from the Kankakee area to East St. Louis. The elder Baldwin was a freelance embalmer who'd dreamed of Carl and another son going into business with him.[9] Carl would have none of it, even though he saw plenty of bodies through the decades in his chosen profession. And some of those corpses related to his coverage of the Sheltons.

To be fair to the petroleum company, the use of the Sheltons by Phillips was no more troublesome in the eyes of many individuals than was the inclusion in the union ranks of numerous ruffians. They had not hesitated to inflict heavy losses on Phillips through property damage and injuries to workers. When the assaults on the drivers did not stop, Mayor Frank Doyle of East St. Louis directed Police Chief Leahy to station officers at the main trouble spot at Eighth and Piggott. Leahy did that, but mysteriously tacked on an order that his officers could not move from that location for any reason. So, while the trucks did begin to pass unmolested by that corner, the unionists congregated there were free to sprint to their automobiles and take off after the trucks without police interference. The drivers still got punched out, just in other parts of town.

For Baldwin and other reporters, the story was all consuming. They hung out with the cops and union fellows hour after hour at Eighth and

Piggott, waiting for a truck to come by and then to watch the labor rough-necks begin pursuit. Each time this happened, the scribes headed for St. Mary's Hospital to await the invariable arrival of an ambulance convey-ing an injured driver.

In between these incidents, the reporters were inclined to visit one of the eighteen or so speakeasies within a short distance of Eighth and Pig-gott. Quite often, remembered Baldwin, a few of the police officers assigned to the hot corner snuck off to join the reporters. At one memo-rable "beer joint hidden away behind a confectionery in a ramshackle frame building," Baldwin wrote years later, "home brew was quaffed and songs sung as a burly police sergeant banged out rhythms on a battered piano. It made the proprietor nervous, all the noise."[10]

As labor's war with Phillips dragged on, Baldwin and others heard that Carl Shelton had decided to resolve the matter by branching out from his guard position with the company to take over the boilermakers' union. The gang leader already had gained influence in several unions on the East Side. With the end of Prohibition coming and official tolerance for gambling an on-again, off-again thing, Shelton fully realized that he had to find other green pastures. Obviously ripe for exploitation in his eyes were the unions and their big organizational drives in the 1930s. Labor racketeering was a natural for Carl, and he became a pioneer in the field just as he'd been in other illicit endeavors. His intrusion could be subtle, pulled off in his velvet-glove manner. Or, if that didn't succeed, there was always forcible entry. Where the volatile boilermakers were concerned, Carl skipped the pussyfooting.

From the onset, Shelton came on strong to Oliver Alden Moore, the business agent for the boilermakers. Take a $30,000 payoff from the Shel-ton gang and get out, Carl demanded of Moore. No thanks, Moore was said to have replied. As president of the East St. Louis Central Trades and Labor Union, Moore was a top labor boss in the area and planned to main-tain the status quo. He was going nowhere. Okay, Shelton reportedly countered, Moore could consider himself a walking dead man. Moore was scared, or so the story went.

Informed of this by sources, Baldwin sought an interview with Moore to hear the man confirm his predicament in his own words. Baldwin got it, in a roundabout fashion.

"Reporters always carried a flask or a half-pint with them," explained Baldwin, "and that's the way I got to interview Oliver Moore. I plied some of his friends with liquor, and they went out of their way to go to him and say that I was an all right guy and he might benefit from an interview."[11]

Consequently, Baldwin found himself late in the afternoon of August 10, 1932, sitting with a very nervous Oliver Moore in a car parked at Summit and Collinsville avenues in East St. Louis. A trio of men armed with pistols stood guard outside the auto.

Moore talked freely to Baldwin of Shelton's bold thrust to seize control of the boilermakers' union, a key step toward making Carl chief of the labor movement on the East Side. Corroborating that he had turned down a $30,000 offer from Carl to pack his bags, Moore added that, in an angry follow-up, Carl had in fact threatened him with death.

"The Shelton gang hasn't been making money out of bootlegging lately," Moore told Baldwin. "They're trying to make a racket out of labor in East St. Louis."[12]

During the interview, Moore went well beyond his previous public statements about his union's side of the drawn out controversy. He contended that the union, devastated by the Depression, had offered to cast aside many of its principles to obtain employment at Phillips, but had been snubbed.

However, the aspect of the interview that stuck in Baldwin's mind was the visible apprehension of Moore at the mention of the Shelton gang. After stating that "word has reached me" that the Sheltons had imported "six carloads of red-hots from Peoria to bump me off," Moore added, "Well, let them try it. They can't intimidate East St. Louis labor."[13]

Still, Baldwin noticed that Moore flinched every time a car passed. Once when Baldwin, who was conducting the interview from the back of the car, looked up from his notes, he didn't see Moore in the front seat where he'd been sitting. Stretching forward, the reporter saw Moore hunched down against the dashboard.

"Didn't you see that car go by?" asked the clearly nerve-wracked Moore. "That was one of theirs. They've been driving past me all day long. I think they're pointing me out to somebody."[14] Moore's fright must have been contagious because Baldwin suddenly "began to get a prickly feeling" on the back of his neck.[15]

Moore took such a quick liking to Baldwin that he invited the reporter after the interview ended to spend the evening with him. Baldwin declined, saying he had a date and it was close to the time he said he'd pick her up.

However, as he shook Moore's hand in departing, Baldwin promised to see the labor leader again the following morning.

12

Strike Three in East St. Louis

Within an hour after he left Oliver Moore, Baldwin and his date were in the grandiose Majestic Theatre in downtown East St. Louis watching Greta Garbo and Joan Crawford in the 1932 classic *Grand Hotel*. After the movie, the pair went to a speakeasy that Baldwin frequented on State Street. He was in the place only a moment or two before he heard the news. Moore had been shot to death.

Stunned but still moving quickly, Baldwin took his date home and hurried to the East St. Louis police station to catch up on the killing's details, which when added to Baldwin's exclusive interview with Moore, gave the reporter one heck of a story. Baldwin learned that Moore, after their meeting, had gone to his union headquarters on St. Louis Avenue, ironically not far from the Majestic. Just about the time Baldwin was getting seated in the theater, twenty-seven machine-gun bullets perforated Moore's body as he turned to leave a group of associates in front of the boilermakers' office. Two of his companions were wounded. The firing, which Baldwin didn't hear, came from a dark sedan speeding by in second gear. Before anybody got a look at the car's occupants, it was gone.

Coverage of Moore's murder in the *Post-Dispatch* was indeed a journalistic coup, although Baldwin got little credit at the time. Since the story was written by a rewrite man from information he had dictated, Baldwin did not get a byline. He thought he'd be commended by Ben

Reese, the gruff city editor of the *Post-Dispatch*, but it was hard to be sure as praise for young reporters was difficult to come by. "You were damn lucky to get that story," Reese told Baldwin, "but just because you had the good sense to try to get labor's side of the story, I'm giving you a $5 bonus...." That was a day's pay for Baldwin, but he considered it little beyond a token gesture.

So it seemed that Baldwin's career was hardly advanced by the *Post-Dispatch* breaking the news of Shelton's bribe offer and threat to Moore. In fact, the immediate impact on the career of Carl Shelton was much greater, especially when the world learned that the labor leader was murdered not even an hour after telling a newspaperman that Shelton wanted to take over the boilermakers' union. East St. Louis was a blue-collar town, and segments of the labor movement were making headway steadily within the East Side's sprawling industrial base. Workingmen may have quenched their thirst with Shelton-supplied brew, but they were incensed at the widespread belief that Shelton had done in Moore, who'd been respected as a tough but straightforward man.

It mattered little that none of the Sheltons or their men was convicted of the murder. One East St. Louis detective, inspecting the expert grouping of the bullet holes in Moore's body, openly insisted that "only one man around here could hold a tommy-gun that steady from a moving automobile. This was a Blackie Armes job." In the wake of the killing, reporters did query Chief Leahy at the police station as to whether or not he intended to arrest Carl Shelton in view of his reported threat to Moore's life. "I called Carl," Leahy replied. "Carl said he didn't do it."[1] However, the snug relationship between the East St. Louis cops and the Sheltons was wearing thin, subjected as it was to constant hammering by pesty Sheriff Munie and a growing number of others, which now included labor leaders.

The day after the murder, Phillips officials expessed shock and regrets. Years later, Baldwin would write that the Moore case was a lesson "all legitimate businessmen should have learned....You cannot do business with a professional gangster without sharing his reputation. If he has blood on his hands, some of it may come off on you." And, Baldwin contended, Carl Shelton "had the softest tongue and the bloodiest hands of any gangster who ever operated on the East Side."

Moore was mourned by labor as a martyr. His funeral was a major event, with hundreds walking slowly and solemnly in the procession behind the flower-draped casket. It might as well also have been a funeral march for the Sheltons on the East Side. Everything seemed to be going wrong.

The handwriting for Prohibition was more than on the wall. Its death became official in 1933. In February of that year, Congress passed the Twenty-first Amendment, which repealed the Eighteenth Amendment. By December, the Twenty-first was ratified by the required number of states, and before the year was over, crowds were thronging to taverns and bars in Chicago and other parts of Illinois to welcome the return of legal liquor. The "noble experiment" for some and insufferable drought for others had lasted nearly fourteen years.

Up to the final days of Prohibition, the Sheltons strove to squeeze every last dollar out of the unlawful manufacture and distribution of booze. They still had a gang payroll to meet, although most of those identified with the bunch devoted lots of time to sundry pursuits independent of the Sheltons that fit their talents. The final straw for the Sheltons on the East Side came when the brothers and their men found themselves the target of a doggedly aggressive strike force that provided Munie with his ultimate weapon against them.

Interestingly, the murder of Oliver Moore helped trigger this development—the coup de grace for the Shelton gang in St. Clair County and the surrounding area. The brutality of the killing caught the attention of Henry Horner, the Cook County probate court judge who was the Democratic candidate for governor in the 1932 election. Horner was on good footing with organized labor to begin with, and his anger at Moore's death gave him a special bond with union leaders in East St. Louis as well as with Munie, a friend of labor.

Furthermore, Horner was a law and order candidate, who in campaign visits to southern Illinois pledged, if elected, to guarantee respect for the law in the region. Horner triumphed handily in the November voting. His victory over former Republican governor Len Small, in tandem with Democrat Franklin Delano Roosevelt's landslide capture of the White House, put a Democrat in the governor's chair for the first time in sixteen years. Horner, the first Jewish governor of Illinois, moved decisively during his initial year in office to fulfull his promise to strike out at crime. A premier step was his plan to bring about a new era of cooperation among state, local and federal law enforcement officers in combating a rash of kidnapping and extortion schemes against private citizens, often well-off individuals.

However, the part of his anticrime effort best remembered south of Springfield was the establishment of what came to be known as the Southern Illinois Crime Commission or, as some labeled it, the Downstate Crime Commission. The name referred to a small but rock solid contingent—set up at the direction or encouragement of Horner and under the command of Munie—with one essential purpose. To crush the Shelton gang.

The special detachment was made possible by Horner's assignment to Munie of two radio-equipped cars and two honest state policemen and by the provision of funding to permit the hiring of two local men with no-nonsense attitudes toward criminals. Although the state budget did not appear to specifically cover the creation of such a unit, Horner apparently drew the money for it out of contingency dollars at his disposal.

Paperwork underlying the commission may have been a little thin; even the origin of the group's name was vague (many credited the press with naming the unit a commission). Beyond that, there was nothing nebulous about the squad. Beginning with the two local persons hired by Munie, Joseph G. Schrader and William Miskell.

Joe Schrader was a former East St. Louis police detective and investigator for a private bankers' group, and all one had to remember about Miskell, a protege of Schrader, was that he was an expert with a machine gun. Schrader was one of the toughest cookies the Sheltons ever encountered on the right side of the law. When he hooked up with Munie while in his mid-fifties, Schrader was already a legend. Born on a farm near Carlyle, he was a telegrapher, barber and railway conductor before landing with the East St. Louis police. After working his way up to detective, Schrader and a partner were credited with the lion's share of major arrests in East St. Louis. Later, the St. Clair County Bankers' Association hired him as a private detective, and he displayed a very germane capability for anticipating robberies and making arrests as they occurred. *Liberty* magazine awarded him a $1,000 prize in its "hero" contest in 1925 for preventing a payroll heist in Venice.

Schrader claimed, and nobody disagreed, to know Carl, Earl and Bernie, along with most of their men, better than anyone else. Moreover, appearing to be in the company of those obsessed with Carl, Schrader was convinced that the gang leader "ran" East St. Louis "in the old days" when it was "almost impossible to walk down Missouri Avenue without bumping into a Shelton red-hot."[2] Carl being a teetotaler fascinated Schrader, as did his observation that Carl "only went on one job in a hundred." Remarked Schrader, "It was Carl's duties to give his henchmen the dirty work to do, and they did it." Like more than a few others, Schrader saw Bernie as a "big dumb ox" and, in contrast to those who found Earl affable, Schrader viewed Earl as "quiet and reserved but dangerous."[3]

To accomplish its mission to eliminate the Shelton gang, the commission—meaning Schrader and Miskell for the most part—employed a novel strategy, certainly one the Sheltons were hardly used to. Shoot first and talk later. It was a technique, wrote an admiring Tom Duffy, "with which the gangsters didn't have the intestinal fortitude to cope....Shelton & Co. couldn't stomach its own medicine." Getting to cover the commission's blitz of the Sheltons, crowed Duffy, "was a college education in how to deal with crime."

Little dust seemed to be kicked up by the commission's quick-trigger approach to its job even though it smacked of an affront to normal law enforcement procedures. As one observer recalled afterward, "Nobody can condone the methods Munie's men used, I suppose. But it's the only way they could have done it." Carl Shelton himself, so one account went, was asked if he was surprised at the tenacity of Munie in that the sheriff always looked to be smiling. "Any man that can arrest you with a smile on his face," Shelton supposedly replied, "can shoot you with a smile on his face."

As the commission hauled in or scared off Shelton gangsters one by one, often with guns blazing, no instance of personal retaliation by Carl, Bernie or Earl was recorded. Nor by Ray Walker, whom Schrader regarded as one of the toughest in the Shelton gang and as having "more nerve than any other member." More nerve even than Blackie Armes. Once, when Schrader was attempting to arrest Walker at a tavern, and he tried to escape, Schrader nicked him in an ear lobe with a bullet.

Walker "stopped and surrendered and gave me no trouble," recalled Schrader. "As a matter of fact, I never had any trouble with any of the Shelton brothers or Walker."[4]

The only close call Schrader had with a Sheltonite involved a gang hanger-on, a small punk named Harley Grizzell. As Schrader was walking early one morning from his garage to the rear porch of his home in East St. Louis, where his wife was waiting for him, Schrader said Grizzell and another fellow shot five times at him from the rear alley and fled. The bullets whizzed by Joe and his wife and ended up embedded in the house. Grizzell was wanted at the time for a $5,000 store robbery at Murphysboro. He later was arrested by Schrader.

Most in the Shelton outfit lived in morbid fear of Schrader, Miskell and company. Even the customary bluster of Blackie Armes wilted before Schrader in an encounter near the end of the Shelton reign on the East Side. It grew out of an arrest by Schrader and Miskell of Armes and two other gang members, one William (Bad-Eye) Smith and hotheaded James Hickey, on vagrancy charges. Hickey, a suspect in numerous bank robberies who'd only been allied with the Sheltons for a short time, fancied himself a very mean character.

When the trio appeared before a justice of the peace in Belleville, Schrader took the witness stand and began to testify about the bad reputations of the threesome. Suddenly, Hickey stood up and unleashed a verbal attack on Schrader.

"You _____!" Hickey shouted. "If I get out of here, I'll kill you! I warn you!"

Armes and Smith, all too aware of Schrader being the genuine article, were aghast. Jumping to his feet, Armes grabbed Hickey and yelled: "Joe, we're not in this! Joe, we ain't sayin this to you! Hickey, you damned fool, shut up! You're signin your death warrant!"

After pushing the impetuous Hickey back into his chair, Armes quickly turned to Munie, who was present. "Sheriff, you're square, but keep that Schrader off us. He'll kill us!"

Munie only grinned. And Schrader? He just sat there, sucking on a cigar and gazing at Hickey, who continued mumbling.[5]

No more than a few weeks afterward, Schrader, Miskell and a deputy sheriff trapped Hickey and other Shelton men in a house on Signal Hill (a neighborhood at the west edge of Belleville), where they were plotting a kidnapping. A gun battle erupted, and Hickey was killed.

The following day, Hickey's wife, Minnie, a resident of the Valley, was brought before Schrader and Miskell. Turning a bright light on her face, Schrader shoved in front of her eyes a headline on her husband's death. Minnie toppled over. It was suggested to Schrader that he might have been too rough on her. His retort summed it all up.

"We don't give any of those rats a break!"[6]

He and his cohorts certainly didn't. By the end of 1934, at the conclusion of Munie's term as sheriff, the Shelton gang was as good as history in the East St. Louis area. When the crime commission was not using the gang's own strong-arm tactics against it, the Sheltons and their men were still harassed, almost day and night it seemed, by suddenly emboldened officers on the once acquiescent East St. Louis police force. One reason may have been that the Sheltons weren't as free with the showering of payoffs everywhere after the death of Prohibition. Or perhaps the cops were shamed into a tougher approach against the Sheltons by the example of Munie.

The law enforcement community also was able to trump the Shelton crowd through vigorous enforcement in 1933 and early 1934 of a new state vagrancy law designed to let police freely hassle and arrest objectionable characters even if they had a "viable means" of making a living. Two of the first charged in St. Clair County under the statute were Jack Britt, a reputed bank robber and close companion of the Sheltons, and Thomas Wilder, a professional gangster and sometimes Shelton adherent. Although penalties for those found guilty under the act were relatively light, police could file charges under the law repeatedly enough to virtually hamstring offenders. To keep up with all the arrests under the vagrancy legislation and to keep track of who was in or out of jail at any given time, one needed a scorecard.

To some in society, the law was questionable from the start because it was seen as according police overly broad authority to detain or incarcerate individuals without just or sufficient cause. One arrest of Earl Shelton by East St. Louis police caused a furor when he was put behind bars for nearly eighteen hours with no specific charge filed against him. An attorney for Shelton requested and obtained the issuance by a judge of a writ of habeas corpus for Shelton on a ground that he was being held illegally.

Under fire in numerous places, the new vagrancy law, which authorities had welcomed as the first "vag act with teeth in it," was declared invalid by the Illinois Supreme Court in April 1934. In its ruling, the court held that the law failed to comply with a constitutionally guaranteed provision of due process.

As far as riding the backs of the Sheltons went, the vagrancy law wasn't the only pain in the fanny. Earl, Carl and Bernie were each accused of federal income tax evasion as the lights went out on their days of dominion in East St. Louis.

In May 1934, Earl and Mrs. Anna Carlson Shelton, identified as his wife, were named in a lien filed in federal court in East St. Louis that charged the pair failed to pay income taxes amounting to $4,359 for the years from 1927 to 1931. When penalties and interest due were figured in, V. Y. Dallman, internal revenue collector for the Southern District of Illinois (and also editor of the *Illinois State Register* in Springfield), said the Sheltons owed $8,714. The lien gave Earl's address as 523 Alexander Place in East St. Louis, although he said he no longer lived there. While the source or sources of the couple's income were not mentioned, the government indicated it based the delinquent tax figure on estimated annual income of $20,000, which appeared to be a ridiculously low amount.

The summer of the following year, Dallman named Bernie in a tax lien filed in the St. Clair County recorder of deeds office in Belleville. The lien alleged that Shelton owed $1,395 in unpaid tax (plus a penalty of $1,309) for the year 1930. Government agents said they assumed his income that year "was derived from gambling and similar sources." The federal filing listed Bernie's address as 826 North Forty-first Street in East St. Louis, but he really was living by then at a "dude ranch" in a rural part of St. Clair County that belonged to the gangster and his spouse.

Carl's turn came with the filing of another tax lien by Dallman right before the end of 1935. In that one, Dallman claimed that Carl owed $9,272 in back taxes and penalties for 1926, 1928, 1929 and 1930. The feds placed his address at 215A Missouri Avenue in East St. Louis, which was an apartment over Nick's Cafe, a Shelton mob hangout. However, Carl was no longer residing in East St. Louis at that point. As far as this case went, records showed that the lien was discharged by Dallman in 1941. It was believed that Carl paid in full what the government asked for.[7]

All of the amounts in these cases may have seemed paltry in view of the reputed income of the Sheltons in at least several of the years involved. Nevertheless, the actions reflected an increasing reliance by the government on the use of income tax cases to make life more miserable for gangsters.

It was an income tax violation case, not all the murder and mayhem he caused, that corralled Al Capone before a federal jury in Chicago in 1931, leading to his conviction and a prison stay. The prosecution's evidence was developed with the help of an impervious Treasury agent named Eliot Ness and his squad of federal revenue investigators, later to be known as the "Untouchables" because they could not be bribed. The person who prepared the case on which Capone was indicted and shouldered most of the work in presenting the evidence to the jury was Dwight Green, mentioned earlier, who'd returned to Chicago from his job in Washington as an attorney for the internal revenue bureau. Green happened to be the best tax person on a staff assembled by U.S. Attorney George Johnson in Chicago to investigate Prohibition period gangsters. Green's reward for his part in sending away Capone was appointment by President Herbert Hoover as the federal attorney in Chicago. Without question, Green was a man on the move in public life in Illinois.

Back to the Sheltons. No longer welcome in East St. Louis—the city Joe Schrader said Carl Shelton had ruled—Carl retreated to Wayne County and the old familiar farmland he knew so well. His holdings there had expanded considerably, a result of shrewd investment by Shelton of part of his take from his nonfarm businesses. Not that Carl wasn't spotted now and then in East St. Louis. He did, after all, still have ties to the largely undercover gambling operations that never seemed to end on the East Side. But in the main, especially after Earl became a guest at the federal prison in Atlanta, the only consistent reminder of the Sheltons on the East Side was the continued presence in the area of Bernie. And that had a lot to do with a woman, Carrie Stevenson, at first his sweetheart and then his wife.

Hardly any of the old standbys were to be found. Some were in hoodlum heaven, others just disappeared into the night and a few, like gang fulcrums Blackie Armes and Walker, ended up like Earl behind bars. Armes, Walker and Buster Wortman, still lesser known in gang circles in spite of a police record a mile long, were convicted in 1934 of assaulting federal agents during a raid on a still near Collinsville the previous year.[8] The agents had been in the process of arresting several men at the still when Armes and the other two arrived on the scene. Attacking quickly, the trio wrested the officers' rifles from them, severely beat the agents and chased them from the still. Armes, Walker and Wortman were apprehended for the crime later, not by federal people but, to no surprise, by Schrader and Miskell. The prison sentences resulting from the incident landed Armes and Wortman on "the Rock," the federal penitentiary on Alcatraz Island in San Francisco Bay.

One of the few Shelton men to quietly exit the world was Jack Britt. Tom Duffy found it little short of astounding that Britt in 1934 "died in bed, peacefully." Pent up in the memory of the *Journal* reporter was the last time he and other scribes saw Britt alive. It happened when he was brought to Belleville by Munie for questioning about the shooting of a star witness in a St. Louis kidnapping case.

As the press congregated, "Britt walked in," Duffy wrote more than a decade afterward, "followed by one of the most beautiful young women our then much younger eyes ever had got into focus. As usual, he was dapper and smiling, yet Jack Britt was a sick man. One look was enough to decide that." While waiting for Missouri lawmen to arrive, Duffy continued, Britt "got the sheriff's permission to take the newspapermen across the street for a beer. He told us then that he thought he was dying. He also told us that beautiful young woman was his bride. Both statements amazed us, no end. 'Treat her right, boys,' he urged. 'She's straight.' We never had the opportunity to do otherwise—we never saw her again, and we never saw Britt again. He died shortly afterward, of a dilated heart they said, here in St. Mary's Hospital."[9]

The service for Britt at the Burke funeral home in East St. Louis was modest for a gangster, another sign that the Shelton heyday in that part of the world was over. Just fifty or so persons showed up to hear a priest, who identified himself as a Britt friend "of former days" but refused to give his name, issue an old challenge. "Let him who is without sin," said the priest, "cast the first stone." Bernie Shelton was a pallbearer, but not many from the underworld were present, probably because law officers were standing conspicuously around the parlor. A chum of Britt asked reporters at the service to leave, and they did so without protest.

Aside from Bernie and one or two other gangsters, the only individual at Britt's funeral singled out for attention was Carrie Stevenson, who simply seemed to infatuate newsmen. Over the years, few of the numerous women entwined with the Sheltons garnered widespread notice outside gangland. Shawneetown's Helen Holbrook had succeeded in getting her name before the public. A few others did too, but none to the extent of Carrie Stevenson.

Her tempestuous years with Bernie added more colorful fodder to the already highly energized goings-on in the world of Sheltonism. Gangster yarns always benefited from the inclusion of a saucy, good-looking gal, and Carrie, the youngish and voluptuous blonde widow of a prosperous rumrunner, Ray Stevenson, filled the bill.

Carrie may have been linked first to Bernie in 1931 when she accompanied him and his lawyer, Harold Bandy, to a St. Clair County courtroom where Shelton was seeking, successfully as it turned out, dismissal of a charge against him of carrying concealed weapons. From then on, the two were an item, as melodramatic a pair as found in any soap opera. Carrie owned and ran The Pines, a popular steak house and motel in the Collinsville area. Bernie was a frequent patron, finding the motel cabins fitting for entertaining his men and their female friends. However, Bernie himself couldn't take his eyes off the proprietress, who with her own money, love of partying, tons of genuine diamonds, fur coats, sequined gowns and long eyelashes was his kind of woman. "Without doubt, she was flamboyant and extravagant," Mrs. Miki Cooper said of her great-aunt, Carrie Strange Stevenson, "but she was not pretentious."[10]

Mrs. Cooper spoke lovingly of her great-aunt during a 1998 interview in Springfield, Illinois, when Mrs. Cooper was cochairman of the Republican Party of Illinois. As far as she and her cousins were concerned, Mrs. Cooper said, Carrie was "like a second mother to some of us," giving the girls diamond rings and the boys classy tie tacks at Christmas. When Mrs. Cooper, a daughter of Saline County coal mine owner Russell Lanham, was a child in the late 1940s, she'd be taken on visits to The Pines, where she more than once tap-danced on the restaurant's piano. Carrie and Bernie had split long before then, so Mrs. Cooper grew up hearing little about Bernie from her great-aunt, who died in 1961.

But there were reminders. Mrs. Cooper recollected a locket of Carrie's on a gold chain that had diamonds shaped in a "C" on the front and a picture of Bernie inside. There was talk about the 1932 Dodge coupe with protective steel plates driven by Bernie when he brought Carrie to visit her sister (the grandmother of Mrs. Cooper) in Eldorado.

Carrie shared Bernie's appreciation of spiffy automobiles. She herself had a Pierce-Arrow, which nearly plummeted her into a watery grave when she accidentally spun it around on the Eads Bridge crossing the Mississippi at St. Louis. The classic car ended up so perilously close to the edge of the span that Carrie, afraid to move it even one more foot, timorously climbed out and let more competent drivers rescue the vehicle.

Carrie and Bernie had two other things in common—a passion for horses and bad tempers. "Believe me," Mrs. Cooper said, "you didn't want to mess with her. She had an air of mystery about her. You never knew what she was thinking."[11]

When Carrie blew her stack, she really exploded. Sheriff Munie and his crew were hit with a full dose of her anger in February 1934, when Bernie was arrested under the controversial vagrancy statute. Storming into the county jail, Carrie demanded Bernie's release. Receiving no satisfaction, she vented her ire on a picture of Munie on the wall behind the chief jailer's desk. Deputies summoned the sheriff from his living quarters next to the jail. Seeing Munie, Carrie let him have an even saltier piece of her mind. Munie promptly ordered that she be booked and lodged in a cell in the women's quarters. "Go on, lock me up," she yelled at the sheriff. "You might as well since you haven't any more on me than you have on Bernie."

Kicking and screaming, Carrie was dragged to Munie's living area, where she was searched by the sheriff's wife in her role as jail matron. Before Mary Munie was finished, Carrie kicked over a chair in the living room and broke a table lamp. When she finally was forced into a cell for women, she ripped off a shoe and, with its high heel, smashed panes of glass in a window. That got her charged with malicious destruction of jail property. The next day both she and Bernie were released on bond. Later in the year, a jury found Carrie guilty of the charge against her. She was fined $100 and costs, which she ended up paying.

Bernie himself did not escape Carrie's wrath. One night, aware that Bernie was dallying with another woman, Carrie shadowed Bernie and the gal and wound up confronting them as they sat together in a car on Broadway in East St. Louis. Flashing a gun, Carrie randomly fired a bullet that smashed into a building. She then beat the other woman on the head with the weapon, compelling her to stagger into St. Mary's Hospital for help. Carrie did not hesitate to admit her actions to police, but neither Bernie nor the other gal would file a complaint against Carrie.

Some trying to keep up with Bernie and Carrie were not aware they'd gotten married, not until she sued him for divorce in 1937. Her divorce papers, which charged Bernie with "extreme and repeated cruelty," said the two were married in January 1935. The marriage was never announced publicly, and, up to the time of the divorce suit, she had continued to use the name Stevenson.

Not as secret was Happy Hollow, the name of the so-called dude ranch that Bernie and Carrie operated not far from the quaint village of Millstadt. Bernie liked to depict the place as his "retirement" retreat, a refuge where he was surrounded by his beloved horses. Some saw it as the last outpost of the Shelton gang on the East Side, and it was true that remnants of the outfit made it in and out. The steady stream of visitors to the ranch went well beyond mobsters, though. Shelton family members came over from Wayne County, and there were paying guests too. Parties at the place were numerous and long.

Of course, lawmen found it hard to believe that Happy Hollow was an innocent recreational center. They'd stake it out, often for days at a time. In January 1934, after watching the ranch for days, Munie, Schrader and Miskell raided it. They were sure they'd find a hidden still on the property, but they came up empty handed. After their scouring proved fruitless, Bernie emerged from the ranch house and approached the raiders.

"All through, boys?" Bernie questioned grinningly. "Then come on in. We've got some fried chicken fixed inside."

Far more often than not, though, Munie and Schrader had scored bull's-eyes in their incursions against the Sheltons. They'd humbled the three gangster brothers, brought them to heel. Most saliently in East St. Louis, the onetime Shelton monarchy.

The extent to which Carl Shelton's status had fallen in the city was underlined graphically by *Journal* coverage of his arrest during an appearance in East St. Louis before the end of 1935.

Under a subhead pointedly noting "Leader of Once Powerful Mob is Riding with Negro in Out-Dated Small Auto," the story began: "Carl Shelton, former mobster and now a gentleman mule farmer near Fairfield, Saturday was the victim of insult and injury at the hands of East St. Louis police."

The article continued, "Shelton, who figured prominently in many southern Illinois killings and fracases of a few years ago, whose influence was a factor to be reckoned with, whose family name was a bugaboo to children and anathema to law enforcement officers, was fined ($100) for carrying a concealed weapon."[12]

The weapon, a .45 caliber revolver, was found on Shelton after his arrest by detectives who recognized Carl as he drove along St. Clair Avenue and knew that he was not on the city's welcome list. The newspaper chided Shelton for not being "in a super-charged limousine, as in the past, but in a 1928 Ford, borrowed from a friend." In addition, the *Journal* made a point of noting that Carl had a passenger in the car, Harry Sterns, an East St. Louis "Negro" (newspapers referred to blacks as Negroes in those days), and that Sterns too was arrested, on a vagrancy charge.

At police headquarters, Shelton was quoted as saying that he no longer was in "the rackets," but was attempting to live a straight life on his "$40,000 farm," where he was raising mules. He also insisted that a *Journal* writer understand that he was not dealing in "white mules" but in "the real thing," which Carl said were "bringing a good price on today's market."[13]

How things had changed.

13

A Break from the Spotlight

Since Clay is the first county north of Wayne County, maybe it shouldn't have been all that surprising that Carl and Bernie attracted so much attention when they journeyed one day in 1935 to the small town of Louisville, the seat of Clay, to buy farm implements. Businessmen came forward to introduce themselves to the brothers while a crowd of onlookers gathered to track the pair's every move. After making their purchases, the brothers felt compelled to ask for directions to leave town by a side street. For them, this was a common occurrence, especially in rural parts. Perhaps Sheriff Munie was right. All the Sheltons had to do to make money was to go from place to place and charge a fee for a handshake and word or two.

The brothers coveted something else, though, after the loss of their East St. Louis base. Hibernation from the notoriety that had plagued their lives since the early 1920s. As the last half of the 1930s moved along, the Sheltons tried to convince the outside world that gangsterism was a thing of their past. Judging by outward appearances, there seemed to be some truth to it.

Bernie, insisting that he truly was retired from the underworld, admitted to nothing more for a spell than the good life he was enjoying at Happy Hollow, the dude ranch he shared with Carrie Stevenson. Carl certainly was spending many hours working his ever-growing land holdings in his home territory. Earl, out of the Atlanta penitentiary and accompanied by a new wife, a woman said to be good for him, also returned to Wayne County, where he farmed his considerable acreage by day and ran a small gambling parlor in Fairfield at night.

The brothers were, for a few years, out of the big-time spotlight.

This also happened to be the juncture when young Jim Zuber became more involved in the lives of his Shelton uncles. His stay with his Grandma Agnes and Grandpa Ben got its start in a very Shelton-like manner. Upon the divorce of his parents, Lula Shelton and James Abraham Zuber, little Jim was in the custody of his mail carrier father, living in Evansville, Indiana. That changed abruptly the day that Carl Shelton, Lula and an associate of Carl pulled up in a car in front of the Zuber house in Evansville. After Lula talked her son into coming out to the car, Carl grabbed the youngster, seated him firmly in the auto and drove off, heading for Wayne County. Young Zuber later understood that warrants charging kidnapping were issued in Indiana, but follow-up action in Illinois was nil. He'd never forget Carl "pushing the car as fast as it would go" across the Indiana countryside, not letting up on the high rate of speed until the auto reached New Harmony, Indiana, and crossed the Wabash River into Illinois.[1]

From then on, Zuber had a window seat to the give-and-take, the to-and-fro, the ebb and flow of life inside the most widely known of southern Illinois' Shelton families. As if paging through a faded family scrapbook, the memories washed over him as he and his wife, Barbara, were interviewed in the summer of 1998 at their handsome brick home on a lake in northern Florida—a house built by Zuber himself, a carpenter. They were the remembrances of a man nurtured in his younger years by strong and affectionate family members, individuals who above all cared deeply about each other.

Zuber's Uncle Carl was a surrogate father and the man Jim idolized more than any other except for his grandfather, Pa Ben. Jim and Barbara named a son after Carl (as did Carl Shelton's brother Dalta). Uncle Carl "maybe didn't know much about reading or writing," Zuber reminisced, "but he could hold a conversation with anyone on any subject. And he really knew how to make a dollar.

"When I was a kid," Zuber said, "Carl told me to take every dollar I could get and put it into land. He believed the mineral rights under the land alone made the buying worth it. If he ever sold land, he never let go of the mineral rights." Some of the land that Carl acquired during the Depression was swampy acreage in the Pond Creek bottoms. Zuber recalled watching Carl dig ditches for drainage. He also went along when his uncle brought pairs of his mules out to pull out stumps and clear the land for farming. Carl drafted the mules when dynamite couldn't dislodge the stumps. When Carl motored to Olney to buy dynamite, he'd take Jim with him. Driving back, Jim remembered, "Carl would tell me to hold the dynamite caps and just sit still and be quiet."[2]

Carl Shelton liked Fords, and that's what he drove. Zuber spent many hours with Carl in his Fords, sometimes on the drives from Fairfield to Peoria, where Carl had business interests. It was not unusual, on these excursions during World War II, for Carl to pick up hitchhiking soldiers and sailors. "When he did that," noted Zuber, "he often bought them meals. Hardly any of them knew who he was." This was a side of Carl not as widely recognized.

"Uncle Carl helped a lot of people," Zuber said, "especially ones who really needed help." Jim guessed that 1940 was probably the year that Carl asked him to haul hogs out of his barn in the Pond Creek bottoms and deliver them right before Christmas to three poor families in the neighborhood. The first restaurant meal of many a person was bought by Carl, and he seldom hesitated to produce a $20 bill for down-and-outers. Some interviewed for this book cited instances of Carl paying funeral or medical expenses for families, no doubt the reason for his depiction in some circles as a latter-day Robin Hood. Charles A. French II, a long-standing banker in Fairfield, was even aware that Carl once offered to let another banker in town wear his huge diamond ring to Chicago so the banker would "look good."

For sure, Carl Shelton had many sides. Some contradictory. One day, Zuber might watch his 6 foot, 2 inches tall, brown-haired uncle sit for a manicure in Peoria. The following day, he'd see Carl getting his fingernails filthy handling farm soil and pigs. Carl's attempt as a young man to play a church organ was followed by a lifelong endeavor to teach himself to play the piano. He did get the hang of simple tunes, Zuber observed, "in spite of his big fingers." Then there was roller skating.

Carl had a passion for skating (an activity also pursued enthusiastically by Jim and Barbara Zuber throughout their long marriage). Carl even bought a portable rink that he'd set up under a tent in Fairfield and other towns. Lula Shelton operated it, at times with help from Shelton follower Charles Harris. In fact, a violent incident at the rink in 1940, while it was open at Fairfield, got Carl both wounded and back in the news.

A fray erupted between Harris and J. C. Anderson, an oil field worker overly attentive to a niece of the hotheaded Harris. After Anderson wounded Harris with a knife, Zuber (who was present) said that Carl tossed a gun to Harris to permit him to defend himself. As the melee intensified, shots rang out. Anderson was fatally wounded, and a bullet struck Shelton in his chest. However, before striking Carl, the bullet hit a steel spectacle case in his breast pocket and lost much of its force. Once again, luck was on Carl's side during a shooting outbreak. Authorities sought to pin the killing of Anderson on Harris, but he escaped any retribution. In the meantime, Carl had posted bond for Harris.

The importance of guns to Sheltons was clear to Zuber right away. He couldn't miss noticing the large revolver that Carl always stuck under his belt at his side. Before Carl slipped for a shave into a barber's chair (shaving was a twice a day ritual for Carl), Zuber would watch his uncle quietly lay the gun on a counter. Out in the fields, Zuber observed Carl shooting rocks off the tops of fence posts. More than once, when riding with Carl in outlying areas, Jim recalled Carl firing shots out of the car at reflectors along the road. Zuber got his share of trigger pulling too. He and others in the family took turns putting rifle shots into an old rusted armored car that Carl had ditched in the Pond Creek bottoms, a haunting relic of the past.

Another thing about Carl that Zuber came to recognize was his uncle's freewheeling way with women. He did not lack for the companionship of females, be they wives or mistresses. After his second known wife, Margaret Bender of St. Louis, died in 1933, Carl was married, for the last time, to a hometown woman, Pearl Vaughan, a comely brunette whose father ran a restaurant in Fairfield.[3]

Durable marriages were not always the case with the Shelton boys, but one that proved to be quite successful was Earl's final marriage. Ironically, her name was Earline. Earline McDaniel. An easy-on-the-eyes redhead, the Tennessee native was working in a St. Louis department store when she met Earl Shelton. They exchanged vows in 1936, and their union lasted until Earl's death a half century later.[4]

In the early years of Earline's marriage to Big Earl, she got a bitter taste of the violence frequently attending her husband's family. But down the line, living in Jacksonville, Florida, substantial financial success came their way, a result of Earl's business acumen in property investments and Earline's handling of the book work. Earl had a talent, Zuber joked, "for throwing a quarter up in the air and having a $5 bill float down."

Earl carried his love of animals, a Shelton trademark as much as guns and sawbucks, to the nth degree. He never went anywhere without a dog in the back of his truck or front seat of his Cadillac or other big cars. For years, his canine companion was Duke, a sorry looking half-breed bull-dog. No lazier creature on four legs could be found, but Duke was the apple of Earl's eye. Earline readily got in a snit, though, when her husband hauled goats, calves and other animals in his splendid cars. Earl understood animals so well he could treat their ills like a veterinarian.

The play given animals meant that younger members of the Shelton family, besides becoming shooters, were expected to learn to ride. Bernie gave Zuber a pony when he was young, but it "was out of a coal mine," Jim said, "and too mean for me." Jim had better luck with Blaze, a horse he learned to ride at Bernie's ranch.

Visits to Happy Hollow left myriad pictures in Zuber's mind, one of the more outlandish being the fifty or so pair of cowboy boots in Bernie's bedroom. The ranch home was on a hill and the barn, cabins for visitors and a swimming pool were down near a creek. To more enliven the setting, the mischievous Bernie kept a coyote chained by a bar at the pool. Even when feeding it frogs, recalled Zuber, "you didn't dare walk up close to the coyote because it was quick to bare its teeth."

The ranch afforded Bernie and his horsemen pals an opportunity to indulge in the upper crust game of polo—news of which gave rise to snide comments that Bernie was going soft. The never-ending party season at Happy Hollow peaked each year with the week of Bernie's birthday, which called for the barbecuing of a cow and days of revelry. Zuber was around for these good times because dark-haired Lula, unlike her more prim and proper older sister Hazel, was an ardent party-goer. Lula

Mae, a "surprise baby" of Agnes and Ben, spoiled said some by her older brothers, liked to drink, cut a rug on the dance floor and stock up on the latest in clothing. Lula was a live wire. It was no wonder she was crazy about Bernie.

One Shelton definitely not a life of the party was Roy. Zuber found Roy the coldest of his Shelton uncles, an individual hardened by his years in prison. Jim wasn't quite sure what to make of the often quietly brooding Roy, who after finally getting out of the pen bought a Packard (his favorite make) and turned his attention, with wife Blanche at his side, to the serious pursuit of farming.

The fifth uncle on Jim's mother's side, Dalta Shelton, short and stocky "Uncle Daltie" to Zuber, was an adept farmer living along U.S. Highway 45 at the edge of the Wayne village of Cisne north of Fairfield. Like Carl, Dalta refrained from drinking and smoking, but couldn't resist skirt chasing. Unlike his brothers, Dalta stayed clear of trouble with the law.

However, Dalta did put in his share of evenings running the poker game at the Farmers' Club, Earl's gambling establishment on the second floor of a Shelton-owned building on the east side of the square in the center of Fairfield. Little Earl Shelton, a son of Dalta, dealt blackjack for a while, and Big Earl oversaw the craps. The task of cleaning the club, actually a three-room apartment over a cafe, frequently fell to Zuber. For the gaming parlor to carry on unperturbed outside the law for the years it did, some local officials had to receive payoffs. Just as certain, the house produced a healthy take, especially since many of the players were well compensated oil field people engaged in the drilling boom in Wayne.

When reporters for the *St. Louis Star-Times* checked up on the club in 1943, Big Earl extended a hamlike hand in greeting them, they said, before insisting that his pursuits no longer went beyond his old home terrain. There, in his words, "everybody knows me and everybody is my friend." With a sparkle in his deep-set eyes, he informed his visitors that he was harvesting plenty of cabbage, both on his farm and in Fairfield. To show he wasn't kidding, he produced a roll of greenbacks from his pocket that looked like a head of cabbage.[5]

Along with oilmen, farmers and miners from the region, more than a few of Fairfield's denizens also made their way up the stairs from the sidewalk to the parlor. As Zuber put it, "The streets may have rolled up in town pretty early, but there'd still be cars sitting out in front of the Farmers' Club. Anyone who didn't know what was running up there had to be blind."

After operating his parlor from early in the evening to the wee hours of the morning, or as long as patrons hung around, Big Earl would catch a few hours of sleep before rising before dawn to work his 350-acre farm down the Merriam Road from his parents' house or to till acreage that he like Carl had bought in the Pond Creek bottoms. The days did not have enough hours to accommodate Earl's enterprises, but tranquillity finally had entered his life.

Carl sought to leave the same impression, but his existence was more complicated. His attention to his farming, as well as to his investments in oil, was quite legitimate. But the brightest of the Shelton clan always was up to more than met the eye. And what it was gradually became clear to more than a few as the 1930s drew to a close.

Moving quietly, if not always covertly, Carl had succeeded in remaining the single most potent individual in the rackets in downstate Illinois, save for St. Clair and Madison counties. At the center of the illegal activity was gambling, and there were few local games from Peoria to the bottom of the state lacking a tie to Shelton by the conclusion of the 1930s. Of course, Carl's hand had been in wagering all along at places where local operators went into gambling after being part of the defunct Shelton bootlegging network. But, even when this was not the case, the gambling usually would succumb to Shelton entreaties, which were backed up by Carl's know-how and reputation, and the perpetual threat of muscle.

Seldom operating games himself, Shelton instead became a partner of local gamblers. One way or another, Carl secured a piece of the action. If he provided little beyond the weight of his name to an undertaking, his take was small. If he did more, like keeping competitors at bay or dispatching guards to prevent holdups or maintain order, his cut could be considerable. The local operators also handed their payoff money to Carl, who distributed it to public officials. Smooth handling of officials simply never ceased to be a Carl Shelton specialty.

Before the early 1930s, many Illinois gangsters were not overly involved in gambling. However, Carl had the foresight, in the heyday of bootlegging, to inject himself into the back street dice games and camouflaged, smoky card rooms in the more wide-open towns. Some of these operations were dubbed sawdust joints because they moved around a lot to avoid law officers not in on the graft. One night a sawdust operation was in a warehouse; the next in a garage. Only after the repeal of Prohibition did a large number of racketeers turn serious attention to gambling. In one state, Nevada, the legislature had made gambling legal in 1931. But, the growth of the gaming industry there was retarded during the next decade and a half in comparison to the illegal but well-appointed casinos and sawdust joints flourishing in Illinois, New York, Florida and some other states. Too, by the mid-1930s, the mob had seized control of the bulk of the gambling in many states.

In Illinois, conventional thought equated the mob with the Capone organization. But Alphonse Capone's tentacles seldom penetrated Shelton territory south of Chicago either in whiskey running days or in the burgeoning gambling era. When the potency of the Shelton gang was at its crest, Capone himself dictated a hands-off policy toward the Sheltons out of reputed respect for the prowess of the brothers, something Capone never had done in regard to other gang leaders in the Chicago area. Interestingly, it was a brazen act of violence reportedly by Chicago gangsters that opened a door to one of the major footholds of the Sheltons in downstate gambling.

The incident happened in 1930 in Peoria. It entailed Clyde Garrison, the czar of gambling in that city at the time. Garrison was the target in October of that year of an apparent kidnapping effort by Chicago mobsters. His wife, Cora, was killed and Garrison wounded by machine-gun bullets when he resisted abduction. Shortly afterward, the shaken Garrison invited the Shelton brothers on the sly to join his gambling network in an effort to halt the apparently intended encroachment by the Chicago underworld. There was no more trouble from elements from Chicago or anywhere else, and Garrison enjoyed a lucrative alliance with the Sheltons during the 1930s. With the opening of the next decade, though, the partnership had cooled, prompting Garrison to retire temporarily from gambling and leaving Carl Shelton free to take complete command of gaming in Peoria. In short order, Peoria became the queen city of his gambling empire.

The gradual but surefooted Shelton ascension in Peoria occurred in vintage Carl fashion—as unobtrusively as possible. The cementing of connections with the right local politicians before going too far. A genial, even cordial approach to one and all, at least in the beginning. Some did-n't catch on until it was a matter of fact that Carl was the new gaming king of Peoria. On the other hand, Shelton links to Peoria had not gone entire-ly unnoticed in the 1930s.

Even when the Shelton gang ruled the roost in St. Clair County, the underworld grapevine held that the brothers also were spawning profitable connections to counterparts in Peoria. Not common knowledge, though, at least south of Peoria, was Garrison's invitation to the Sheltons to make themselves at home in Peoria. In May 1932, the talk of the town in East St. Louis was a running machine-gun fight in the city one night that month between occupants of two automobiles. Two Madison County policy game operators were said to be in one car and Bernie Shelton and sidekick Jack Britt in the other. Bernie and Britt, as well as one of the two in the other auto, were reported wounded. However, police couldn't find any of the sup-posed participants for questioning. Bernie, so the story went, took refuge in Peoria, where he received care in a hospital or private home.

The evolution of Carl Shelton into the downstate gambling lord coin-cided with the beginning of the wildest decade of the twentieth century in Illinois in unlawful, yet unfettered, gaming. Wagering would be more widespread in the state later in the century with the legalization of bingo, the state lottery and riverboat gambling, in addition to the already sanc-tioned betting at horse racing tracks. Nevertheless, the atmosphere then was tame in comparison to the dangerous nimbus surrounding the both sleazy and glamorous wagering houses of Illinois in the forties.

The rapid expansion of legalized gambling in the state, starting in the 1970s, occurred with the approval and cooperation of Illinois' ruling polit-ical elders. In turn, their campaign coffers were stuffed by contributions—all required by state law to be made public—from the corporations and individuals controlling the various gaming enterprises. Back in the 1940s, the explosion of illegal gambling also couldn't have happened without a tacit green light from major state officials. They too, like their brethren decades later, were rewarded handsomely by gambling interests. Not with publicly disclosed donations, but through under-the-table payoffs, often made to go-betweens in out-of-the-way places after the setting of the sun.

The explosion of gambling in Illinois in the forties was ignited after the election of 1940, a pivotal one in state politics. Eight years of Democratic gubernatorial control ended when Republican Dwight Herbert Green defeated for the state's top office Democrat Harry Hershey, the Taylorville attorney who had assisted in the Christian County prosecution of Carl, Earl and Bernie for the 1924 Kincaid bank robbery.

Green, forty-three years old and a native of Ligonier, Indiana, who gained name recognition in the prosecution that sent Al Capone to prison, had made an unsuccessful bid to unseat Mayor Edward J. Kelly of Chicago, a Democrat, in 1939. Green's strong showing, though, boosted his standing in the GOP. Winning the Republican nomination for governor the following year with little difficulty, he ran as a reform candidate opposed to campaign finance corruption and to alleged tolerance of crime and gangsters by Chicago Democratic leaders. In beating Hershey, Green led the GOP state ticket to victory in all races except for secretary of state, where Democratic incumbent Edward J. Hughes survived. Green had it all going for him, right down to his chiseled good looks.

When Green became governor, World War II had been under way for more than a year. Before the end of his first year in office, the United States entered the war. Life for many Illinoisans became topsy-turvy with the disordering of families and the suspension of other normalcies of society. An upshot was a heightening in the appeal of gambling, which mirrored the uncertainty that so many suddenly felt in their lives. Another thing was that the wartime economy put extra money into the pockets of many persons for the first time since the dawn of the Depression.

With wagering on the upswing, with increasing numbers of individuals testing their skill or luck at cards, dice and the slots, support broadened for the outright legalization of gambling in Illinois. Some individuals of this persuasion backed the governorship of Green in spite of its good government tone. One of the more prominent of these persons was O. D. Jennings, a Democrat and frequent host of Green at his Mississippi plantation. It also happened that a Chicago company headed by Jennings manufactured mechanical vending devices and close to 20 percent of the slot machines in the United States.

Folks like Jennings did not get their way on legalization, but gaming advocates did see one problem for gambling go down the drain after Green took office. Before the Green administration came in, outgoing Illinois Attorney General John E. Cassidy, a Peoria Democrat, obtained through a St. Clair County circuit judge the issuance of an unprecedented antigambling injunction designed to shut down handbooks, stop the distribution of horse race information and curtail gaming clubs, slot machines and pinball operations throughout the state. The injunction, which named 1,400 defendants, threatened to nip the Illinois gambling boom in the bud by making it much more difficult for officials to turn their faces away from wagering sites with a wink of an eye. The injunction was a sword hanging over the gambling industry's head. However, in 1942, an Illinois appellate court ruling reversed the circuit court injunctive action, holding that a court of equity could not enforce criminal law by injunction. The injunction subsequently died after Attorney General George F. Barrett, elected to the office in the 1940 election, failed to appeal the apppellate court ruling to the Illinois Supreme Court. The gamblers could breathe a sigh of relief.

As is often the case, there was more to the story. But it didn't come out until years later—not until the mollycoddling of gambling by top Illinois officials became a scandal inflamed by the brutal death of none other than Bernie Shelton.

Only then did it become known that an intent for the injunction's demise was discussed at a secret meeting of representatives of gamblers and state officials at the Broadview Hotel in East St. Louis in September 1941, nine months after Green became governor and fellow Republican Barrett was sworn in as the state's chief legal officer.

At the get-together, the gambling reps were told that the state would get rid of the injunction in return for regular payoffs to state officials by gaming operations. A system for the payoffs was outlined and agreed to by those present. Gamblers were to be divided into groups, each of which would select a person to pick up the payoff money from each operator in the group. In turn, these collectors would deliver the payoffs to collectors for the state officials at designated times and places. The scheme was put into practice shortly after the Broadview confab. Before it ceased seven or eight years later, millions of dollars were funneled through it.

A principal figure in the delivery of the payoffs was Carl Shelton. For years following the East Side meeting, Shelton paid $2,000 each month to a state "collector" as insurance against interference with the dice and poker games, slot machines and related enterprises run by Shelton followers in Peoria and across the Illinois River in Tazewell County. Accompanied by one or two bodyguards, Carl would leave Peoria and drive toward Springfield. At some point, he'd stop at a predetermined rendezvous, get out of his car and cross the road to hand the cash payoff to a "special investigator" for the attorney general or another state official waiting in an auto. The routine seldom varied, except for changes in the meeting place.

The payoffs may have constituted naked bribery, but to Shelton they were part of the cost of doing business. Carl was raking in the dough again, and he did not want big wheels with the state or Illinois highway patrolmen butting into his affairs. Like Governor Green, Carl was on a roll.

14

Roaring Peoria

If Carl Shelton had been a politician, and he certainly had some signs of being one, Peoria would have been his last hurrah.

Already a wide-open town on the Illinois River before Carl moved in, Peoria became a downright gambling mecca during World War II. The presence of Shelton loomed so heavily over the city in that period that one local official got little argument when he wagged that "you couldn't spit around here without you asked Carl."

Shelton even attained a semblance of social acceptance in a circle or two in Peoria, something he'd desperately sought, mainly in vain, a decade earlier in East St. Louis. Peoria never pretended to be as ruthlessly rough-and-tumble as East St. Louis. Carl called the shots on the gaming and other vice in Peoria with the aplomb of any other chief executive, succeeding greatly as he liked to do in staying aloof from the unruly aspects of his business. He pulled this off in Peoria better than ever before. If a situation got ugly, Carl had Bernie on hand to bring dissenters into line. Ray Walker was there too.

The Peoria bearing Carl Shelton's imprimatur was a study in sharp contrasts. Often a target of unfair put-downs by know-it-all outsiders, Peoria just as easily might have been pictured as a little San Francisco in central Illinois. Like Frisco, Peoria was a world of opposite extremes contributing to a full-bodied community encompassing the bawdy with tasteful grandeur. Visitors to Peoria were struck by the graphic disparity between the genteel life of the rich on the bluffs above the Illinois River and the drab existence of those confined to the sometimes ill-smelling industrial sectors down along the waterfront. A bluff and valley place in more than geography. No question. A city of churches, and at the same time, a cornucopia of saloons. A repository of civic-minded highbrows and a bunch of lowbrows, along with everything in between.

The Peoria that Shelton latched onto was Illinois' second largest city with a population of more than 100,000. It also boasted one of the state's most impressive collection of industries, bolstered for years by brewers and probably the best known distilleries in the land. Then there were the farm machinery manufacturers and Peoria's later claim to fame in the making of giant earth-moving equipment. Additionally, when Shelton held sway, Peoria had up to 200 firms turning out almost every product imaginable. Little of this was divorced from the river. Indeed, the need to satisfy the provocative tastes of those plying the Illinois and its commerce helped give rise to the worse side of Peoria.

For a town so vibrant, Peoria got a bum rap from coast to coast. President Theodore Roosevelt was said to have once proclaimed Grandview Drive to be "the world's most beautiful drive," but accolades were few in comparison to the potshots.

One magazine scribe was driven to say that outside of Brooklyn no place in the United States was slandered as routinely as Peoria. It seemed to be an unending open season on Peoria for comedians, old hoofers, vaudevillians and anybody else looking for a metaphor for hayseed or bumpkin. Why the constant ridicule? Perhaps too much was read into the fact that Jim and Marian Jordan—the husband-wife team playing cornball Fibber McGee and his long-suffering wife, Molly, on an immensely popular national radio show—were from Peoria. But who really knew?

Peorians took the lampoonery in stride since they apparently had little choice anyway. Not all liked it, though. A Peorian writing in the *Chicago Tribune* lamented that her town had been a victim of so much false advertising and mawkish jokes that "some people don't even believe it exists."[1] On the other hand, this writer hardly ducked the seamy side of her hometown.

Peoria, she wrote in 1974, "used to be the sleaziest, the orneriest, the rottenest and rip-snortingest town this side of...well, this side of Chicago and that side of St. Louis. Its sins are legend."[2] That didn't leave much to the imagination.

Many from Peoria did not argue with the labeling of their town as sin city, a gangsters' paradise or, and this one popped up a lot, "Roaring Peoria." Offense may have been taken at the debunking of Peoria as a hick place, but not at its depiction as a haven for gamblers and loose broads. The truth was the truth.

An interesting thing about it was that Peoria always had a considerable number of residents taking satisfaction in the city's tolerance of gambling and brothels. When Carl Shelton surfaced in town, illegal wagering was welcomed with open arms, by none more so than the politicians and officers of the law. As with many of his predecessors, Shelton flourished because he either bought influence over local authorities or, at the very least, had their tacit approval.

Such fraternization between vice chieftains and elected officials was accepted in Peoria because of its "liberal" tradition. To describe one as a liberal back then in Peoria, as well as in East St. Louis and even Springfield for that matter, meant something different than in the rest of the nation. Liberals in those major downstate cities stood for a wide openness that willingly endured, if not encouraged, gambling and other unlawful activity as long as economic vitality was enhanced. There were always "good" groups of citizens to combat the liberals, but in Peoria—at least up to 1945—the liberals often prevailed for the reason that their ranks contained, besides criminals, many leading politicians, businessmen and labor stalwarts. To a number of these "liberals," Carl Shelton was not a problem, but instead a firm hand in the Peoria business world. Some didn't object to sitting down with him in public either.

Shelton might never have gotten a foothold in Peoria if other outside gangsters had not launched a string of successful or attempted kidnappings of local gambling operators—incidents that terrified not just the victims, but also their political defenders. The botched move in 1930 to snatch Clyde Garrison, a partner in the operation of the Windsor Club on Fulton Street, one of the biggest gaming houses in the Midwest, particularly tripped alarms because the attack left his wife dead. After that, Garrison needed no more convincing of the need to import muscle to protect the still locally controlled gambling industry in Peoria. His hunch that Carl and his boys were right for the job turned out to be a good bet. For a while.

Prior to the 1940s, Carl danced to Garrison's tune, protecting the interests of Garrison (and other Peoria gamblers) from outside predators, but not usurping Clyde's role as the local gaming kingpin. The Garrison-Shelton relationship, many called it an alliance, was lucrative for both. However, rapport between the two went noticeably sour amid the gambling upswing in Peoria with the advent of World War II, the coming to power of the administration of Governor Green and the return to the city's mayor office of an ancient, genuine liberal.

Pinning down the precise reasons for a falling out between shady characters is seldom easy, as the Shelton-Birger split illustrated. The best that insiders could grasp in regard to this split was that Shelton moved to join Garrison in the political power brokering end of the game. Since this was a strong suit of Garrison, he resisted. But not for long. Realizing he lacked the firepower to engage Shelton, Garrison exited the Peoria gambling scene and went into the wholesale liquor business. Carl, then in his early fifties, had the field to himself.

For four years, from 1941 to 1945, Carl never had it better. And, lo and behold, that period just happened to coincide with the last mayoral term of Edward Nelson Woodruff, the most prolific and undoubtedly colorful politician Peoria had ever known. As they say, Woodruff was one for the ages. A descendant of a pioneering Peoria family and longtime head of an ice company, Woodruff served, off and on, as mayor of Peoria for a total of twenty-four years, commencing in 1903. A profane Republican with the visage of a fox, a man who suffered defeats as well as victories at the electoral box, Woodruff was nevertheless a beloved municipal leader without parallel in his day.

When Woodruff died in 1947, the eulogy in the *Peoria Star* for the city's "most honored citizen" typified an endless stream of tributes.

Said the *Star*, "In his many active years, Mayor Woodruff was a positive character who generally achieved his aims. He did more for Peoria, and did it well and for less money, than any other mayor in the city's long history. He was mayor during most of the prohibition years, when the city received no money from liquor licenses. Neither was there income during those years from parking meters or other sources which now bring money into the city treasury. Taxes were low, and yet streets were improved, bridges were built, police and fire departments were efficient, and all the city's bills were paid with reasonable promptness and without grumbling.

"Mr. Woodruff attained a wide reputation in those years as a wizard in municipal finance. He was known and supported as the business man's candidate. High and low supported him...."[3]

In its news columns, the *Star* added the following observation on Woodruff: "Always liberal, and in no sense a reformer, he held as a fundamental political philosophy that some degree of vice is inevitable in every community, but that it should be rigidly controlled." Judging by his final stint in office, Woodruff no doubt held this tenet close to his heart. He was a true-blue Peoria liberal.

Not far from his eightieth birthday when voters returned him to the mayor's seat in 1941, Woodruff was soon at the helm of a city where wagering sites seemed to outnumber restaurants, banks and even churches. For years, Peoria had housed a core of respectable gambling houses like the Empire on South Jefferson, with its large jackpot-paying baseball pools. But now every cigar store and other joint offered slot machines, horse betting, back-room poker and other inducements that might snare a sucker's dollar. Carl Shelton and his crew set up shop in the Palace Club, which was located, quite appropriately, right across Madison Avenue from City Hall. All kinds of gambling were offered at the Palace, but players had to be wary. Individuals coming out too far ahead sometimes were roughly relieved of their winnings after leaving the premise.

Some former Peorians looked back with shame on the windup of Woodruff's stewardship of the city. "Everybody knew that the politicians were running our city on profits from gambling and prostitution," wrote one woman. Decent people, this person went on, "wouldn't go within 100 yards of City Hall and its smelly spittoons. Bums cluttered its steps and threw their empty whisky bottles into the courthouse yard...." As for the whores, the woman added that "in high school our dates used to drive us on a dare through the redlight district. I can still remember those women standing in the doorways."[4]

Woodruff's benign attitude toward the unseemly doings did have qualifications. First off, he was said to be personally honest. Furthermore, his liberal philosophy notwithstanding, he advocated the zoning and licensing of gambling and prostitution principally for their potential to enrich the city's coffer. At the very least, the gambling operators and the tools of their trade were subjected to assessments or fines—the dollars from which supposedly went into the municipal treasury. For instance, during Woodruff's last term, gamblers paid a levy on slot machines—$20 a month for each machine—that reaped the city close to $170,000. Payments were documented in records and published in the press. Of course, crap tables, roulette wheels and just about every other thing used in gambling were targets of a city fee or periodic fine. There was a spell when prostitution overlords regularly deposited goodly sums of money at City Hall, dough that was applied to street cleaning (so the public was told).

As far as the fuss by the do-gooders over the brothels was concerned, old Ed thought it was just so much nonsense. What the heck, as he liked to say, "you can make prostitution illegal, but you can't make it unpopular."[5]

Unpretentious was a word often used to describe Woodruff. And it showed, from his modest residence to his private hangout, a decrepit stern-wheeler bought by Woodruff and converted into a crude clubhouse along an isolated stretch of the Illinois River. This retreat, given the humble name of Bum boat by Woodruff, became a political rendezvous for governors and Woodruff's local cronies alike. Get-togethers in the old hull produced strategy for the governing of Peoria as well as games of rummy, at which Woodruff was a fine player. Carl Shelton may or may not have made it to the Bum boat, but, whether he did or didn't, he and Woodruff were close to kindred spirits.

Woodruff's accommodation of the unlawful side of Peoria included no tolerance for violence. Thus, he had to be pleased at the great success of Shelton in maintaining order among the unsavory elements in the early 1940s.

Carl's far-flung business network required the enlistment of various individuals to carry out or oversee this or that particular endeavor. He mixed in aboveboard activities, such as the Shelton Amusement Co., with illicit pursuits. Headed by a trusted follower, Jack Ashby, the amusement firm handled jukeboxes and other mainly legal coin-operated devices. Only Carl had all the pieces of his weblike system in his head. Carl alone had the complete picture of who did what here and who covered bases over there.

Too, Shelton seldom was without an extra ace or two up his sleeve. Not until after Carl was gone from Peoria was it learned that he'd had supposedly silent associates in his slot machine operations. At least one such individual happened to be a respected civic leader and key figure in various legitimate businesses. This particular person, it was alleged, was especially sought out by Carl as a dependable businessman to keep straight books on the slot machines and advise Carl on the ins and outs of life in Peoria. The individual steadfastly denied ever doing anything untoward in his relationship with Shelton. However, the knowledge Shelton gained from engaging persons like this in Peoria was especially useful to the gangster in his reach for acceptability.

Carl's longing for respectability in Peoria ruled out the unbridled antics of the old days in East St. Louis when Carl's men chased scantily clad women into the streets at night and did about anything else they pleased to terrorize neighborhoods. Shelton allowed none of this in Peoria, beginning with the neighborhood around his own smartly appointed residence in the 1940s. Jean Whalen, who with her husband Bo was a next-door neighbor of Carl, attested to that.

In an interview decades later for a newsletter, Mrs. Whalen remembered when she asked her "tall and very good looking" new neighbor, who introduced himself as Carl Shelton, what he did for a living. After replying with a term she didn't recognize, he then explained, "That's another name for slot machines."

Subsequently, after Bo Whalen mentioned he'd heard of the Shelton gang and wondered whether the neighbor "might be some shirt-tail relation," a Peoria newspaper ran a story about the outfit that made it clear the gang's leader was their neighbor. Shortly after the paper came out, Carl was at the door of the Whalens. After confirming that the couple had read the story, Shelton was quoted by Mrs. Whalen as saying, "I'm not here to deny anything. It's true. We are what we are. But I want you to know we will never do anything to make you sorry we moved in next door. Whatever we may have to do, we won't do it here."

True to Carl's promise, the neighborhood remained trouble free. In Mrs. Whalen's view, few even knew that Carl lived there. For one thing, she recalled, Shelton's home contained "a battery of telephones," but not in his name. If attention ever was called to Shelton's residence, Mrs. Whalen guessed it was caused by four cackling chickens appearing in his backyard after one of his visits to his southern Illinois farms.

And speaking of the chickens, she couldn't contain her surprise when Carl told her he didn't know how to kill them. When she demonstrated the neck wringing way of doing it, she was surprised that he looked amazed. How ironic, she thought, that this man apparently knew how to kill people "but not chickens."[6]

If anything dented Carl's composure during his Peoria reign, it was a tragic incident far from the city. On November 16, 1943, while driving from Peoria to Wayne County, Carl struck and killed a nine-year-old girl, Violet Christine Varner, on State Route 121 by Decatur. Carl, who was accompanied in his car by Bernie, said the child ran onto the road, and he was unable to avoid hitting her. After the impact, the Shelton auto overturned and righted itself. Neither Carl nor Bernie was seriously injured. "Unlike other matters," Zuber recalled, "Carl talked about that. It wasn't his fault, and he paid the funeral bills. But it really never stopped bothering him."[7]

The end of Carl's hold on Peoria, which was inevitable, occurred rather quickly and with hardly even a whimper from Shelton himself.

Nineteen forty-five was a municipal election year in Peoria. Fed up with the city's grandiose reputation for vice, a growing number of people were stepping forward, protesting they'd had enough. Much of the ire, including the army's, was aimed at the prostitution. Woodruff still thought that most in town didn't want change, but he discovered that he'd fallen out of favor when he lost in a bid to retain his office. He was replaced by voters with Carl O. Triebel, a laundry operator who, like Woodruff, was a Republican from an old Peoria family.

Triebel became known as a reform mayor, although he didn't lay claim to the title. The label seemed appropriate to many, though, as a result of his crackdown on open gambling and the other stuff that had tarnished his city's image. Triebel maintained he did not approach the mayor's office feeling he was under a voter command to reverse the wide openness, but he recognized right away that the greed-inspired alliance between the underworld and politicians was cancerous for Peoria. Shortly before he took office, Triebel made his intention clear to Carl Shelton.

This happened when Shelton sent a representative, Ferd (Fish Mouth) McGrane, to call on Triebel and lay groundwork for the new days ahead. Based on an account in print numerous times and also repeated verbally, the exchange between Triebel and McGrane went as follows.

"I've come about the slot machines," said McGrane.

"What about them?" asked Triebel.

"We'll handle them for you."

"You'll what?"

"We'll take care of them. How much do you want out of them?"

Nothing, Triebel replied.

"All right. Then we'll pay something into your campaign fund."

"That won't be necessary," Triebel retorted.

"No, why?"

"Because," concluded Triebel, "there are not going to be any slot machines."

McGrane was stunned. A few minutes afterward, Carl got Triebel on the phone and made an appointment to see him. Here's what transpired according to the most common version.

"I hear you couldn't get together with McGrane," said Shelton.

"That's right," answered Triebel.

"Did you mean what you said?"

Triebel nodded his head.

After gazing at Triebel, Carl smiled and said, "Well, I guess that'll give me more time to farm."

Triebel, who also had farming interests, sat with Shelton thirty minutes longer, talking agriculture. They then shook hands and Carl departed, never to see Triebel again.

Shelton had been in this situation before. With Sheriff Jerome Munie. When Munie had ordered the gangster to get out of St. Clair County, Shelton argued with him, but eventually acquiesced to Munie's demand. With

Triebel, there was no haggling and, as the Peoria mayor later learned with relief, no harboring of hostility toward Triebel by Shelton. Not resisting Triebel may have seemed strange for most in Carl's position. However, going back to his early days as a bootlegger, Carl had adhered to a maxim that retreat usually was in order in any place where a top local official said no to the payoffs necessary for Shelton to operate without hindrance. Furthermore, by this stage, he openly yearned to spend more time tending to his rewarding farm and oil interests in Wayne, working toward the realization for himself of a Shelton version of landed gentry.

Triebel's stand may have led to the seemingly overnight dethronement of Carl in Peoria, but not to an end of the Shelton family presence. Bernie was not to surrender the field so readily. The baby brother of the Shelton boys served notice, and proceeded to show, that he fully intended to fill Carl's shoes in the administration of vice in the Peoria area. The jump appeared easy enough for Bernie because it was he—the pug-nosed brawler with the terrible temper and ungovernable hair—who struck fear in the hearts of friends and foes.

In the city of Peoria, pressure from Triebel forced gambling underground. But not so in Peoria County, where Bernie secured a free hand with the rackets through financial arrangements with certain county officials. Under Bernie, the Shelton headquarters was moved from downtown Peoria to the Parkway Tavern, an unimposing bar on Farmington Road only feet outside the Peoria city limits. Farther out on Farmington, Bernie was living with a touch of baronial splendor on property he'd acquired and named Golden Rule Farm. His private world at Golden Rule, a more than worthy successor to Happy Hollow, the ranch he'd shared with Carrie Stevenson down near Millstadt, included a remodeled, two-story farmhouse, landscaped grounds and, Bernie's pride and joy, prized palomino horses.

With Bernie in command in the Peoria region, some assumed Carl truly was out of the Shelton gang picture. Others were not so sure. Carl still lived part of the time in Peoria (his wife, Pearl, called Peoria, not Fairfield, her home). He huddled off and on with Bernie and the latest bunch of Shelton followers at the Parkway, functioning at the very least as a senior adviser to the vice network he'd fostered. Too, south of Peoria, Carl, and not Bernie, remained the godfather to many of the numerous gambling operations, big and small-time, strung through the largely rural parts of central and southern Illinois. Carl never had rebounded in Madison and St. Clair counties, where underworld honchos aligned with the Chicago crime syndicate were in control. However, the Chicago and St. Louis area mobsters recognized that any expansion plans in Illinois had to take into account the mystique and still very real presence of Carl, Bernie and, yes, Big Earl.

Nevertheless, Carl's step back from his highly visible role in Peoria was an appetite whetter for those with covetous eyes on Shelton territory. Like sharks smelling blood, the Chicago and East Side gangsters sensed the Sheltons finally were vulnerable. After years of a hands-off policy toward the Sheltons, the Chicago outfit figured the time, at long last, had arrived to put the kibosh on the independence of the Sheltons. Being businessmen, the Chicagoans would ask their St. Louis area emissaries to offer the Sheltons a deal that would bring them peacefully into the syndicate fold. If that didn't work, there was the murderous alternative.

By the end of World War II, the Chicago syndicate, or outfit as its hoodlums called it, had expanded from the foundation built by Al Capone into increasingly diverse and rewarding undertakings, things like legitimate businesses and labor unions on top of the rackets. New territory always was needed to feed the growth. As a result, the Chicago mob had enhanced its hand in underworld dealings across the country. Chicago took a backseat to nobody. In hooking up with St. Louis area mobsters, the Chicagoans inherited or won over the services of some tough characters who'd once marched, but no longer, to the tune of the Sheltons. Two of the most prominent were Buster Wortman and Blackie Armes. Overtures were extended to Ray Walker to desert the Sheltons, but he remained loyal to the brothers.

The defection of Wortman and Armes came in the early 1940s after the end of their federal prison incarceration for assaulting federal agents during a raid on a still near Collinsville in 1933. When the two were inmates together at Alcatraz, the Chicago mob was able to woo the pair through the provision of certain favors which made penal life more bearable. In addition, when Wortman and Armes got out of prison, Carl Shelton did nothing for them, or so they said.

Few developments more colored the history of St. Louis area gang-sterism in the 1940s than the rise of Wortman. Acting as an agent of Jake (Greasy Thumb) Guzik, a successor to Capone as Chicago outfit over-lord, Wortman displayed head of the class potential in purely old-fash-ioned strong-arming. Aided by former Egan mob stalwarts Frank (Cotton) Eppelsheimer and David (Chippy) Robinson, Wortman crudely, but convincingly, muscled his way to the top of the again booming East Side gambling business—rejuvenated, just as in Peoria and elsewhere, by the granting of almost statewide political immunity to gamblers by the Green administration.

Carl Shelton might have been proud of his onetime underling had he not now viewed Wortman with a jaundiced eye. In one of his first suc-cessful moves, Buster bulled his way into the operation of the Hyde Park Club, a casino in Venice, where the handbook, one of several wagering attractions, grossed more than $6 million yearly. Wortman also soon had a piece of many of the large handbooks in downtown East St. Louis, where voices could be heard on loudspeakers giving morning lines, scratches, quarter calls and results at racetracks from New York to Cali-fornia. So prosperous were these bookmaking enterprises that one of their sites was the first commercial operation, outside of movie theaters, to be air conditioned in East St. Louis.

Encouraged by the Chicago syndicate, Wortman scored a major coup by wresting control of the Pioneer News Service in St. Louis from Bev Brown and Gully Owen, the old Cuckoo bondsmen. Pioneer was a major racing wire endeavor that provided information on a private line to 250 St. Louis area handbooks (at which $25 million a year was bet). When Mis-souri officials clamped down on Pioneer's operation, Wortman moved its headquarters to Fairmont City on the East Side, where gambling contin-ued to be treated as a virtually legitimate business.

Of course, and this was a big rub, attempts by Wortman to expand in Illinois beyond the East Side brought him up against the Shelton sphere. When a gambler in central or southern Illinois wanted racing wire service or a Western Union racing news ticker, he had to first get approval from "the brothers," meaning the Sheltons. "How do you stand with the broth-ers?" was the initial question always put to a gambler. The wise guys in Chicago coveted that privilege only for themselves.[8]

A concerted effort to undermine the Sheltons was mapped out in a visit to Chicago in 1944 by Wortman and Eppelsheimer. Word soon circulated that Carl or Bernie, either one, was worth $10,000 to whomever brought one of them to Chicago alive. But nobody could get close to the Sheltons, who had grown contemptuous of most St. Louis area gangsters in addition to Wortman and darn near incommunicado where Chicago hoods were concerned. So it then became known that Carl or Bernie was worth $10,000 dead or alive. Stimulated by that offer, a crew of Chicago gunmen set a trap to ambush Carl and Bernie at the Parkway Tavern. Carl's old sixth sense for smelling a rat was as keen as ever, though, and several carloads of Shelton henchmen ended up at the bar instead of Carl and Bernie. The Chicagoans beat it back to the Windy City.

Farther south, Wortman was trying his best to disrupt the Sheltons. In September 1944, Ray Walker, who refused to side with Wortman, was shot at and wounded by two men riding in an auto in Herrin. Walker identified one of the assailants as his erstwhile gangster ally Blackie Armes. Three months later, the violent life of Armes—a life of black deeds committed mainly in the service of the Sheltons—came to an end in a shoot-out at the Herrin nightclub of Thomas Propes, a cousin of Walker. In an exchange of shots ignited by an argument between Armes and Propes, Armes was killed by Propes, and the club operator himself was fatally wounded. Ray Dougherty, another Herrin gangster in the tavern and a cousin of Armes, was suspected of firing the shots that finished off Propes.[9]

The death of Blackie Armes did not alter Wortman's campaign against the Sheltons. Before the demise of Armes, gangland guns already had finished off a group of individuals, who either weren't in tune with Wortman's upstart dominance of the East Side, or who had not satisfactorily disavowed their past association with the Sheltons. The latter included top-notch burglars Norman Farr and Harley Grizzell, the hood who'd once had the guts to fire shots at Joe Schrader. Wortman's ranks also were bolstered by new recruits with exceptional insight into the Sheltons. One was former Sheltonite Roy (Tony) Armes from Herrin, a brother of Blackie, and another was Charles Harris, the onetime back-home chum of Carl and his brothers whom Shelton partisans would come to view as the ultimate betrayer—the traitorous quisling of the Shelton story.

By 1946, a war to eliminate one by one real or perceived Shelton followers reached the Peoria area. While the triggermen in the killings (probably hit men from St. Louis or Chicago) eluded authorities, not much mystery surrounded the supposed allegiance of those slaughtered. Shelton associate Frank Kraemer, a slot machine operator and tavern owner, was shot to death by an unidentified gunman in February 1946 as he sat in the large home on his country estate along Farmington Road. Seven months later, the bullet-riddled body of Joel Nyberg, a convicted felon described as a Shelton muscle man by the Kefauver committee, was found on a golf course. A month after that, Phillip Stumpf, an often-arrested slot machine man tied to the Sheltons, was fatally plugged by slugs from a .351 caliber rifle while driving his car home from a bar on Big Hollow Road.

With each murder, the protective ring around the Sheltons shrank further. When the killings went unrequited, as far as anyone could see, an impression deepened that the Shelton brothers were living on their past reputation; that they no longer could defend their friends. In addition to shying away from their old fatal bloodshed ways up around Peoria, the Sheltons also had begun to lag on the political payoff front, at least at the state level if not locally.

Although Carl certainly had kept Woodruff placated and continued to make his monthly payments to state "collectors," the Sheltons refused to contribute to a $100,000 campaign fund raised by Illinois gamblers for Green in his bid for re-election in 1944. The reason for the hesitation was hard to figure. Maybe, some surmised, it had to do with Clyde Garrison. While having ceded the Peoria gambling scene to Carl and Bernie, Garrison was believed to be involved in the solicitation of the $100,000. If so, Carl wouldn't have needed any additional excuse for boycotting the sizable kitty.

Whether the Sheltons did or did not contribute as much at the state level as requested in 1944, their relationship to the Republican officials running Illinois government still seemed intact. That happened to be the year in which the Sheltons followed advice from Attorney General Barrett's office and incorporated Big Earl's Fairfield gambling house as a nonprofit corporation under state law in order to deter official interference. Carl himself applied for the charter for the Farmers' Club at the office of the Illinois secretary of state, contending in the application that the purpose of the club was "Recreation—checkers and card games."[10] It was not unusual for patriotic or fraternal organizations operating clubs for members to turn to not-for-profit incorporation. Otherwise, such clubs might be bound by closing laws and other regulations applying to strictly commercial establishments.

If Illinois voters were greatly riled at the unrestrained gambling in their state, if they were repulsed by the blatantly open activities of the Sheltons and other underworld figures, the outcome of the 1944 election did not show it.

Winning second terms was not always easy for Illinois governors, but Dwight Green pulled it off, albeit by a narrow margin. Green's Democratic opponent in the gubernatorial contest was State's Attorney Thomas J. Courtney of Cook County, who in an odd coincidence had Chicago living quarters in the same place as Green, the Edgewater Beach apartments facing Lake Michigan. Courtney went to bed thinking he'd been elected. Green, who stayed up until the southern Illinois vote was in, knew otherwise. The tally was close, but Green scraped by with slightly more than 50 percent of the vote, winning a razor-thin plurality of 72,271.

Green carried ninety counties, including Peoria. Even in Democratic-leaning counties where gambling was rife, Green did quite well. Barrett was reelected attorney general, also by a close margin, and all other Republican candidates for state offices, except for the nominee for secretary of state, were victorious. Consequently, the 1944 balloting left the top of Illinois government still under GOP domination. Before long, more than adversaries were viewing Green as the leader of a powerful political machine, one fueled in no small measure by the considerable tribute exacted from the blossoming gambling industry.

As Green's second term rolled along, inquiries showed that nearly every third county in Illinois, from Cairo to Chicago and from the East Side to the Indiana border, had gambling of some kind. South of Chicago, Madison and St. Clair counties remained headliners, right along with Peoria, Tazewell and nearby Mason County. The emergence of large casinos in Alexander and Pulaski counties also brought deep southern Illinois more heavily into the picture.

In short, Illinois was a mother lode of gambling in the United States. A golden goose for the industry.

However, as Green's second four years in office moved into the homestretch, the big city racketeers still were not fully exploiting the gambling craze throughout the state because of the continued hovering of the Sheltons over central and southern Illinois. It was frustrating for the urban mobsters. They just knew the Sheltons, viewed by the syndicate as stubborn hayseeds past their prime, were only skimming off the top, not really cashing in by controlling, for instance, everything bought and used in a tavern or gaming parlor, from the peanuts and towels to toilet paper. After the Sheltons had refused to bow down to the Chicago-St. Louis gangster alliance, the eradication of Shelton adherents had followed, leaving the brothers more penetrable. But all the killings in the world could not erase the Shelton influence as long as Carl, the head of the Shelton octopus, remained alive. Attempts to kill him at Peoria or trap him elsewhere had failed. But his luck couldn't last forever.

When Carl began spending more time in Wayne County after Triebel became mayor of Peoria, the odds on eliminating Shelton grew longer, or so it was assumed. Getting rid of anyone in his own lair, let alone Carl Shelton, was hardly easy. But all was not harmonious for Shelton on his home front—far from it, in fact. On one hand, as his farming prospered and his Basin Oil Well Service Company of Fairfield appeared to be doing well, Carl seemed headed for his golden years solidly established as a bona fide and successful businessman. Many in his neck of the woods accorded him utmost respect if not outright status as a celebrity. But this was not true of a number of his neighbors in the Pond Creek area, especially its bottoms.

With Carl increasingly on the scene, one squabble followed another. Many stemmed from heated animosity between Carl and some members of an extended family of "Pond Creekers" known as the Harris-Vaughan clan. The differences were exasperated by the close tie to the Harris-Vaughan group of Charles Harris. As a natural outgrowth of his hostility toward the Sheltons, Black Charlie evolved into a protector of those on the outs with Carl or Big Earl. The wrangling might have been dismissed as true to form feuding and fussing between old hillbilly families, but the inclusion of Black Charlie made the situation much more flammable.

One reason given for the Harris split from the Sheltons had a familiar ring. After years in Leavenworth following his conviction on a counterfeiting charge in Detroit during his rum-running days with the Sheltons,

Harris figured the brothers owed him more than their continued friendship and the dropping of a business crumb now and then. How often that had been heard. Harris' grudge, nursed slowly, passed the point of no return when Harris felt that Carl had swindled or undercut him on the ownership of some Wayne County farmland. When Harris trailed other former Shelton associates in establishing a relationship with Buster Wortman, the East Side mobster gained an ally posing an unusually dangerous threat to the Sheltons. More than just another lethal figure, Black Charlie was a killer who knew the Shelton boys' native turf inside out.

If the Sheltons truly came to regret crossing swords with any one person in the twilight of their gangster years, it had to be Black Charlie.

Born in 1896, Harris could legitimately claim to be a descendant of the first-known white settler in Wayne County. He took pride in his middle name, Bryan, because he said it came from William Jennings Bryan, the "Great Commoner" from nearby Salem who ran unsuccessfully for president in 1896. Harris did not appreciate his nickname, usually attributed to his dusky look and dark hair. He once contended the Shelton boys stuck him with "Black Charlie" to "demean him." He himself, he added, "wouldn't have done that to anybody."[11]

When he wasn't angry, when his quicksilver temper was in check, Harris often was a little charmer. The word little was accurate because Black Charlie was not a big man. He had to look up to almost everybody he encountered.

For a brief, but incisive, take on Harris, the words of long-standing Fairfield newspaperman Jack Vertrees rang true in a story on Harris late in his life that Jack penned, but never published. Here is what Vertrees said in part:

"Black Charlie. To many a midwesterner, that name brings to mind a modern day Jesse James or a slightly tarnished Superman. Among Pond Creekers on closer ground to Black Charlie, there is division too—some count him a twentieth century Robin Hood, helping the oppressed, while others tag him ruthless killer.

"Have you met him? Here he comes. You look at the small figure approaching—maybe five foot six, no more than that—stylish in a pinstripe suit, gray felt hat and fresh polished shoes. You ask yourself...this man...he can weigh no more than 135 at most, his hair gray-streaked...is this the man the FBI lists with 21 killings to his credit?

"He tips his hat...and the words come out with soft politeness. 'Good morning, Ma'am.' The smile is there. God, how long since a man tipped his hat? And when he smiled, a gold tooth flashes in the sunlight flooding Main street. His face is wind-spanked leathery, his complexion dark, almost swarthy. Is that where the name Black Charlie comes from? Or from deeds, killing for pay as reputed, even men he did not know but somebody wanted dead.

"'A lovely day, Ma'am,' speaks a voice without trace of ten years spent at Leavenworth. The pleasantries continue. He extends his hand, a hand roughened by years breaking rocks in a prison quarry. The hand doesn't seem to fit the pinstripe suit, even with expensive rings on both hands. His head turns for a moment and you notice the tiny hearing aid behind his left ear. His deafness has been a lifetime problem caused by natural body malfunction...or some close range gunblast in some close moment. His body mold is lithe, lean and you imagine that he could move like a cat—like killers have to do.

"Then you notice the eyes. Out of place, like his hands...the eyes are gray, unflinching marbles of steel, and you notice, and feel uncomfortable, despite the politeness."[12]

The end of Carl Shelton was presaged by two happenings in 1947, one of which—a step-up in the bickering between Shelton and his neighbors—treaded on the toes of Harris.

The event that didn't involve Harris was the murder of Ray Dougherty, the relative of the Armes brothers who was suspected of killing Herrin tavern operator Thomas Propes in 1944. The body of Dougherty, who was shot to death, was found on the banks of Crab Orchard Lake near Carbondale. Like the Armes fellows, Dougherty was a Shelton follower early in his gangster career. At the time of his death, though, Dougherty was closely aligned with Roy Armes, who had taken the place of his murdered brother, Blackie, as a Wortman lieutenant. Coroner Sam Simmons of Williamson County simply linked the unsolved murder of Dougherty to "trouble between gangs," but suspicion was strong that the killing may have been a first step in a planned resurgence by Shelton loyalists.

Rumors suddenly were running wild that the Shelton brothers, reasserting their old pride, were shoring up their hold on wagering in outlying areas of Illinois as well as contemplating an attempt at a comeback in the East St. Louis area. If true, the murder of Dougherty had to be a warning sign of the Sheltons' intent. Or, in the eyes of the syndicate, it meant that no more time could be lost in disposing of Carl, not if a new outbreak of gang warfare was to be avoided.

For that reason, the Chicago and St. Louis gangsters had to be delighted at the antagonism between Carl and his Pond Creek neighbors—especially when the quarreling turned violent in 1947, an upshot of the alleged stealing of some of Shelton's blooded black angus cattle. In searching for the culprits, an incensed Carl, aided by Ray Walker and Little Earl Shelton, meted out a heck of a beating to an individual said to be a nephew of Harris. Subsequently, that same individual was shot and seriously wounded in an attack by unknown assailants in the countryside between Fairfield and Albion. Black Charlie was enraged. Within hours of the shooting, Harris was seen huddling anew with St. Louis underworld associates—meetings to be viewed with great interest after October 23, 1947.

October 23, 1947. A pivotal day for the Shelton family, and gangland history in Illinois.

Ironically, Carl Shelton had made an appointment to confer that day with Frank Borah, a Fairfield acquaintance, to discuss the making of a will. Borah remembered afterward that, in lining up the appointment, Shelton had seemed on edge, openly fearful that he might be in real danger. Anxiety was gnawing at Shelton, Borah recollected. However, before meeting Borah on October 23, Carl intended to dispense with some farm business.

For that reason, he was driving up Pond Creek Road in his army surplus jeep at eight o'clock in the morning with Walker and Little Earl following in a truck. It should have been a routine exercise.

As Walker related later, "We didn't think anyone knew we were going out in that neighborhood that morning. We had taken Carl in the truck to his brother Roy's farm to get a jeep he had left there. Then we started to town, where Carl was going to get a tractor and haul it to one of his farms."

However, before leaving Roy's place, Walker continued, the men heard automobile horns blaring up around the area of the small bridge on Pond Creek Road that the trio soon would cross. Although he did not "think so much of it at the time," continued Walker, "there would be a long honk and two shorts and so on. Somebody said: 'What's all that honking for?' But we set out."

When the small convoy reached the bridge, hell broke loose. The volley of gunfire exploding out of thick brush and trees...Carl toppling out of the jeep...Little Earl and Walker leaping from the truck and scurrying toward a ditch near the bridge. And, after reaching the ditch, Walker hearing the voice of Carl pleading: "Don't shoot me any more, Charlie. It's me, Carl Shelton. You've killed me already."

Then came the reply—another burst of gunfire echoing through the lonely countryside.

15

A Gang under Siege

Hours after the gunfire on Pond Creek Road, an episode on the eve of Jim Zuber's seventeenth birthday, he was called out of class at Fairfield High School. His cousin, Little Carl Shelton, a brother of Little Earl, needed to see him. When he approached his waiting cousin, Jim was startled by the troubled expression on Little Carl's face. Without hesitation, Carl told Jim that their Uncle Carl had been shot. The two immediately left the school building. Once outside, Jim got the rest of the news from his cousin. Uncle Carl was dead.

The pair hurried over to Nale's Funeral Home, where Lula awaited them. She led her son and nephew to a back room at the place. There, Jim was struck by the rawest experience of his young life. He'd known Grandpa Ben was dying a few years earlier, but Jim was not prepared for this. The body of his uncle was laying back down on a table, naked except for a hand towel over his private parts. Jim couldn't hold back the tears as he observed "the bullet holes all over Uncle Carl's body."[1] He'd never forget the sight—the focus of his nightmares for years to come.

The trauma was only beginning. From the funeral home, Lula and Jim went out to Grandma Agnes' house. Agnes didn't know Carl was dead, and when Lula told her mother about it, the old woman screamed and screamed. Let it be anybody but her beloved Carl, Agnes pleaded. Anyone but Carl. Within hours, neighbors and friends started coming silently to the door of the small home, each bringing food. Before long, food was piled all over the house.

Back in town, Fairfield vibrated wildly with excitement at the death of the most famous, or infamous, person tied to the city. How could it not be the talk of the town? Strangers streaming through Fairfield, many just naturally curious but some downright nosy, added to the hub-bub. Too, out-of-town reporters seemed to be everywhere, hustling to scoop up as much detail as possible about a story already hitting front pages throughout the state.

The slaying of Carl was the second major story that year to come out of southern Illinois. Back in March, the nation had mourned the death of 111 men in a blast at Mine No. 5 of the Centralia Coal Co. at the south edge of Centralia. It was the country's worst mine disaster in twenty-three years. On a less serious note, the hot talk in the barber shops and general stores had centered on Jackie Robinson joining the Brooklyn Dodgers in 1947 to become the first black major league baseball player.

To reconstruct the killing of Carl Shelton, law enforcement officials and scribes pretty much had to go on what Ray Walker and Little Earl said they saw.

Based on what the pair told law officers and stated in testimony at a coroner's inquest, they got a partial picture of the ambush scene as they jumped from their truck trailing Carl's jeep and scrambled into the ditch. The attackers' car was sitting on the other side of the road near the bridge, parked in a lane by the underbrush from which the first shots rang out. Walker and Little Earl saw the auto again when the assailants drove away—a view clear enough to convince them it was a black, 1946 model Ford sedan with a sun visor over the windshield.

Walker and Little Earl crouched in the ditch, doing nothing to assist Carl because neither was armed—something many found hard to believe, especially in the case of the normally gun-toting Walker. When the two heard the voice of Carl pleading for the ambushers to stop shooting, Walker peered up out of the ditch and saw Carl still on the road, walking or stumbling around. While yelling at Carl to retreat back into a ditch, Walker said, he got a glance at a man standing across the road from Carl, an individual of medium weight wearing a gray suit, hat and dress shirt but no tie. Walker was sure the man, whom

Ray did not recognize, was holding either a shotgun or rifle. A new hail of bullets spraying every which way sent Walker back to the bottom of the ditch.

After the gunfire finally stopped and the attackers' car had spun onto Pond Creek Road to head south, Walker and Little Earl cautiously emerged from the ditch in time to see a man running up the road. Both swore it was Charles Harris. Little Earl testified that Harris stopped at one point, turned around and pointed a gun at him and Walker. Walker added that they didn't know for sure whether Harris fired the weapon, described by Walker as a "long gun," but he noted that "something knocked down the right front tire of the truck." After Harris resumed his flight from the scene, Little Earl and Walker got into Carl's jeep and drove through back roads to Fairfield to summon help. As it turned out, the testimony of other witnesses at the inquest, under questioning by State's Attorney Virgil W. Mills of Wayne County, also put Harris in the vicinity of the shooting right after it occurred.

A good two hours passed after the killing of Carl before Walker and Little Earl could notify law officers and return to the scene of the shooting. They were accompanied by Wayne County Sheriff Hal Bradshaw, Lieutenant Ben Blades of the Illinois State Police and Big Earl. Little Earl had a notion that the body of Carl might not be found, that the gunmen may have returned to pick it up. However, the men found Carl's body in the ditch by the bridge on the east side of the road. His feet were about a foot from the top of the ditch and his head and face were downward. Blades and the sheriff suggested that the body be left there until pictures could be taken. But Big Earl protested, saying that he didn't want his brother laying there "like that."

In picking up the body, the group saw that it had been shielding a gun. Big Earl identified it as Carl's revolver. Opening up the weapon, Blades saw that five of six shells had been fired. Searching the ground on the west side of the bridge, Blades and Bradshaw found numerous empty cartridges and shells, some a government issue type that could be used in an automatic pistol or submachine gun. After the body was taken to the funeral home, it was determined that at least seventeen rifle, handgun and machine-gun bullets had entered Carl, causing twenty-five bullet holes in his head, body, arms and legs.

The reputation of the Sheltons being what it was, fear was rampant that vengeance would be visited with due haste on those suspected of having a hand in the slaughter of Carl. At the same time, apprehension was almost as heavy that the killers, encouraged by the elimination of Carl, well might be eyeing more Sheltons for the mortuary before the clan could impose its own retribution. New gang warfare inevitable, blared the media. More violence almost surely loomed in the offing. Some even worried about the funeral of Carl turning into a hornet's nest. There was nothing to that, though.

No trouble materialized at the late Sunday afternoon funeral, which was the largest event of its kind Fairfield had witnessed.[2] The numerous law officers present, including seven Illinois state cops, ended up doing little more than directing the enormous amount of traffic generated by the occasion. Overwhelmed, the officers said they'd never seen so much traffic at a funeral. Spectators lined the streets of Fairfield as the cortege made its way to the town's First Methodist Church from the home of Agnes Shelton, where the body of Carl had lain in a $2,500 bronze casket purchased by Shelton for himself a year earlier. After the church service, the throng of onlookers ignored a drizzle to continue hugging the streets as the cortege proceeded to the family burial plot in Fairfield's Maple Hill Cemetery. Because darkness had fallen, the headlights of cars illuminated the setting as Carl was laid to rest beside his father.

If one ignored the shoulder holsters worn by some Shelton relatives and friends, the observance of Carl's death was a fit tribute for a pillar of any community. At his mother's home, more than 100 floral pieces, many very expensive, consumed the inside and overflowed onto the porch. On the wall across from the casket, Agnes had hung an old-fashioned, framed motto, "The Way of the Cross Leads Home." Instead of Carl's gangland friends, the pallbearers for the funeral were highly respected citizens.

In fact, only a few characters from Shelton's gangster career, far fewer than expected, were spied among the close to 1,200 persons jammed into the flower-bedecked church for his final rites. (Hundreds more stood outside.)[3] The *Wayne County Press* reported that the "floral display at the funeral exceeded by far anything ever seen in Fairfield."[4] The *Press* also noted that "(big) city newspaper photographers were standing on the steps of the church to take pictures of the casket when it was carried in."

Although the Shelton family had granted the photogs permission to snap shots of the flowers and casket in the church before the family entered, the *Press* pointed out, "one rude city photographer sought to make a picture of the family as they entered and was rebuked by a family member."[5]

Those persons managing to squeeze into the sanctuary heard Elder L. Curneal, a Baptist pastor and longtime friend of Carl's, stress Shelton's early Protestant roots and then add that "in later life, while not an active member of any church, he (Shelton) was generous in his support of many churches, always manifesting a willingness to help them discharge their financial responsibilities." Curneal also said of Shelton that those "who were most intimately acquainted with him knew best of the many charitable acts that he quietly but willingly performed." All in all, Curneal concluded, Carl Shelton was "our friend and neighbor," a member of a family "long known," a son of parents who "had a good Christian home."

Mindful of the anxiety in the community over the strong chance of further bloodshed in the wake of the funeral, Curneal pointedly declared before ending the service that "nothing is solved by vengeance and wrath—only more vengeance and wrath will follow."

Although his words were hard for many to believe, Big Earl moved to ease the tension gripping his part of the state when he said his family's only reaction to the slaying of Carl would be to let the law enforcement process "take its usual course." At the start of the inquest into the murder, Big Earl seemed confident that the testimony of Little Earl and Walker alone would be sufficient to lead to the indictment of Black Charlie for complicity in the killing as one of the shooters. Or, at the very least, as the finger man who'd set up Carl for the other gunmen—believed to be four—in the ambush.

A spate of stories on the murder contended without hesitation that Harris almost certainly had a hand in the killing because only someone very familiar with the Pond Creek area could have picked such a perfect spot for the ambush. While Harris was the only individual placed at or near the scene of the shooting to be named publicly, the quartet of shooters were automatically assumed by reporters and their sources in the law enforcement world to be gunmen tied to Chicago Caponites and their St. Louis-area allies. However, true to gangland tradition, the identities of the gunmen remained cloaked in mystery. Much play was given, though, to a report that a new fund of $20,000, a tidy sum in 1947, had been raised by major gambling interests opposed to the Sheltons to finance the killing of not only Carl, but also Bernie, Big Earl and Walker.

The Harris factor was anything but easy to deal with. Empathy for Black Charlie obviously was felt by many around Pond Creek and other sections of the county, who had long awaited the day when somebody would knock the browbeating Sheltons down a rung or two. Few were surprised to learn afterward that Sheriff Bradshaw had appointed Harris a "special deputy" so Charlie could guard from further attacks the Harris nephew who'd been beaten and then shot after quarreling with Carl. Too, State's Attorney Mills advanced a theory, for a while, that the death of Carl was a result of nothing more than "a face-to-face duel down there between Carl Shelton and Harris—no ambush at all."

Years after the dust had settled, David Dickey, a former Wayne County treasurer, recollected Bradshaw once telling of the quandary the sheriff found himself facing in the days after Carl's killing.

"Hal never forgot Ray Walker backing him up against a wall in the courthouse, shaking him hard, rattling his head against the wall and telling him (Bradshaw) what he was supposed to do and not do in investigating the murder," Dickey recounted. "Ray told Hal what he'd do to Hal if Hal didn't handle it right.

"Well, Hal said he replied that he didn't doubt Ray could carry out this threat. But, just so there'd be no misunderstanding, Hal said he told Ray that if it came to following Ray's orders or being dead, Hal would rather be dead."[6]

As it turned out, the inquest into Carl's death did result in the delivery to Bradshaw by Walter Young, the Wayne coroner, of a warrant for the arrest of Harris. The warrant was issued after the inquest jury recommended that Harris be held for a Wayne County grand jury investigation into the murder. Harris had fled from his farm home after the shooting, but was arrested in a bus depot in Tulsa, Oklahoma, after the issuance of the warrant. He was accompanied in Tulsa by a niece, whom Harris said he was taking to Arizona for nurse's training. However, Harris also told authorities he had left the Fairfield area because of fear of reprisals by the Sheltons. Still, Bradshaw and several deputies encountered no resistance when they journeyed to Tulsa to bring back Harris, who waived extradition.

On his return to Illinois, Harris boasted that he was not afraid to go on trial for the killing of Carl. He did concede being in the vicinity of the shooting when it happened, but only by chance coincidence. He denied any connection with the murder, contending that "I thought Carl and I were getting along fine." Nevertheless, after Bradshaw brought Harris home, the sheriff sought to keep the location of Harris' confinement a secret to preclude any clashes, especially since Big Earl, now joined in Fairfield by Bernie, was demanding to talk to Harris. No meeting occurred. After Harris was released from Bradshaw's custody on a $7,500 bond to insure his appearance in event of a grand jury indictment, he went into hiding in the Pond Creek area with relatives and friends constantly at his side.

There would be no trial for Harris because the grand jury returned no indictment. Harris was released from the bond and became a free man after the grand jurors apparently determined that the testimony they heard from Little Earl and others was insufficient to charge Harris or anyone else with the murder of Carl. Mills maintained to reporters that he had presented all the evidence on hand at that time to the jurors, but he said they could not draw any firm conclusions from what they heard.

Big Earl, angered by the verdict of the grand jury, lamented that "Charlie Harris helped kill my brother, and I know it. I wanted the law to take its course." Nevertheless, he held that he "still wanted to" stay within the law on the matter, a stance that belied the image of the Shelton gang in previous decades. Law officers still expected a new wave of violence to break out. But, it didn't happen, and legions of crime watchers were left wondering if the Sheltons finally had run out of gas. With Carl gone, would the remaining Sheltons and the remnants of their once widespread followers fade into the night like old has-beens? Was it possible, lawmen speculated, that the Sheltons might not even be heard from again?

The answer was no. That would become resoundingly clear in the year after Carl's death. The Shelton penchant for bringing upheaval to the lives of others was far from over. One to attest to it, albeit begrudgingly, would be the governor, Dwight Green.

The more immediate upshot after the death of Carl, though, was mild by Illinois underworld standards. In the weeks following his killing, some Shelton associates shut down their gambling houses. Or, they handed over control of their operations to the Chicago-St. Louis mob combine, which was flushed with a new burst of energy by the departure of Carl. Buster Wortman, the increasingly strong syndicate kingpin on the East Side, a man not viewed by many as an innocent bystander in the elimination of Shelton, had a much freer hand to broaden his expanse well beyond St. Clair and Madison. Some of this was pulled off with minimal strong-arming now that the shadow of Carl Shelton no longer hovered.

Although he left no will, an inventory of Carl's estate produced some rather modest figures in view of the huge sums he reportedly had pocketed through the years from the rackets. The inventory revealed that he held about $60,000 in real estate and another $36,000 in personal property at the time of his death. The real estate included 475 acres in Wayne County, another 1,000 acres in adjoining Hamilton County valued at $25,000 and various oil and gas interests in Wayne. His personal estate included, for the most part, farm machinery, oil well equipment, tax purchase certificates and two vehicles (his jeep valued at $300 and a 1947 Buick worth $2,600). He had only $1,000 in life insurance and just $9.20 on deposit at a Fairfield bank.

Where, it was commonly asked, was all of Carl's money? Rumors abounded about obscure lockboxes, a hidden safe in Peoria and well-concealed bank accounts. If there was any truth to the talk, the public never found out about it.

The ground hardly had settled over Carl's grave before he ascended—rightfully so, many agreed—into the folklore of southern Illinois. In the months after his slaying, jukeboxes in parts of downstate, a lot of them under the thumb of Shelton people, were blaring a mournful ballad about the gang leader and his demise. "The Death of Carl Shelton," composed and copyrighted by Big Earl and a country minstrel from Fairfield, Fred Henson, ignored the sordid side of Carl's life in seeking to elevate him to the celebrated status of, say, valiant railroad engineer Casey Jones. The chorus of the ballad, sung by Henson to his own guitar accompaniment, tugged at heartstrings by wailing that Carl had left his "dear old mother" in lonesome sorrow in "her little country home," but wound up expressing hope that she might again meet "her darling" in "a better world some day." Darn if the song didn't catch on.

Carl's departure still left one especially troublesome fly in the syndicate ointment south of Chicago. Bernie.

While Carl lived on in jukeboxes and gangland mythology, Bernie lived on in the same way he did before his brother's death—running the still entrenched Shelton gaming enterprises around the city of Peoria. Said by associates to believe he had what it took to fill Carl's shoes, Bernie also threatened to stop the hemorrhaging of the Shelton influence and financial stake in various gambling operations farther south in Illinois. This greatly disappointed the Chicago and St. Louis gangsters, who almost took for granted that their encroachment into Shelton territory would proceed unimpeded with Carl no longer around. The mobsters approached Bernie with an olive branch, but he brushed off the overture.

There'd be no Shelton surrender, not even a retreat, where Bernie was concerned. Not with gambling humming along so well in the state. The syndicate could go to hell.

The outfit's response was predictable. Bernie had been a marked man before the killing of Carl, and the Chicago-St. Louis combine made it known that nothing had happened since to change the situation. Word raced through the netherworld that reward money for the murder of Bernie remained in the fund that had been raised for the elimination of Carl and Bernie (and of Big Earl and Ray Walker too). The big city mobsters wanted it spent.

For a time, at least through the early months of 1948, Bernie showed he was quite capable of protecting the Shelton hold on Peoria-area gaming. Payoffs to certain individuals in the region, with the clout or know-how to discredit Shelton antagonists, were continued or resumed from the days when Carl oversaw the always crucial bribery part of the business. Backing off was the last thing on Bernie's mind, according to a person who witnessed one payoff meeting between Shelton and an important, but secret ally. Bernie was said by the observer to have excitedly exclaimed, "I'm going to be boss of Peoria County, and nobody's going to stand in my way."[7]

True to his words, Bernie was no pretender to the title of Peoria underworld chief. But he didn't stay in the saddle very long. As if the price placed on his head by the syndicate was not enough of a problem, an old Bernie Shelton pitfall—tavern fighting—also helped trip him up.

Bernie was lucky to have escaped prison in the late 1930s for allegedly slugging and shooting a packinghouse worker from East St. Louis named Frank Zimmerman during a brawl at a Cahokia bar. Shelton never got untangled, though, from the outgrowth of a fight at his Parkway Tavern on Memorial Day in 1948.

The clash reportedly started when Richard Murphy, a navy veteran from Peoria, objected to the ejection from the tavern of another patron who was drunk. Fisticuffs ensued on the Parkway parking lot, resulting in the beating of Murphy by Bernie, Walker and another Shelton follower, John E. Kelly. One account from witnesses had the trio pistol-whipping Murphy. During the fracas, A. L. Hunt, proprietor of a popular drive-in located across Farmington Road from the tavern, came over to halt the one-sided fight. Hunt, who was no friend of Bernie's, said that Bernie retaliated by shoving a pistol against him and marching him back across the road. As a result of the brawl, a Peoria County grand jury voted indictments on June 25, 1948, charging Bernie, Walker and Kelly with assault with intent to kill, a felony.

The tavern altercation might have been dismissed by some folks as a minor incident, but not by the man who spearheaded the grand jury investigation, Roy P. Hull, the state's attorney of Peoria County. In the Illinois primary balloting in April of that year, Republican Hull had been defeated in his bid for nomination for re-election to his post in the upcoming November general election. One of those opposing Hull happened to be Bernie Shelton, which didn't set too well with Hull. And, of course, the wrath of a jilted lover can seem mild compared to that of a scorned politician. Much more would revolve around the indictments of Bernie, Walker and Kelly, as revelations a few weeks down the road were to show.

Meanwhile, the primary election that had turned out badly for Hull produced for Illinois voters one of the more interesting races for governor in the nation. Green was nominated by the GOP for a third term as Illinois chief executive. Although burdened by the political baggage that any governor of eight years would have accumulated, Green still shaped up as a formidable candidate because of an abundance of campaign cash (thanks in part to gambling industry dollars) and his control of a well-ensconced political machine. Furthermore, his Democratic opponent, Adlai Ewing Stevenson, was not as familiar to Illinoisans. Although he came from an old political family, Stevenson was an aristocratic blue blood with a long record of public service mainly tied to Washington. He wanted to run for the United States Senate in 1948, but party honchos in Chicago prevailed upon him to seek the governorship, partly to fend off another Democratic gubernatorial aspirant they did not want. Too, Stevenson had a clean face, making him perhaps a salable commodity to those in the electorate who felt the Republican overlords in Springfield had become too fat and overbearing.

To unseat Green, the highly principled Stevenson adopted a conventional campaign tact in attacking the incumbent governor for supposed mismanagement of Illinois government. Republicans sought to dismiss Stevenson as an egghead, unable to connect with the average Joe. Green supporters also believed, as did many others, that the governor stood to benefit from the shirttails of the seemingly strong GOP candidate for president in 1948, Governor Thomas E. Dewey of New York. A goodly share of Democrats also saw it this way. Sort of lackadaisical about the Stevenson candidacy to begin with, they felt he needed some unforeseen break to boost him into serious contention with Green. Something had to happen to rock the Illinois Republican boat.

A scandal stirring up public indignation might do it. Chicago was always a likely place for a thing like that to erupt. But one could pop up anywhere. Springfield was often a possibility. Or maybe East St. Louis or Rockford. Or, for that matter, Peoria.

Peoria was unquestionably a time bomb.

Had the syndicate fellows any sensitivity to political timing or any real regard for the sitting governor whose administration so coddled the vice rampant from one end of the state to the other, they would have called off the dogs on Bernie Shelton till at least the November election was over. Why throw gasoline on a tinderbox already regarded as Green's most likely Achilles' heel? But, in its pursuit of Shelton and the gambling profits he still controlled, the mob was impervious.

Most individuals privy to underworld doings were aware of talk that Bernie had not fallen into one trap set for him by gunmen at the start of July, a few days after the return of the assault indictments against Shelton and his associates. The attempt on Bernie's life was to have occurred while he was on his way to Muscatine, Iowa, to sell some of his palomino horses. Two cars filled with gunmen reportedly had waited for Shelton to pass along a highway near Galesburg, Illinois.

However, Bernie took another route to Muscatine and avoided the trap. Whether he did so by design or by sheer luck, no one knew. Word of the plan reached the ears of Sheriff Earl Spainhower of Peoria County through an erroneous report that Shelton had been ambushed and killed. The report was believable, at first, because Wortman-aligned gangsters from the St. Louis area had been spotted a few days before hanging around the Peoria area. The report soon proved to be false, though, when it was learned that Shelton had returned safely from Iowa without anybody firing a shot at him.

Nevertheless, the underworld grapevine insisted that Bernie's days were numbered.

The next attempt to kill him was planned for July 26, a hot summer Monday. Bernie had left his Golden Rule Farm home (also called Golden Rule Acres) at ten o'clock in the morning and driven to the Parkway to confer with Alex Ronitis, a bartender at the place. Bernie wanted Ronitis to follow him to a Peoria auto agency, where Bernie intended to leave his car for some work. Ronitis then would return Shelton to the Parkway.

After Shelton spent about forty-five minutes handling a bit of business in his private office at the tavern, he and Ronitis started to walk out together. However, Ronitis stepped back into the bar to get a pack of cigarettes, leaving Shelton to stride alone to his sedan in the parking lot.

Bernie was unaware, as he approached his vehicle, that he was in clear view of a well-dressed man crouched or laying in thick undergrowth near the base of the steep, wooded hill behind the tavern—an incline rising up to St. Joseph's cemetery above Farmington Road. The man had with him a .351 caliber Winchester automatic rifle, a gun used for big game.

The weapon was quite fitting because, in gangster lingo, Bernie certainly was big game.

16

1948—A Year of Upheaval

While Bernie was heading from his tavern to his auto late on that bright July morning, James Albert McGill, a nineteen-year-old student at Bradley University in Peoria, was engaged in a tennis doubles match on a court across Farmington from the Parkway. McGill, from Springfield, had patronized the Parkway because of its fit-for-a-king hamburgers. On one of those visits, Bernie introduced himself to McGill. They exchanged small talk, with McGill exercising caution "not to let on that I knew he was a celebrity...of a certain kind."[1]

As McGill raised his racket, with his back to the tavern, to slam a serve, he heard a shot. A single shot.

"I spun around right away," he said, "because I knew exactly what it was. It sounded like a high-powered rifle, like I'd heard on a military firing range. I saw this man falling, and I was sure it was Bernie. Then I saw this movement in the trees and brush over to the west of the tavern. Within moments, I could see this guy going up the hill fast, or as fast as he could."[2]

McGill ran to his nearby car, followed by the other three tennis players, all photographers for the Bradley newspaper. Grabbing cameras from inside the auto, the three photographers took off for the scene of the shooting. McGill, however, jumped into his 1937 Chevrolet, peeled off to the east on Farmington and raced up a hill to reach the cemetery above the Parkway.

McGill got to St. Joseph's in time to see a man on the run jump into a dark-colored sedan being driven by another fellow. Then the car, in McGill's words, "shot out." McGill, who had a police-sanctioned weapon in his vehicle by virtue of his job as a night clerk for a burglar alarm firm, pursued the other car. "My tires were squealing, and they knew I was following them," McGill related. "I kept them within sight a good mile, even though they were running stop signs. But their car was well tuned, and they just finally outdistanced me. I don't know what I'd have done if I'd caught up to them. I was young and feisty, but I don't know...."[3]

Later, investigators were told by two workmen at St. Joseph's that, shortly before the time of the shooting, a dark green car, quite likely a Chevy sedan, entered the cemetery. Two men, both attired smartly, were in the auto. The workers remembered watching the car head for the northwest section of the cemetery, where a path led down the slope toward the Parkway. They did not recall seeing the auto leave the cemetery.

Another individual who heard the shot was the ever vigilant A. L. Hunt. Glancing out a window of his office at the restaurant, Hunt told the press he saw Shelton fall across the bumper of his car, then slowly get up and stagger toward the tavern door. Hunt telephoned the sheriff's office.

Ronitis was about to open the tavern door to step back outside when the shot sounded. After hesitating for a few seconds, he opened the door and saw Bernie kneeling by his car. Ronitis started to move toward Shelton, but the gangster waved him off. So Ronitis held the door open as Bernie stumbled across the parking lot and into the tavern. Plopping on to a bar stool, Bernie mumbled to Ronitis and another bartender, Edward Connor, "I've been shot from the woods." They saw he had a bad chest wound.

Connor called for an ambulance. When it arrived, Bernie insisted on walking to it. Once inside, though, he laid on a stretcher. On the way to St. Francis Hospital, Shelton spied through a window a green Chevrolet trailing the ambulance. "Watch that car!" he yelled to ambulance attendant Earl Stevens. The driver was directed by Stevens to speed up, and the ambulance pulled away from the car. Shelton apparently feared the Chevy contained his would-be killer or killers, which, if true, did not square with McGill's belief that he had chased the auto occupied by the shooter.

After arriving at the emergency room at St. Francis, Bernie asked an attendant to remove his shoes and trousers, predicting that he was going to die. And, he did—a few minutes before noon. He was forty-nine years old.

The examination at the hospital revealed that the bullet struck Bernie near his heart and passed through his body, exiting the right side. The rifle from which the fatal shot was fired was found by sheriff's deputies in underbrush high up on the slope behind the tavern. Bernie's assassin had discarded the weapon in making his escape. Farther down the slope, at the spot where the killer had waited to draw a bead on Bernie, a discharged cartridge fitting the rifle was picked up. The rifle was subjected to fingerprint and ballistics tests, which led nowhere. (Law officers did notice, though, that Shelton slot machine associate Phillip Stumpf had been shot to death on a road near Peoria in 1946 with bullets of the same caliber as the one that killed Bernie.)

As with the killing of Carl Shelton, the murder of Bernie was never to be solved. Authorities concluded that, although Bernie's quarrelsome nature earned him numerous enemies, his killing was a well-planned, professional execution carried out for business reasons and not the result of anger prompted by any barroom fight. The judgment was probably on target, but it hardly set well with the rest of the Shelton clan and its friends.

"Who did it? Was it that dirty dog who killed Carl?" asked a distressful Agnes Shelton, by then eighty-six years old, according to most accounts. A livid Big Earl declared that "the law" could have prevented Bernie's death by solving Carl's. "I talked my head off after Carl was killed, but what's the use?" Earl complained. "We get no protection from the law." He said that Ray Walker and other remaining Sheltonites would tell Sheriff Spainhower and other officials what they knew, but added that he, himself, intended to try to get to the bottom of Bernie's murder.

First, though, the family had to undergo another funeral ordeal, only nine months after the burial of Carl. Plans initially called for Bernie to be interred in Fairfield, but the Peoria woman who became his last wife, Genevieve Paulsgrove, opted instead to have the funeral and burial in Peoria. The proceeding was remindful of Carl's.

As with the body of Carl, Bernie's was laid out in a $2,500 bronze casket. It was placed for viewing in the expensively furnished front room of Bernie's farm home. The room overflowed with floral wreaths that Peoria florists said were ordered from all parts of the country. Visitors to the wake, judging by the license plates of automobiles parked around the house, came from Missouri, Indiana and Kentucky in addition to Illinois.

At the Boland mortuary, where the body was taken for services, several hundred persons crowded into the funeral parlor, while curious spectators lined the curbs outside. After the soloist's final number, "The Old Rugged Cross," the Reverend E. L. Fernandes of Peoria's Arcadia Avenue Presbyterian Church endeavored to cast Bernie in the best light possible by noting that, although his weaknesses could not be condoned, he was a generous man, especially where underprivileged children and animals were concerned. After the minister said what he could to comfort the family, a funeral procession of about forty cars, most of them expensive models, trailed the body to Parkview Cemetery, which happened to be in close proximity to the site of the gangster's murder.

The most lasting images associated with Bernie's final hours above ground had to be of the woeful figure of his mother. Agnes needed to be assisted from the funeral parlor by Walker and Jack Ashby. At Parkview, they had to virtually carry her to and from the grave site. Of course, there was the obligatory *Associated Press Wirephoto* of a weeping Agnes hunched over one end of the casket at the cemetery.

The descent of Bernie into Parkview's earth—at a site eventually to be topped by a reddish granite tombstone—failed to bring about the result desired by those who wanted him out of the way. Bernie's personal estate may have been valued at only $13,000 according to his will filed in probate court (a gross undervaluation in the opinion of many persons), but he bequeathed a legacy of impact on the lives of many who'd crossed his path. Devastation was perhaps a more fitting word. For a tumultuous period in 1948 after his murder, Bernie was every bit the hell-raiser in death that he was in life.

As the *Peoria Journal Star* put it, the killing of Bernie "precipitated a series of reverberations which shook Peoria's official circles for months and echoed throughout the state and nation."[4]

When the dust settled, the era of big-time gangland dominance in the Peoria area was dead or heading for the door. The syndicate never realized anything close to the fruits of victory it anticipated with the elimination of Bernie. That was ensured by a radical turnabout in Illinois political life, a topsy-turviness that just might not have happened when it did if the gambling world of Bernie Shelton had not been shattered. Rats scurried out of woodpiles, and skeletons fell from closets.

In the simplest terms, the assassination of Bernie finally provided the break needed by those wanting to bring to a head their strong dissatisfaction with the moral climate in Illinois during and after World War II.

When a number of individuals upset with vice and corruption complained to public officials and were ignored, they followed a time-honored American tradition of going to newspapers. What this meant in downstate Illinois was that some contacted hometown papers, while others became anonymous sources for a few bigger out-of-state dailies with a track record on Illinois issues. Like the *St. Louis Post-Dispatch*.

The Pulitzer paper's penchant for investigating skulduggery in Illinois had been widely recognized since the 1920s when the *Post-Dispatch* outstripped its competitors in revealing inside stories of the Shelton-Birger war and of other unsavory happenings. Well before the death of Carl Shelton, reporters for the *Post-Dispatch* had been assembling information from informants, including Virgil W. Peterson, director of the Chicago Crime Commission, on the rapidly growing Illinois gambling industry and its accompanying graft. The effort was intensified after Carl Shelton was laid to rest, partly because underworld sources told *Post-Dispatch* men that Bernie and other Sheltons also were marked for murder.

Carl Baldwin was even dispatched by City Editor Raymond L. Crowley to stay day and night in Fairfield for what amounted to seven weeks after the killing of Carl, waiting for the next murder. Baldwin didn't stumble over any new bodies, but he did glean increased insight into the Illinois gaming trade from Shelton associates, who were shook up by the murder of Carl and suddenly not so tight lipped with the press. Baldwin spent so much time hanging around the Merriam crossroads that Agnes Shelton had invited him in for more than one of her home-cooked meals.

However, the *Post-Dispatch* reporter in the forefront was Ted Link. By this stage, Link—who finally had reached the *Post* staff in 1939 after stints at the old *Star* and other St. Louis newspapers—was a crime reporter par excellence, a worthy successor to the newspaper's legendary John T. Rogers. Like Rogers, Link's bird-dogging of criminals had gone beyond the St. Louis region, earning for him, like Rogers, a national reputation.

No moviemaker or novelist like Raymond Chandler could have fashioned a more suitable fictional model for what Link did than the hard-boiled Link himself. Not that Link began with the idea of becoming a criminal investigator, or even a newspaperman for that matter. He intended at first to be an architect, to follow in the footsteps of the grandfather for whom he was named, Theodore C. Link, the highly regarded architect who designed the castlelike Union Station and other St. Louis buildings. But he got sidetracked early on into short-lived ventures, such as selling stoves on the road. Only after he landed his first newspaper job with the *Star* did he realize he'd discovered his labor of love.

Link's early years with the *Post-Dispatch* were interrupted by World War II. Enlisting in the Marine Corps in 1942, he served as a sergeant and combat correspondent in the Pacific and was wounded in the fighting on Bougainville Island. After returning to the newspaper in 1945, Link embarked on the most productive period of his career, a span extending well into the 1950s. During this time, the *Post-Dispatch* was awarded the Pulitzer Prize for 1951 for articles on corruption in the then Internal Revenue Bureau that were based largely on a Link investigation. Link pieces on Miami as the gang capital of the United States in early 1950 had brought the reporter to the attention of the Kefauver crime investigating committee. It was mainly at the suggestion of Link that the panel lost no time conducting at Miami that year one of its widely publicized hearings. At the conclusion of the hearings, Senator Kefauver wrote that "in numerous instances, the first leads on the connections among the underworld, conniving politicians and corrupt law enforcement officials were supplied to committee investigators out of Ted Link's voluminous files."[5]

After Link died in 1974, he was extolled in a memoir by Carl Baldwin, who was perhaps Link's chief rival among *Post-Dispatch* investigative reporters and a person who had a sometimes cool relationship with Link. "Suave and handsome, with dark features...Link probably was the closest thing St. Louis ever had to a TV-type private eye," wrote Baldwin. "Gangsters like Earl Shelton and Ray Walker had a certain romantic admiration for him, and he was chosen as the receptacle for their information."[6]

Many who knew him considered Link as much flatfoot as reporter. Some swore he had more contacts in the underworld than the police. But the cops fed him too. He had access to inside dope in numerous police departments and investigative units of federal and state governments.

As his son, Theodore C. Link Jr., put it, "My father had the capability to get information from both sides, the lawbreakers and the law officers. Without doubt, dad was a private investigator as well as a reporter. He certainly knew the right people to talk to. And, if he couldn't find them, they usually found him."[7]

It was after the death of Carl Shelton that the circle of people talking to Link was broadened to include Big Earl, Bernie and a number of their followers. The Sheltons were aware, of course, that Link was digging hard to expose the drive by the Capone mob, a Shelton enemy after World War II, to expand its control of organized crime to St. Louis, Kansas City and other spots like Denver and Louisville. Too, Link shared the Sheltons' distaste for Buster Wortman and the crime empire he structured on the East Side, once Shelton territory, as the St. Louis area agent for the Capone crowd. Also figuring into the Shelton-Link equation was the Sheltons' memory of the *Post-Dispatch* role in helping to get Carl, Earl and Bernie off the hook from their conviction in the Collinsville mail robbery case two decades before.

With the passing of time in 1948, more than one rival reporter was heard to complain that Link had sacrificed reportorial objectivity by going to bed with the Sheltons. There was a smidgen of truth to it. After Bernie was killed, Baldwin was to note, Link and the remainder of the Shelton hierarchy lived, ate and slept together for days.[8] Led by Big Earl, the Shelton gang survivors realized their days in organized crime were numbered, and they came clean with Link on payoffs to officials by themselves and other gamblers. They knew a lot about other graft also. This information, when added to what Link and other *Post-Dispatch* reporters had dug up beforehand, produced a series of disclosures, most under Link's byline, of widespread corruption in Illinois, implicating state, county and city officials. Specifics about payoffs by gamblers to local officials and to "collectors for the state" finally were revealed, as was tickling of palms on state contracts. The great degree to which unfettered gambling and prostitution flourished in many counties was vividly spelled out.

The single most sensational disclosure came August 6, 1948, when Link revealed in the *Post-Dispatch* that an effort was made to collect a $25,000 bribe from Bernie Shelton in the weeks before his murder.

Far from a run-of-the-mill payoff allegation, discussion of the bribe sought from the gangster was documented on secret phonograph records of a conversation at Shelton's home between Bernie and a man named Roy D. Gatewood, who depicted himself as a representative of State's Attorney Hull. The purpose of the bribe was to bring about dismissal of the felony indictments against Bernie, Walker and John Kelly charging them with assault with intent to kill in the beating of Richard Murphy at the Parkway.

Bernie, but not Gatewood, a onetime candidate for Peoria County sheriff then in the advertising business, knew that their conversation on the attempted $25,000 shakedown was being recorded. Afterward, Shelton placed the four records in a bank vault and instructed his wife to give them to Link "if anything happens to me."[9] As he directed, the records were removed from the vault and delivered to Link by Shelton associates under heavy guard after Bernie was killed. They were played, and a stenographic transcript was made.

Although the *Post-Dispatch* was first to publicly disclose the existence of the records and their content, it was learned later that several newspaper people in Peoria were given a chance to listen to the recordings in the days before Bernie's assassination. They were not permitted to publish anything about the records, though, reportedly on orders from the Sheltons.

Obtaining the recordings was a work of ingenuity, an undertaking that would have made J. Edgar Hoover or James Bond proud. After meetings between Bernie and Gatewood began in late June, the Sheltons set their mind to secure a record of the proceeding. Jack Ashby, the Shelton Amusement Co. manager and an army veteran with radio and jukebox expertise, bought an expensive recording device and wired Bernie's house on Farmington for sound. A microphone was placed in a table model radio on a sun porch and wires were run to the recording machine in an adjoining room.

The challenge then was to get Gatewood, who'd been conferring with Bernie in out-of-the-way places, into the sun parlor. This was accomplished when Gatewood drove to Bernie's home on June 26—the day after the grand jury voted to indict Bernie, Walker and Kelly. Gatewood expected Shelton to join him in his car, but he was maneuvered by Bernie into the sun room, ostensibly because it offered cool relief from the hot weather. Gatewood didn't know that Ashby was at the recording instrument in the next room, accompanied by his wife, Mary, and Genevieve Shelton.

When the transcript of Bernie's chat with Gatewood was made public, juicy reading followed. As the two got around to the bribe, those listening to the records heard Bernie protesting in his southern Illinois twang, "Twenty-five thousand is a lot of money." This was especially so, argued Bernie, because "you know damn well, Roy, that he is framing me." To that, Gatewood replied, "Sure, I know he is framing you. Just like my wife said, she heard him. The wife said: 'What is the matter with that cheap, no good, rotten _____?'"

Nevertheless, Gatewood continued, "He said, '$25,000.' I said, 'What?' I said, '$25,000, man, what are you talking about?' Just like that I said it to him. He said, 'That is the way it is.'"

At one point Bernie asked if the person to whom Gatewood was referring was the state's attorney. Answered Gatewood, "That's right, our state's attorney."

If the requested bribe was not forthcoming, Gatewood advised Shelton to "stay hid out, because they are going to get you down at this jail and make you sweat in there for a week." Bernie, who had posted $6,000 cash bond for his trial appearance, retorted, "I got a lot of bond." And he had something else to add, on the subject of sweating. "They are all liable," he said prophetically, "to sweat with me."[10]

When questioned by Link about the recordings, a flabbergasted Gatewood said he wanted to see his lawyer. As for Hull, he denied soliciting money from Bernie. In an open letter to Peorians, Hull declared that he and his staff "have been maliciously charged with an attempt to solicit a bribe from a group of underworld persons commonly known as the Shelton gang." On the other hand, Hull did tell Link that Gatewood was a close friend who "may have facetiously remarked to Shelton that he could square the case, but he certainly had no authority to do so." Hull also insisted to Link that the indictments against Bernie, Walker and Kelly were not born out of a desire by Hull for revenge against Bernie. The tavern fight simply offered Hull an opportunity, he maintained, to go after gangsters whom he regarded as a blot on the Peoria scene.

It was after the death of Bernie Shelton, and especially following the revelation of the Gatewood recordings, that corrupt officials in Illinois, a number of them in Governor Green's administration, had to feel under siege by the *Post-Dispatch*. Day after day, its headlines trumpeted case upon case of vicious political-criminal alliances besmirching public morality in the state. The breakdown in law enforcement went so far, the articles contended, that the State Police even furnished chauffeurs from its ranks for hoodlums and gamblers. New informants seemed to come out of the woodwork every night, but none more talkative than Big Earl and the dwindling number of Shelton associates. They fingered crooked officials, who'd accepted dough from Carl and Bernie, and provided records to substantiate the allegations. A result was that light also was shed on ties between gangsters and officials in other parts of the Midwest.

As for the Peoria area, Link revealed that Bernie Shelton had paid $300 a month to state officials to prevent their interference with his Paradise Club, a gaming casino in neighboring Tazewell County. Many of the payments, which Bernie duly noted in writing, were picked up at the Parkway by George Chiames, owner of a pool hall in Peoria and an "area collector" for state officials. Link disclosed further that Chiames also happened to be on the state payroll of Attorney General Barrett, receiving about $400 monthly as a sales tax investigator.

Link also reported that Sheriff Spainhower received slot machine payoffs with regularity in addition to his acceptance of a $7,200 fund from gamblers to help cover his election campaign expenses in 1946. Link's source on this story was Renard McDermott, identified as a stepson of Carl Shelton and a right-hand man for Carl in the slot machine business for years. McDermott also maintained that Carl gave Spainhower a pearl-handled revolver as an election present, which Spainhower denied just as much as he did everything else Link wrote about him.

While Link focused on Peoria, other *Post-Dispatch* writers were getting into print detailed disclosures about gambling and other questionable activities elsewhere in Illinois.

Springfield and its organized crime boss, the reticent Frank Zito, came under close scrutiny by a surefooted digger, Roy J. Harris. Harris, who in 1949 worked with the *Chicago Daily News* in a Pulitzer Prize-winning investigation of Illinois newspaper publishers and editors on the state payroll during the governorship of Green (their principal service had been to print handouts from GOP party headquarters), conducted one interview during his 1948 gambling inquiry memorable because of its candor. Under questioning by Harris, Sheriff Meredith J. Rhule of Sangamon County acknowledged he knew about commercial gambling and intended to let it continue. Although he declined in the interview to confirm or deny he accepted graft from gamblers, Rhule stated to Harris, "If some night club operator wants to make me a present because he likes the color of my eyes, well, why shouldn't he?"[11]

Based on his findings, Harris concluded that payoffs from gambling and other vice in the Springfield area to city, county and state officials for "protection" amounted to the incredible sum of $10,000 per week. The payoffs were routed through a local "syndicate" run by Zito.

Baldwin, sometimes aided by another dogged *Post-Dispatch* tracker of shady characters, Selwyn Pepper, often appeared to be in more than one place at the same time. In vice-ridden LaSalle County, Baldwin reported on a citizenry indignant at the escape from prosecution of eight public officials indicted on charges of nonfeasance. In Mount Vernon, Baldwin confirmed that the Capone crowd had set up headquarters in the Jefferson County community for gaining the say over rackets in southeastern Illinois. Mysterious strangers were surfacing in Mount Vernon, a number of them henchmen of Wortman and the others gangsters from Chicago.

Down in the basement of the state, Baldwin brought out that law officers in Alexander and Pulaski counties had retreated to the sidelines while outside mob factions battled for control of profitable gambling dens that no longer could rely on Sheltonites for safekeeping. Baldwin's snooping so ticked off the hoods that a group of them schemed to give him a beating during one of his incursions into Cairo. When the muscle men arrived in the town to do the job, though, they discovered that Baldwin had departed a half hour earlier.

Link didn't have to be reminded of the perils in prying into the underworld. The more productive his Illinois investigation, the more rumors circulated that he was marked for death. This led him to often register at one hotel but sleep under a phony name at another. In going places he

avoided the beaten paths. Just hanging around the Sheltons was dangerous in itself. "Once," Baldwin recollected, "Link was drinking at a bar,
standing between Big Earl and Ray Walker, when the two gangsters
became engaged in a heated dispute. It got so hot each drew a pistol, and
there was the startled Link in the middle."[12]

As the summer of 1948 moved on and Illinoisans' consciousness of
vice and graft in their state spread widely, two very predictable out-
growths occurred. One, ministerial and chamber of commerce groups,
fueled by public anger, sought investigations by special grand juries and
special prosecutors all over the landscape.

Second, the Stevenson gubernatorial campaign was beginning, in the
language of southern Illinois politicos, to smell the meat "a cookin'." A
breakthrough was at hand. The newspaper assault against official tolera-
tion of vice in Illinois had the Green machine rocking on its heels. Since
his own hands were clean, Stevenson was free as a bird to tear into the
governor for allegedly perpetrating an atmosphere of sleaze that was drag-
ging Illinois' image through the mud. And, the greatest supplier of ammu-
nition for Stevenson was Peoria, where the murder of Bernie Shelton was
unleashing a torrential backlash.

The Green campaign had hoped early on that its negative press on the
Peoria situation might be limited to the *Post-Dispatch*. But, this proved to
be wishful thinking when many newspapers felt they no longer could
ignore the unfolding story of corruption in Peoria, especially after the
divulgence of the Gatewood recordings. When the *Chicago Daily News*
city editor, Clem Lane, ordered young reporter Fred Bird down to Peoria
to find out what all the commotion was about, Bird joined the ranks of
other reporters suddenly assigned to a story that was almost totally a *Post-
Dispatch* exclusive.

Years later, Bird recollected the challenge he faced in "going to Peoria
for the first time to cover this wild scandal involving some very important
people and these Shelton folks, whom I really knew nothing about." Bird
came across few persons who'd give him any information, not even the
Western Union worker who sent Bird's copy to Chicago. "When I asked the
Western Union chap about the origin of this big odor hanging over downtown Peoria," Bird said, "he just wisecracked that he didn't smell anything.
However, I did finally learn the smell was from this large distillery."[13]

More than one reporter trying to track the *Post-Dispatch* disclosures were fed scraps of catch-up info by Link—just enough crumbs to keep up the interest of the reporters and their papers. Such a tactic served to highlight to an even further degree the way out ahead coverage by the *Post-Dispatch*. "Without question," acknowledged Bird, "the story was all sewed up by this fellow Link, a smooth old-timer who knew the score about everything."[14]

For the most part, Bird and other reporters seeking to confirm the *Post-Dispatch* revelations ended up filing color stories on the electrified atmosphere in Peoria. Bird did venture once to the late Bernie Shelton's home, where the reporter was told he'd find Big Earl. However, after arriving and knocking hard on the front door, Bird was confronted by "a rather tough looking fellow at the house who abruptly chased me away." Venturing out to Shelton's home day or night, where big lights lit up the place for hundreds of yards surrounding it after dark, was risky because gunmen inside the house had their sights trained on visitors from the moment of their arrival.

The scandalous state of affairs in Peoria intensified September 3, 1948, some two months before the general election, when a Peoria County grand jury under the direction of a court-appointed special prosecutor, Verle W. Safford, indicted Hull, Spainhower and Charles Somogyi, an investigator for Hull, for malfeasance in office through failure to suppress gambling. Hull was named in a second indictment for allegedly attempting to obtain a $25,000 bribe from Bernie Shelton, and Spainhower also was hit with a second indictment, charging him with perjury. The latter charge was leveled because the jury maintained the sheriff testified falsely before it that he was not socially active with Carl Shelton and members of his family, a relationship that was said to include partying with the Sheltons at Carl's home on Knoxville Avenue in Peoria. An irony was that the thin-faced Hull himself had requested the grand jury inquiry into the alleged bribe solicitation, as well as into the gambling in Peoria County.

During the jury's sessions, Link was called to appear three times before the panel. After the indictments were returned, the reporter was singled out for high praise by Safford, a former president of the Peoria Bar Association, in a letter to the *Post-Dispatch*. "Due to Mr. Link's very thorough investigation and previous delving into the matters under consideration," wrote Safford, "his suggestions and information were most valuable...." Other witnesses appearing included Big Earl and Ashby, who played the Gatewood recordings to the jury. Gatewood appeared voluntarily, but declined to testify. Subsequently, he returned and testified under a guarantee of immunity.

Far from settling the dust in Peoria, the indictments worked an enraged populace into an even bigger lather. In a report with the return of the indictments, the grand jury stressed that its upcoming expiration hardly negated the need for much further investigation of the reported ties between officials and racketeers in Peoria County. Future grand juries were urged to take up the cause.

In addition, even before the outgoing grand jury finished its work, the Peoria Association of Commerce requested in a strongly worded letter to Green and Barrett that they "take prompt steps" to appoint a special assistant attorney general to undertake a wholesale investigation of the deplorable conditions creating "a disturbed public confidence" in Peoria. Almost daily since the August 6 article on the alleged $25,000 bribe, the letter stated, "the *Post-Dispatch*, a St. Louis newspaper, has published prominent and extended news stories revealing widespread official bribery, extortion and corruption in the Peoria area." Consequently, the commerce group concluded, urgent need existed for "an immediate, vigorous and thorough investigation and prosecution of every phase of these charges regardless of how long it takes, who it may involve or what it costs."[15]

Up to this juncture, Green repeatedly had brushed off requests, or outright pleadings in certain cases, to take action to assist those local authorities honestly wanting to combat gambling and corruption. His stance, not unlike that of some previous governors, was that law enforcement was essentially a local responsibility. However, with the scandals becoming a political tempest, Green and Barrett switched gears abruptly in mid-September.

Prompted by the letter from the Peoria business association and by similar exhortations from Springfield, Barrett—after huddling with Green—ordered state investigations immediately in Peoria and Sangamon counties. He appointed a special assistant attorney general to head each inquiry. The one for Peoria was James A. Howe, former mayor of Oak Park, and for Sangamon, Oliver H. Bovik, a onetime staffer for the

Cook County state's attorney. For his part, Green agreed to assign state policemen to assist Howe and Bovik, a move equated by skeptics with sending foxes into a henhouse.

Demand for the Sangamon inquiry was particularly prompted by the brutal murder in August 1948 of Leonard Giordano, a dice table man at the Pad, a roadhouse north of Springfield. In line with gangland tradition, Giordano was knocked out with a blackjack, his jugular vein slashed and his neck punctured by a bullet. His body was found in a ditch off U.S. Highway 66, north of Springfield. Days later, his friend and roommate, Joseph Teresi, a bartender at the Pad, was found shot to death. Although a coroner's jury ruled Teresi's death a suicide, many saw it as another gang hit. Whatever, the deaths did nothing to ease public alarm over the violent forces tied to gambling in Sangamon. By the time Bovik arrived in the county, though, Sheriff Rhule had reversed his earlier position and begun to put a lid on open wagering in Sangamon.

As it worked out, the investigation in Peoria County under Howe was the major attention-getter. The Howe inquiry opened at the same time a new grand jury in the county began a fresh investigation under the direction of Hull (even though he was under indictment) into disclosures of wrongdoing. Although at first each was billed as a proceeding independent of the other, the two investigations would dovetail, leading in the end to jury conclusions under the guiding hand of Howe.

The jury output was a humdinger. Although intended to boost the beleaguered Green and his ally Barrett, it did just the opposite.

To grasp what the grand jury and Howe zeroed in on, one had to go back to a tense situation the night of July 30, 1948, in Link's ninth-floor room at the Pere Marquette Hotel in downtown Peoria. Four days had passed since the murder of Bernie Shelton, and Link was trying to assist Big Earl in his private effort to track down the killer. Based on information picked up by Shelton folks, a Peoria gambler and Shelton camp follower named Peter J. Petrakos may have been a finger man for those plotting to bump off Bernie. Suspicion about Petrakos was further aroused when he failed to get in touch with the Sheltons after the murder, even though he was a close acquaintance of Bernie.

Link made the first contact with Petrakos after Bernie's death, finding him at his apartment in a building owned by Clyde Garrison, who was trying to resurface in Peoria area gambling as a Johnny-come-lately ally of the Chicago mob. Denying to Link that he'd become a stool pigeon for Garrison, Petrakos, a son of a Greek immigrant, told Link that he "loved" Bernie and would do anything to help solve his murder. Consequently, he agreed to meet Big Earl on the evening of July 30 in Link's hotel room. He entered the room with Ray Walker and Jack Ashby after going along with a telephone arrangement to meet them ahead of time on the street in front of the Palace Theater.

Exactly what transpired in the hotel room remained subject to conjecture. Link, who stayed in the room during the four-hour questioning of Petrakos, maintained it amounted to little more than an ordinary interrogation. He did report afterward that, at one point, Big Earl shook his finger at Petrakos and said firmly, "I want to know who killed my brothers. The law hasn't helped us. Tell us the truth, Pete."[16] In reply, Petrakos professed to know nothing about the killings of either Bernie or Carl.

He preferred to talk instead of his affection for Bernie and of services he'd performed for the Sheltons. "Remember the time I moved the body?" Link quoted Petrakos as asking Earl. Later, Earl told Link that the question was "a figure of speech" and did not pertain to a human body.

Petrakos, who smoked cigarettes, paced the floor and sometimes squatted on his heels during the meeting. Afterward, he asserted that Earl threatened at least once to wrap him in a sheet, hold him out the window and give the sheet a small slit with a knife each time he gave what Earl believed to be an untruthful answer to a question. Lucky for him, Petrakos noted, Link objected to the sheet strategy. Link's protest, added Petrakos, may have saved his life.

When Petrakos left Link's room in the early morning hours, he was described by Link as "nervous and shaking."[17] At the same time, Link insisted that Petrakos never was restrained from leaving the room and that, when the meeting ended, all on hand, including Petrakos, were amiable. Petrakos even volunteered on departing, said Link, to get back to Earl with "anything I hear." After leaving the hotel, Petrakos took a cab to his apartment and, within a few hours, drove with his wife out of Peoria. When he appeared again in Peoria weeks later for questioning by investigators, he was flanked by a man who was a bodyguard for Garrison.

Moving to the Howe inquiry in Peoria weeks down the line, Carl Baldwin got an early idea of where Howe was heading when he called in the *Post-Dispatch* reporter for questioning. "Are you and Ted Link associates of gangsters?" Howe queried Baldwin right off. Baldwin gave an evasive answer that he felt saved him from being summoned later as a witness before the new Peoria County grand jury. But that first question tipped off Baldwin to the goal of Barrett and his man Howe—nothing short of the indictment of the *Post-Dispatch*. More than that, as Howe proceeded to gather information from others enroute to his takeover of the grand jury inquiry, word leaked out that little of substance was being found to give credence to the hullabaloo over gaming and graft in Peoria County.

Yet, hardly anybody was fully prepared for the actions taken by the jury on October 23, 1948, a week and a half before the election.

Link was charged in indictments returned that day by the jury with kidnapping, conspiracy and intimidation in the questioning of Petrakos in Link's hotel room. Also indicted on the charges were Big Earl, Walker and Ashby. According to the indictments, the four men "conspired, combined and agreed feloniously, willfully and without lawful authority to seize, confine and imprison Peter J. Petrakos against his will on July 30, 1948." The defendants committed these acts, it was alleged, to "obtain a confession by Petrakos in a homicide," the unsolved assassination of Bernie Shelton.

Just as astounding, the grand jury reported simultaneously that it uncovered no evidence to back up charges by the *Post-Dispatch* that state and county officials had been handed payoffs by gambling interests. The report censured the Peoria Association of Commerce for "accepting the untruths carried by the *Post-Dispatch*." Link was condemned for "obtaining his information from known hoodlums." The *Post-Dispatch* was criticized for printing information obtained in such a manner. In the windup of their report, jury members said they found it "incumbent upon us" to commend Barrett and Howe "for their outstanding public service to this community and in the thorough, complete and competent investigation they have conducted" into the gambling and corruption allegations.

Green and Barrett had struck back at their tormentor. Their surrogate, Howe, had convinced the latest grand jury to extract a pound of flesh from the *Post-Dispatch*, and in so doing, hopefully divert attention away from the matters targeted by the paper's gumshoes. Voices suggesting that the jury obviously was manipulated by the special prosecutor didn't appear to bother Green advocates. Domination of grand juries by prosecutors was a fact of life in American jurisprudence. Besides, more than a few individuals had viewed the previous grand jury's indicting of Hull, Spainhower and Somogyi as politically motivated. So, Green partisans reasoned, fair was fair.

But the world didn't see it that way.

Few newspapers were as sacrosanct as they liked to be perceived, but indicting a reporter for any reason short of murder was close to a sacrilege at that point in the nation's history. And the Howe-inspired jurors declaring Peoria County to be clean as a hound's tooth smacked of incomprehensible audacity. Many who had been giving Green the benefit of the doubt found the jury's actions just too much to stomach. Pundits sensed in the final days before Illinoisans went to the polls that numerous Republicans might be joining the majority of political independents in casting votes for Democrat Stevenson.

The normally unflappable Link displayed anxiety when he was arraigned at Peoria on the kidnapping charge. His nervousness increased when the judge was reluctant at first to accept a *Post-Dispatch* check for Link's $11,000 bail because it was billed by the issuing bank as a secretary's check instead of a cashier's check. To have not made bail, although Link did, would have subjected him to a stay in a jail run by a sheriff whose indictment was partly based on the work of the reporter. Big Earl, Walker and Ashby, the codefendants of Link, also posted bond.

The discomfiture of Link had to pale, though, in comparison to the jitters that his indictment ended up causing Green and Barrett and their troops. The charges against Link ignited a storm of protests not just in Illinois but also across the United States. Newspaper editorials blasted the grand jury action as an attack on the freedom of the press to investigate corruption. Even the Green-leaning *Chicago Tribune* rallied to Link's support. Sigma Delta Chi, a national professional journalism organization, would condemn the development as a "brazen attempt" to "intimidate and gag the press."

As for Link's own newspaper, the *Post-Dispatch* came out with an editorial the day after the indictments declaring that the Green machine could not bully the paper into silence. Furthermore, editor Joseph

Pulitzer directed that the editorial and a cartoon by editorial cartoonist Daniel R. Fitzpatrick lampooning the indicting of Link be published as advertising in newspapers in Chicago, Peoria, Springfield and other Illinois cities on October 26 and 27, 1948. The ad was headed, "For the Information of the Voters of Illinois."

If Green, Barrett and company thought the performance of the grand jury might play well in Peoria, they guessed wrong. The *Peoria Journal*, for one, savaged Barrett, Howe and the jury for staging a sham in the city. A ludicrous whitewash was how the *Journal* saw it.

"From the time Mr. Howe arrived in Peoria...to begin what Mr. Barrett promised would be a 'thorough and exhaustive' investigation of charges of alleged vice and corruption," the *Journal* editorialized, "it was evident that his (Howe's) efforts were designed to bring about a whitewash of the gamblers and racketeers and the public officials who might be involved with them." Sure enough, the *Journal* went on, the jury did have "the effrontery to claim or admit that it was unable to find any evidence of the existence of organized rackets." But hardest of all to swallow, the newspaper stated, was that Barrett and Howe had the gall to "have written into a whitewash grand jury report a glorification of themselves in the form of a commendation for the type of investigation they carried on."

By failing to find not one individual to indict in connection with vice in Peoria County, the *Journal* reasoned, the grand jury in "the eyes of the law abiding, decent citizens" did in truth indict one person, George Barrett. The attorney general "stands indicted before the people of Illinois for his utter failure to represent the best interests of the people of this community and the people of the entire state, the very people whom he is calling upon to return him to office on November 2," the paper concluded.[18] To underscore its contempt, the *Journal* ran front-page pictures of Barrett and Howe with halos around their heads.

The Illinois electorate did not return Barrett to office on November 2, 1948. Dwight Green and many other Republicans went down to defeat also. The election that day produced one of the greatest Democratic avalanches in state history. In the all-important contest for governor, Stevenson swamped Green by 572,067 votes, a record at the time. Along with Carmi attorney Ivan A. Elliott's victory over Barrett, Democrats won all the other state offices on the ballot. University of

Chicago professor Paul H. Douglas, a Democrat, ousted Republican C. Wayland Brooks from a seat in the United States Senate and, in a surprise to many, President Harry S Truman managed to edge Thomas Dewey in the presidential balloting in Illinois by 33,612 votes, a thin margin. Without the strong showing of Stevenson, Democrat Truman most likely would not have carried Illinois, a state that turned out to be crucial for Truman in his upset victory over Dewey.

Stevenson went on to establish a record as governor that would propel him to national prominence. Twice, in 1952 and 1956, he was the Democratic Party's unsuccessful candidate for president. In the race for the White House in 1956, the vice-presidential candidate on Stevenson's ticket was Senator Kefauver, who had become widely known as a result of the work of his crime investigating panel. Stevenson still was in the nation's eye in the early 1960s, when he served as United States ambassador to the United Nations. However, when Stevenson became his party's candidate for governor in 1948, few would have predicted that such a distinguished journey in public life lay ahead for him.

Going into the final days of the campaign, Democratic politicians in Chicago appeared resigned to the likelihood of a Stevenson defeat, believing that Dewey would win the state by a margin substantial enough to carry Green with him. The old Democratic pols didn't see Stevenson getting across his pledge to reclaim Illinois government from the grafters and lawbreakers around Green and to abolish the shakedowns, kickbacks, padded payrolls and political lugs marking Green's last years in office. But, analyst after analyst detected a swing toward Stevenson after the Link indictment, a trend labeled "a sudden wave" by *Chicago Sun-Times* columnist John Dreiske. The surge to Stevenson was so obvious to Jacob M. Arvey, the Cook County Democratic boss, that he suddenly predicted a Stevenson victory by 400,000 votes.

Voter sentiment was no more clear than in the so-called gambling counties, where Stevenson won the major ones and ran well in all. In spite of a large concentration of Republicans in Peoria County, Stevenson carried it. In addition, Peoria countians put a Democrat, Michael A. Shore, in the state's attorney's office. All other Peoria County offices at stake in the election went to Republicans. Stevenson also won staunchly GOP Sangamon County, where an investigation by a grand jury tied to Oliver Bovik, the special assistant attorney general sent into Sangamon by Barrett, also failed to return any gambling indictments. The incumbent state's attorney in Sangamon, Democrat John W. Curren, who'd directed that whitewash grand jury inquiry along with Bovik, was beaten for re-election by Republican George P. Coutrakon, a crime-fighting attorney from Springfield. And so it went in other parts of the state, where new faces were put in office by voters right and left.

Of course, the headliner was Adlai Stevenson. To many, it was somewhat ironic that his ace in the hole in defeating Green was the issue of crime in the state, since Green himself had earned his early reputation as a key figure in the successful prosecution of Al Capone. Yet, to repeat the view of numerous political observers, the crime issue really didn't register with many voters until the uproar over the indicting of Link. But, going a step further, the Green machine never would have had Link indicted if not for his tenacious digging along with other *Post-Dispatch* reporters into gambling and other wrongdoing tolerated by Green's administration. However, to take it one more step, the role of the *Post-Dispatch* and Link may have been far less muckraking if not spurred by the murder of Bernie Shelton. So, in a tracing of causes and effects in the election of Stevenson, one very important line well might have been drawn from his political ascendancy back to the grave of the gangster in Parkview Cemetery.

Stevenson carried out as governor his pledge to crack down on flagrantly open vice. After greatly revamping the corrupt State Police, he did not hesitate to send in troopers to shut down gambling dens when local officials still refused to do so. While open gaming was not completely wiped out, Stevenson's drive against it did more than anything else to reap him nationwide recognition.

As noted earlier, Link proceeded from his Illinois exposes in 1948 to build a national reputation in investigative reporting, based in part on his feeding of the Kefauver committee. He continued to pursue underworld figures up to his death, never forsaking in his attire the wide trousers and wide-brimmed hats that had gone out of vogue years before.

In 1960, Link made front-page news of a different kind when he was charged with murder in the shooting of Clarence W. Calvin, a handyman once employed by Link at his country home near St. Albans, Missouri. Link said he had wanted to question Calvin about a fire that had destroyed the country house. However, insisted Link, he felt he was forced to shoot Calvin in self-defense when the handyman moved toward him with a switchblade knife and three-pronged hoe. The reporter was acquitted by a jury after a trial at Hermann, Missouri.

Back to Peoria and 1948, Link, Big Earl, Walker and Ashby never went to trial on their indictments for allegedly kidnapping Petrakos. After gathering dust in a filing cabinet in the Peoria County Courthouse, the indictments were dismissed in February 1949 by Circuit Judge John T. Culbertson at the request of the county's new state's attorney, Michael Shore. After reviewing the situation, Shore said he concluded that "convictions could not be sustained in these causes," partly because the whereabout of the only witness against the four men (assumably Petrakos) was no longer known.

Culbertson also dismissed at the same time the perjury indictment against Sheriff Spainhower on a technicality, namely that in referring to a trip Spainhower took to the Kentucky Derby in 1947 with Carl Shelton the indictment inadvertently referred to Carl as Bernie Shelton. Since Circuit Judge Henry J. Ingram earlier had thrown out the malfeasance indictment against Spainhower, the sheriff was free of all charges. In the end, all the Shelton and gambling-related indictments returned by the two Peoria County grand juries in 1948 were dropped or permitted to die on the vine because of insufficient evidence in the various cases. Of those involved, Hull was regarded in some circles as the one charged most unfairly—a prosecutor who, in his zeal to punish Bernie Shelton, may have been a victim of a clever trap or frame-up. When Hull died in 1981, a *Peoria Journal Star* article on his death did not even mention his indictment. Instead, it gave the World War I veteran and University of Michigan law graduate credit for attempting to prohibit gambling in Peoria County, a move that in the words of the article "involved the infamous Shelton gang."

The indictments never were viewed by a number of onlookers as anything more than a politically motivated hodgepodge. Looking back years later, the *Journal Star* appeared to agree, saying they were "complex, chaotic and contradictory."[19] If it was true that the indictments of the first grand jury reflected the investigation of the *Post-Dispatch* and the work of the second jury satisfied the Green machine's desire to counter the investigation, then the only conclusion to be drawn, figured the *Journal Star*, was that from "the legal standpoint, the battle of the grand juries ended in a draw."[20]

Not arguable was that the death of Bernie Shelton precipitated the close of Peoria's gang era. It also led to the end of the road for the Shelton gang, or what was left of it, on the broad criminal stage in Illinois. Ray Walker made noises about trying to assume the mantle of Shelton influence once wielded by Carl and then Bernie, but there were not enough pieces left to pick up. Big Earl, the last of the Shelton boys who'd been feared in their heyday, seemed reluctant to venture away from Fairfield. Most of the remaining members of the family were around there, too, trying to recapture a semblance of order in their lives in old, familiar home territory. But even that was wishful thinking.

17

Terror in Fairfield

Since the movie never was made, the world didn't get a chance to see what actor would have been chosen to play Carl Shelton. It was true, though, that Frank Sinatra and several of his "rat pack" pals, including Dean Martin and Peter Lawford, flirted with the idea of doing a film in the 1960s about the Shelton boys and their gang. Had Sinatra—who himself was very familiar with some gangsters—gone ahead with the production, part of the movie was to have been shot in Fairfield and Wayne County. After all, only so much could be done to reconstruct Fairfield on a West Coast studio lot.

Although played out in sundry places, the Shelton melodrama had its backdrop in the Fairfield area. Whether folks there admitted it or not, and certainly some could have cared less, a Shelton thread ran through that neck of the woods. Because of the undertakings of Carl, Bernie and Big Earl, Fairfield was more than just another dot on the map. At least to outsiders.

As the years of the twentieth century neared an end, the legacy of the family of Agnes and Ben was a distant memory to many in or around Fairfield. But it was there, and when some from the town were asked by inquisitive strangers to talk about it, they did not shun candor. One such individual was Judith Puckett, a communications and humanities teacher at Frontier Community College at Fairfield, who was questioned about the Sheltons on a summer afternoon in 1998.

Puckett's grandfather, Ora Hubble, and father, Sam Puckett, both served as mayor of Fairfield. As she was growing up, she realized that her town was known in the outside world for two things—the Shelton gang and the Farmer's Store on West Main Street, a well-known supplier of women's and men's apparel. As for the Sheltons, Puckett said she doubted "the image of Fairfield was hurt by them.

"To the people who lived here, the Sheltons were viewed by many as normal people in an abnormal business. They've never stopped being a subject of discussion, but now, all these years later, the Sheltons seem like another time altogether. An intriguing time, yes, but gone. Sure, it remained very emotional for some of those touched directly, but for most of us, it's in the past. No question, though, they were legends."[1]

Fairfield at the end of the twentieth century—a quintessence of small town America. An embodiment of a way of life fundamental to the early character of the country, far afield from urban sprawl. A place where traditional trappings were not sacrificed, even through the stagnant cycles of the region's up and down oil industry and other economic upheavals.

Driving through western Wayne County (named for American Revolutionary general Anthony Wayne), the stretch of Highway 15 between smallish Wayne City and Fairfield offered a view of a true agrarian landmark, a hulking old barn of blackened boards with faded lettering, "Chew Mail Pouch Tobacco—Treat Yourself to the Best." From the north, the road to Fairfield passed both rusty and new oil field equipment, old farm windmills and a turnoff leading to the Wayne County Coonhunters Club.

As an official "Illinois Main Street Community," Fairfield, population 5,400, remained stubbornly faithful to a more relaxed pace of life, one unadorned save for the same old refrains, the main street stuff. The Christmas and homecoming parades. The festivals. Queen contests. Star-spangled concerts in the summer by a municipal band. The great pride in Fairfield High School.

County courthouses anchor many Illinois towns, and Fairfield was no exception. Along with the old stone and brick bank building boasting a pointed spire at the corner of Third and Main streets, the redbrick courthouse remained Fairfield's architectural gem. Its clock tower with a pyramidal roof was clearly visible from several directions. A memorial tablet on its lawn proclaimed to one and all that Wayne County Republicans gave Abraham Lincoln his first endorsement for their party's presidential nomination in 1860.

Fairfield's venerable newspaper, the *Wayne County Press*, was long identified with the family of Thomas O. Mathews Sr., the paper's widely respected editor and publisher in a span exceeding four decades. More than just a newspaperman, Mathews was a devoted civic leader; a man who had a leading hand in bringing about community improvements before chronicling them in his paper. Mathews was Fairfield's person for all seasons. Then there was Jack Vertrees, a salt of the earth kind of fellow.

When the *Press* rehashed the twentieth century in Fairfield in a special issue prior to the start of the next millennium, a retelling by veteran columnist Vertrees of the Shelton story with all its "tentacles of crime" got major billing.

Jack Wesley Vertrees was a southern Illinois success story in his own right. A son of a Fairfield house painter, Vertrees served in the army in the Pacific in World War II and received a Bronze Star Medal for heroism in action on Okinawa. After earning a journalism degree at the University of Illinois following the war, Vertrees spent two years at a newspaper in Hancock County before accepting an offer from Tom Mathews to work for the *Press*. By the time the year 2000 rolled around, Vertrees had put in nearly half a century at the paper as a reporter, photographer and editor, as well as columnist. His homespun column, "Random Thoughts," which often featured Jack's dog, Koko, was must reading in Fairfield.

In making the rounds in Fairfield with Vertrees, it was hard to not notice the deference paid to a man who forwent a bigger journalism market for that of his hometown. Newspapering was a very personalized vocation in Fairfield, just like other things in the life of Vertrees. His office at the *Press* was covered by pictures of country singer Barbara Mandrell, who called Jack to sing happy birthday to him on his fiftieth. That may or may not have had something to do with the fact that Mandrell's mother had worked at The Grill, a Fairfield restaurant that had been operated by the family of Jack's wife, Kay Cox.

Vertrees knew some of the Sheltons. He also was acquainted with Charles Harris. When Vertrees started at the *Press*, the era of the Sheltons in Fairfield, and in Illinois for that matter, was at an end. The way the curtain came down on the Sheltons was fresh on every person's mind in Fairfield at the time because it was traumatic—a nightmare of shootings, bombings and fires aimed at the remaining members of the family on their home terrain.

As Judith Puckett put it in a bit of understatement, "The things that happened with the Sheltons in their final years here were not viewed by many people as very entertaining."[2]

Nobody understood that more readily than Puckett's grandfather, Ora Hubble, a Fairfield merchant as well as straight arrow mayor of the town from the end of the 1940s well into the 1950s. The oil industry was booming then, and Fairfield was enjoying a prosperous, lively period. However, escape from the shadow of the Sheltons seemed impossible. Someone, or some persons, wanted to kill off more of them.

The climactic wave of terror involving the Sheltons erupted full scale the night of May 24, 1949, when Big Earl was wounded by one of three bullets fired through a window of Shelton's Farmers' Club by an unknown gunman. The window at the rear of the second floor gambling establishment on Fairfield's courthouse square was the only one at the parlor not painted black. To get into a position to see the interior of the club through the window, the assailant climbed a ladder to the roof of a car firm next to the club. From there, the attacker had a clear view of Big Earl's back as he sat on a stool at a card table. Little Carl Shelton, who was in the place at the time of the shooting along with his brother, Little Earl, told authorities later that his uncle had been playing poker but had laid down his hand and was conversing with friends when the bullets crashed through the window. As Big Earl, struck in the back, staggered to his feet, the gunman scrambled down the ladder and disappeared.

After a hasty examination by a doctor in Fairfield, Big Earl was rushed by ambulance to Deaconess Hospital at Evansville, Indiana. He was diagnosed there as having suffered from blood loss, but was not in danger of dying. An operation at the hospital failed to find the bullet in Shelton, although a doctor believed it had lodged under a shoulder. As Big Earl began to recover, Wayne countians, who'd hoped that Shelton-related violence had ended the year before in Peoria, went on alert for the worst.

Initially, the Chicago-St. Louis gambling syndicate was seen as the likely culprit in the attempted assassination. Apparently, some law officers concluded, the syndicate never could be at ease with its inroads into the control of vice in old Shelton territory as long as Big Earl, and perhaps other Sheltons, remained alive. After all, underworld sources had insisted, following the murder of Bernie, that a price still remained on the heads of Big Earl and Ray Walker.

However, other motives for the shooting also were advanced. One was that Charles Harris was the gunman, or the arranger of the attack, because of his hatred of the Sheltons. Of course, this possibility did not necessarily rule out mob involvement, it was noted, since Black Charlie also might have been doing the bidding of Buster Wortman in going after Big Earl. Another suspicion, harder to swallow, was that the shooting may not have been divorced from a reported falling out between Big Earl and his brother-in-law, Guy Pennington, then the husband of Lula Shelton. The animosity supposedly came about when Big Earl was said to have suspected that Guy secretly worked with dry forces in defeating the Big Earl-aligned wets in an election in Fairfield to legalize liquor. The drys prevailed after pamphlets denouncing the "Shelton-Pennington gang" for leading the fight for the wets were dropped over Wayne County from a plane. Nevertheless, Big Earl had his doubts about Pennington's true feeling on the subject, since the known bootlegging interests of Pennington in Wayne would have suffered with a wet victory.

Still, it was hard for many to accept that a dispute between Big Earl and Pennington actually would lead to an attempt to kill Shelton. About four weeks after the shooting, a roadhouse speakeasy run by Pennington two miles south of Fairfield was first bombed and then burned to the ground. Although Big Earl received some suspicious looks, the destruction was seen by most as having been carried out by Pennington himself for twisted reasons or, as Sheriff Bradshaw suggested, by citizens angry over the continued operation of the roadhouse in defiance of the law in the dry county.

The next shattering of the calm in Fairfield occurred in the early morning hours of September 9, 1949, when numerous residents were awakened by furious gunfire outside the Elm Street home of Little Earl. The twenty-nine-year-old Shelton, who'd been working at Big Earl's farm, as well as serving as a bodyguard for his uncle, was lucky to escape death. Again. He'd emerged unscathed, along with Ray Walker, from the bullets flying every which way during the assassination of Carl Shelton two years before. And, in World War II, Little Earl had served with valor in an army armored division. Besides being wounded in the invasion of Sicily, he was badly burned in an oil fire on the ocean caused by a sinking troop transport. When he pulled up in front of his house in the dark of that September morn, he might have thought he was back in the war.

As his Buick stopped, a storm of bullets riddled the front door on the driver's side. Somehow, Little Earl, although hit, threw himself on the floor of his car, a move that probably saved his life. As the auto of his attackers pulled away, Earl managed to draw his gun from a shoulder holster and get off several shots. Afterward, Earl told Bradshaw and the new state's attorney of Wayne, Gerald Mayberry, that in the light of the headlights from his car he could see his assailants were in what appeared to be a black sedan and that one of them, Earl contended, was Black Charlie Harris. Furthermore, Earl claimed to have noticed the license number of the gunmen's vehicle, a number that turned out to be issued to Harris.

After his attackers sped off, a blood-covered Earl was rescued by his wife, Eleanor, after he managed to crawl out of his car on the side facing his house. As had been Big Earl, Little Earl was conveyed to Evansville's Deaconess Hospital, where he was found to have been struck by eight shots, most hitting lower parts of his body. Fairfield police said Earl's car contained twenty-one bullet holes coming from two types of weapons, one presumably a machine gun. For that reason, the cops did not doubt there were at least two gunmen. Miraculously, Little Earl survived the assault.

In the aftermath of this shooting, events followed a script similar to the one after Carl Shelton's slaying. Based on what Little Earl said he saw, Harris was charged in a warrant with assault with intent to kill Little Earl. Harris denied knowledge of the crime, and local lawmen were inclined to believe him, thinking it was not likely Little Earl could have seen much of anything because of the darkness. About five weeks after the wounding of Little Earl, the charge against Harris was dismissed in magistrate's court when Shelton failed to appear for the prosecution of the case. Mayberry said that Earl had informed him that he had no witnesses to back up his identification of Harris.

Mayberry also quoted Little Earl as recalling that he was not believed when he insisted in 1947 that Harris participated in the killing of Carl Shelton. Harris was named at the coroner's inquest in the death of Carl as a suspect to be held for a grand jury inquiry into that murder. However, the jury refused to indict Harris in spite of the words of Little Earl and Ray Walker that Black Charlie had a hand in the crime.

The attacks on Big Earl and Little Earl bolstered a growing recognition in Wayne County that the surviving Sheltons were relics of the past. Outsiders could continue to speculate about the horrific revenge surely to be inflicted on Shelton foes, but the home folks knew better. Black Charlie had no competition for the title of the most feared individual in the county, and hadn't had since the death of Carl Shelton. Local officials certainly seemed to give Harris a wide berth. And the Sheltons? It was getting hard to see them as little more than toothless tigers, sitting ducks for their enemies. But as long as they stayed around, there seemed to be little chance of peace.

The year 1950 saw a resumption of open season on the Sheltons. In May, Big Earl was hit in the right arm, but not seriously wounded, when he and Little Earl were motoring through the Pond Creek area, inspecting oil drilling operations on property owned by Big Earl. Little Earl, who was not injured, said the gunfire came from one or more persons hidden on a bank overlooking the road. Two weeks later, on June 5, Little Earl's luck prevailed again when he received only a slight nick from a rifle and shotgun fusillade fired by would-be assassins. This attack came as he and an associate, Dellos Wylie, were sitting in Shelton's car in front of a garage a few miles west of Fairfield that the two men recently had purchased. The assailants, it turned out, had awaited the arrival of Shelton in a carefully camouflaged spot in undergrowth across the road from the garage. At the first burst of gunfire, Earl and Wylie managed to get out of the car and make it into the garage. When the hidden gunmen kept firing, Wylie tried to escape from the building. He was immediately cut down by bullets in the back, leaving him severely wounded.

If a crowning blow to the Sheltons was needed, it came two days later, early on the morning of June 7.

Roy Shelton, by then in his mid-sixties, was shot and killed as he was driving a tractor on farmland owned by Big Earl near the Pond Creek Road, only a mile or so from the spot where Carl was ambushed and killed. Roy was plowing a field when a lone gunman, hidden behind brush in a muddy slough at the edge of the parcel, got off at least five rifle shots. As one bullet hit his spine and another lodged in his groin, Shelton toppled from his still moving tractor. As the tractor started to run in a circle, the plow blades ran over Shelton, turning his body into a bloody hulk. However, medical people later were of the opinion that Roy was dead before he hit the ground.

Frank McKibben, a farmhand working in the field with Shelton and a witness to the murder, said he "could see the fire coming from the brush, but couldn't see who was shooting." According to McKibben, the gunman fired twice at him when he ran over to stop Shelton's tractor so it would not "run over Roy's body again." As a result, McKibben was forced to duck behind the tractor after turning it off. No more shots were fired. The murderer was not apprehended.

The slaying of Roy brought about near frenzy over the anti-Shelton violence. Although he was in trouble almost continuously from the time he was a young man and spent many of the years of his life behind bars—much more so than his celebrated brothers Carl, Bernie and Earl—Roy was a decidedly lesser light in the family. Hard to get along with, yes. But part of the Shelton gang? No.

It seemed a stretch to blame Roy's death on the mob. A more common guess was that his murder was at the hand of someone in the local community. Harris automatically came to mind. And if not him, then quite possibly some other "Pond Creeker," one of those in the bottoms with no use for the Sheltons because of their aggressive accumulation of thousands of acres and constant bickering with neighbors. Or, perhaps the killer was a relative of a Shelton gang victim back when the brothers ruled their vice kingdom with an iron hand. One thing seemed clear. Roy's murder was taken as definite confirmation that the Sheltons were marked by one or more enemies for nothing less than outright extermination. Anybody with a tie to the Sheltons also seemed to be fair game.

As with the funeral of Carl, a horde of onlookers was attracted to Roy's. More than a dozen state policemen were called to Fairfield to help local law enforcement personnel protect the remaining Sheltons, as well as ensure order among the more than 1,000 showing up for the service in the chapel of the Dixon and Crippin Funeral Home. Since only about 250 could squeeze into the chapel, the rest congregated on the lawns of the funeral parlor and nearby courthouse.

Those in the chapel heard the Reverend Kent Dale of Fairfield's First Christian Church express sorrow that "tragedy has again stalked across our smiling fields and green country lanes. Once more, fear casts her pall and grips the hearts of our citizens."[3] Afterward, many of those present joined Roy's family in the all too familiar cortege to Maple Hill, where he was to be buried next to Carl and Benjamin. Before the crowd drifted out of the cemetery, those closest to the grave site observed a hysterically sobbing Agnes Shelton being helped to her son's coffin. Giving it a last pat with her hand, she cried, "Good-bye, Roy."

Ma Shelton was soon to bid adieu to another son, Dalta, for a while. Within two months after the burial of Roy, Dalta was gone from Wayne County. Word of his departure got out through a weekly newspaper notice that his farm by Cisne had been sold. Those few who knew where he went clammed up, not wanting to jeopardize his safety. In time, it was learned that he ended up in Florida.

Sheriff Bradshaw and certain others suggested that, in order to avoid further imperilment of Fairfield residents, the remaining Sheltons consider hitting the road. But Big Earl and Little Earl nixed the idea, vowing to not be driven away. Big Earl's resolve to stay, though, was dampened when a homemade bomb wrecked his $35,000 home at his Hill Top Farm before the year was out. Big Earl and his wife Earline were fortunate to survive.

The pair were in bed when the would-be killer tossed a tin can filled with nitroglycerin through a picture window at an early morning hour. Awakened by the breaking of glass, Big Earl related, "we ran into the living room, and Earline was talking to the sheriff's office on the telephone when there was a terrific blast. It blew me into the bedroom, and Earline went flying into the bathroom. By the time we pulled ourselves together, the whole living room was in flames. There was no use trying to save anything. The flames raced through the house and we were lucky to get out."[4]

Losing his home was the final straw for Big Earl. A month and a half later, in January 1951, Earl and Earline, along with Little Earl and his family, left southern Illinois. Like Dalta, they went to Florida, to the Jacksonville area, a locale frequented often by Big Earl in his liquor-running days. Most newspapers that trumpeted the departure of Big Earl were in the dark on his destination. With Agnes, Lula and Jim Zuber about the only Sheltons left in Fairfield, some city residents who assumed the Shelton haters finally may have been satisfied began to breathe sighs of relief. Others just held their breaths.

For the first five months of 1951, there was a hiatus from the violence. During that period, parcels of land in Wayne and Hamilton counties in Carl Shelton's estate sold for a total of $69,900 at an auction sale in the Wayne courthouse. Shelton deeded his land to his widow and other relatives, but they were said to be unable to divide the acreage. So the land was put up for auction, with the estate retaining the oil and other mineral rights. The largest single purchase was the $27,000 paid by a Wayne farmer and oil well owner for a tract in Wayne. Another major buyer of acreage in Hamilton, as well as in Wayne, was businessman Carl Wittmond from Brussels in Calhoun County, a future member of the Illinois House of Representatives.

Wittmond quickly realized that he'd gotten more than he'd bargained for in acquiring some of Carl's land. When he tried to get it farmed, he complained that he "couldn't get nobody to rent it...they wouldn't even go on it...I couldn't get no service on it...."[5] This was almost to be expected since anyone brave enough to work the land of the departed Sheltons took a chance on losing his life. No one knew that better than Edward Hillary (Little Hill) O'Daniel Jr.

O'Daniel, a son of a respected Wayne County farmer, was twenty-nine years old on June 6, 1951, when he paid a price for attempting to farm, under a lease arrangement, Big Earl's acreage where Roy Shelton had been murdered. William O'Daniel, a brother of Little Hill, related what occurred that June day during a 1998 discussion, when William O'Daniel, then living at Mount Vernon, was an Illinois state senator.

"Hill had prepared the land for the planting of corn," O'Daniel said, "and was standing with two other men by a pickup truck on the acreage that day. Suddenly a shot from a high-powered rifle cracked over their heads. The two men with Hill jumped behind the pickup for shelter. The shot had come from a wooded place on a hill overlooking the Pond Creek bottom area. Hill, he just stood there and laughed. Then a second shot came, hitting the dirt where Hill was standing. Hill still didn't move. Then a third shot came, and it went through the upper muscle of Hill's left arm, completely through the arm. With that, Hill jumped behind the pickup with the others because it was clear that whoever was shooting intended to kill him. The two men then got Hill to the Fairfield hospital as fast as they could."[6] Little Hill survived the wounding. Nobody was ever arrested for the shooting.

The O'Daniel family had done business with the Sheltons for years. William O'Daniel also pointed out that his family had gotten along well with everybody on both sides of the Shelton-Harris feud. On the day of Little Hill's wounding, William O'Daniel said, "Hill got a visit in the hospital from Charlie Harris. He (Harris) told Hill that he didn't know who shot him, and that Harris liked all of us in our family. But, Harris told Hill there were people who wanted to make sure that the Sheltons didn't get any income off their land."[7] Little Hill never returned to the acreage where he was shot.

Being seen at oil well drilling sites on Carl's properties also could be hazardous. Snipers often shot at motors on the rigs, causing considerable damage. Lelan Russell, a Fairfield High School graduate, recalled the anxiety gripping his father, Red Russell, when his job as drilling superintendent for an oil company required him to check on projects on Shelton acreage at all hours of the day.

For night stops at wells on Shelton land, Red Russell would drive a light truck instead of the big Buick he normally drove because "the Buick was like a Shelton car and dad didn't want to be mistaken for a Shelton," explained Russell, who coached high school basketball at Norris City before going on to become executive vice president of the Illinois Oil and Gas Association. "The last thing dad wanted was to get shot."[8]

A day after the O'Daniel shooting, the elaborate $7,000 barn near the ruins of Big Earl's home at Hill Top was burned down by an unknown arsonist or arsonists. The blaze, coming on the heels of the O'Daniel incident, substantiated the apprehension of many in Fairfield that the break from violence early in 1951 was only temporary.

Three weeks after the fire, right before the end of June, 1951, gunfire erupted again in Fairfield—this time in broad daylight in a residential neighborhood on Ninth Street. An ambusher armed with a machine gun fired upon Lula and Guy Pennington. Both were hit, and both flatly identified Charles Harris as the shooter. By the time Jim Zuber was notified, at the Fairfield lumberyard where he worked, about the attack on his mother and stepfather, they had been admitted to the Fairfield hospital.

Dashing to the hospital, Zuber found his entrance momentarily blocked by a law officer demanding to know if Jim "knew who did it." Without hesitation, Zuber replied, "Charlie Harris did it."[9]

Later, Zuber would pass on that his mother "remembered that she had seen Charlie at the Post Office in Fairfield, and she hadn't spoken to him. So he must have felt slighted, and that's all it took."[10]

Alarmed that Harris might enter the hospital at anytime to finish off Lula and her husband, strategy was mapped in due haste to get the two and the other Sheltons remaining in Fairfield out of town as inconspicuously as possible. Death already was in the air. Within hours of the wounding of Lula and Guy, a man who was thought to have witnessed their shooting was mysteriously murdered in a bootlegging joint operated near Fairfield by Ogie Pennington, a brother of Guy. Subsequently, the building was torched and destroyed. The tension in the Fairfield area was suddenly so thick that it was almost palpable.

Amid the rampant unease, some started pointing fingers. Contributing greatly to the ceaseless violence, contended the Reverend Eugene Leckrone, a Methodist pastor and head of the Fairfield Ministerial Alliance, was the indifference of citizens refusing to assist law enforcement officials in any way. "When the good people laugh at the laws," said Leckrone, "the bad people disobey them."[11]

State's Attorney Mayberry struck a similar theme when he told the *St. Louis Globe-Democrat* that individuals who might know something about the acts of violence "just don't want to talk." Added Mayberry, "It seems a little unusual that no one sees anything." However, when Leckrone suggested that many persons apparently were afraid to tell what they knew, Mayberry countered that it was more likely that most individuals viewed the onslaught against the Sheltons as none of their business.

As Leckrone and Mayberry sounded off, the plan to get the remaining Sheltons out of Fairfield was set in motion. Although neither had recovered enough to leave the hospital, Lula and Guy quietly left the facility at dawn with Zuber only a few days after their admission. Wasting no time, Zuber drove the pair, along with his Grandma Agnes, to the apartment of his girlfriend, Barbara Wallace, in Mount Vernon, thirty miles to the west of Fairfield. They were joined there by Little Earl, who'd come up from Florida. With Little Earl driving Lula and Guy, and Zuber taking Agnes in his Studebaker, they departed for the Ohio River town of Henderson, Kentucky. There, the party rendezvoused with Big Earl and Earline, who also had journeyed up from Florida. From that point, they all traveled to Florida. No members of the family of Ben and Agnes who'd been in the public eye were left in the Fairfield area.

Based on the account by Lula and Guy of their shooting, Harris again faced a charge of assault with intent to kill. And once again, nothing came of the charge. With the Sheltons gone, the bullets stopped. But not the fires. Apparently intent on erasing visible reminders of the Sheltons in Wayne County, the Shelton antagonists had, along with everything else, turned into pyromaniacs.

A month before the end of 1951, the abandoned Shelton homestead at the Merriam crossroads, last lived in by Agnes, was burned to the ground. In March 1952, an arsonist eliminated the two remaining structures at Big Earl's Hill Top Farm. One was a small frame tenant home and the other a vacant concrete house which once was the residence of Ray Walker. These fires were set after Big Earl supposedly asked Governor Stevenson for help in protecting his property. However, the office of Stevenson, a person extremely busy in a year he'd be running for president, insisted that no such request was received.

Ironically, during Stevenson's first year in office, groups of Fairfield ministers and businessmen went to Springfield more than once to solicit assistance from the governor after Big Earl allegedly threatened Mayberry with death if he interfered with operation of the Farmers' Club. However, no state action resulted, in part because Stevenson was in the process of reorganizing the State Police.

Mayberry himself requested a helping hand from the State Police in 1949 in his investigation of the Shelton shootings occurring that year. The request was turned over to another unit in the Illinois Department of Public Safety, the Division of Criminal Identification and Investigation. Two years later, James Christensen, the division superintendent then, but not in 1949, noted in an internal report to Michael F. Seyfrit, the department director, that Mayberry's request apparently was ignored. Added Christensen, "It is my opinion (that) assistance should have been given when it was requested and that the cause or motives of all these shootings could have been determined."[12]

The location of what had been the Farmers' Club was involved in the grand finale to the attempted annihilation of anything Shelton-related in Fairfield.

It occurred shortly after nitroglycerin and dynamite caps were stolen during a break-in at a storage facility between Fairfield and Mill Shoals of a firm that shot oil wells. When Red Russell found out about the theft, his son Lelan recollected, "he predicted that something was going to be blown up."[13] Red was right.

A little more than an hour after midnight on the morning of July 15, 1952, Fairfield was rocked by an explosion that extensively damaged the building on the city square that had housed the upstairs Farmers' Club. The blast was attributed by law officials to a nitroglycerin bomb placed at the front door to a recently opened restaurant on the first floor of the building, said to be the last one in Fairfield owned by Big Earl. While no injuries were reported, the explosion heavily damaged adjoining garages and broke windows in buildings all around the square, including the Brown Hotel a block away. Fearing the Fairfield National Bank was blown up, Elmer Brown, the latest sheriff of Wayne County, said he "ran all the way over barefooted from the jail."[14] He soon was joined on the square by hundreds of residents, who had been shaken out of their sleep again by violence tied to the once powerful Shelton family.

It was the last time it would happen.

18

And the Years Went On

A gnes was resilient. One had to give her that. Few persons about to enter their ninth decade could have reckoned with being exiled from a place like Wayne County to the bustling city of Jacksonville, Florida, by the Atlantic Ocean. She did, at least, have with her in this new land what was left of her family. That helped her cope, if anything could, with the heartbreaks she had endured in the home from whence she'd come. Three sons lost to bullets, and almost another son and a daughter too. In her new world, hopefully, she'd at least find solace from the killings and those devastating newspaper headlines.

The change in America in the lifetime of Agnes was incredible. Abraham Lincoln was president when Agnes entered the world (assuming that she indeed was born in 1862), and Dwight Eisenhower, seventeen presidents later, was in the White House during the last years of her life. She witnessed the evolution of the horseless carriage, the flying machine and newfangled inventions beyond belief. Television was one. Agnes liked it. However, according to her grandson, when she watched TV in the house in Jacksonville that she shared with Lula, Agnes donned her finest dress and put on perfume. The primping was necessary, in her mind, because she thought that those people she was observing in live productions on the screen also could see her.

Some things in her life didn't change though. Right up until she died in 1957, Agnes refused to waver from her insistence that her sons were good boys, every one of them.

Not until newspapers revealed her death did many followers of the Sheltons' exploits know for sure that the Jacksonville area—known to Floridians as their First Coast—was the place in which Agnes and the other Sheltons who'd fled Wayne County had settled. She died thirteen years after Benjamin Shelton did. Although space for burying her next to her husband was available back up in Maple Hill, Agnes was interred in Oaklawn Cemetery at Jacksonville.

Three years after her death, Dalta died in Jacksonville from cancer.

Big Earl, the last of the Shelton brothers, hung around a lot longer. He was ninety-six years old and in declining health at the time of his death and burial at Jacksonville's Riverside Memorial Park in 1986. Off and on during the last thirty-five years of his life in Florida, where he prospered in real estate developments, he was haunted by fears that his old enemies in Illinois might renew their deadly interest in him. But, as far as was known, nothing materialized along this line.

Earl did encounter difficulties throughout the 1950s, however, when negotiations for the sale of his farm and other acreage in Wayne County oftentimes broke down when prospective buyers got cold feet. One of Ted Link's last stories on the Sheltons related that oil speculators eyeing Earl's land had to tread carefully, mainly as a result of continued hints by Charles Harris that anyone wishing to stay healthy needed to avoid undertakings in Wayne County that would be financially helpful to Earl. Nevertheless, it appeared that Big Earl's existence in Florida was quite calm in comparison to the turmoil surrounding the lives of some of those who either did or tried to make Earl as miserable as possible during his final years in Illinois.

The leading example was Harris, a person who, in the words of Jack Vertrees, was "thought of by nine out of ten people around Fairfield to have been involved one way or another in just about every shooting of a Shelton."[1]

With the Sheltons gone from Wayne County, Harris himself emerged as a major farmland owner, bringing more than 1,000 acres under his name, an appreciable number of which had belonged to various Sheltons.

Harris also remained a self-anointed guardian of the Pond Creek area. However, this role became strained because of his combative nature. As a onetime Pond Creek resident put it, "Charlie was the watchdog down there. But it was like the old western story about how the hero ran out of enemies and began fighting with his friends."[2]

The tide began to turn against Harris in 1963 when he was tried for the murder of a neighbor, H. S. Taylor, widely regarded as the unofficial "mayor of Pond Creek." Taylor acknowledged to his friends that his life was in danger after he won a civil judgment against Harris for damage to Taylor's crops by hogs straying from Harris' land. Not long thereafter, Taylor was found shot to death in his car on a Pond Creek road. On the heels of Taylor's murder, Harris showed up at the Fairfield hospital with a bullet in his arm. According to ballistics tests, that bullet came from a pistol belonging to Taylor that was found under his body. Harris was charged with the killing, but was acquitted at his trial by a Wayne County jury and set free.

The next round turned out differently for Harris. In 1964, the charred bodies of Jerry Meritt, who testified against Harris at the Taylor murder trial, and Betty Newton, reportedly a woman friend of Harris, were found in a burned Pond Creek house belonging to the Meritt family. Both had been shot. Charged in the double killing and also with committing arson, Harris dropped out of sight. After the FBI placed him on its most wanted list, Harris finally was apprehended by agents who found him sleeping in a vacant house in a wooded section of the Pond Creek bottoms.

This time, Harris did not stroll out of the courtroom a free man. Wayne countians, no longer enamored with Harris, wanted a no-nonsense prosecution of Black Charlie. They got it from State's Attorney Willard (Bill) Pearce and Richard C. Cochran, a Fairfield attorney appointed a special assistant prosecutor by Wayne officials to assist Pearce in preparing the case and presenting it in court. The result of the Pearce-Cochran effort was a jury conviction of the sixty-nine-year-old Harris in late 1965 on both the double murder and arson charges. He was sentenced to serve sixty to seventy-five years in a state prison. He ended up spending more than fifteen years behind bars before being released on parole early in 1981. He lived the last three or four years of his life with a relative in Kansas, although he did manage several visits back to Wayne County before he died. By then nobody was afraid of him anymore.

A dark cloud over Wayne County was lifted on December 22, 1965, the day Black Charlie was taken from the county jail before dawn for the ride to the Menard penitentiary. Jack Vertrees, with his newspaperman's desire for recording history, requested permission to accompany Harris on his possibly last departure from Fairfield, and neither Harris nor Sheriff Eugene Leathers of Wayne objected. Jack made the trip in the front seat of the sheriff's car conveying Harris. Leathers was driving and Black Charlie sat in the backseat, handcuffed to a sheriff's deputy, Harry Lee. Following the vehicle was a State Police car manned, as Vertrees remembered, by troopers Bob Lee and Harold Jones.[3]

Harris, after obtaining consent from those in his auto, puffed on cigars all the way to Menard. While taking a long look at Christmas decorations in Mount Vernon and other places through which the small convoy passed, Harris meandered from one subject to another. He didn't think the death penalty was a deterrent to criminals, and he thought it was a shame that American farm boys received training in weaponry during the world wars that made them killers. And he had notions about the nation's space exploration program and preachers, and heaven too. As for the Sheltons, Black Charlie mentioned them only in voicing his belief that they had pinned on him the nickname he so disliked.

When the law officers, after arriving at Menard, were escorting Harris to the prison's front gate, Vertrees retrieved his camera from under his seat in the car and captured one last photo of the convicted killer. Moments afterward, Black Charlie became inmate No. 33156. The diminutive Mr. Harris did not appreciate that picture one bit, Jack later learned.[4]

Unlike Harris, Frank (Buster) Wortman never returned to prison after his federal penitentiary days in the 1930s. Wortman came darn close, though, as a result of a long-running battle with the Internal Revenue Service over alleged tax evasion. Wortman may have been the undisputed boss of the underworld in Illinois south of Springfield after the decline of the Sheltons, but he managed little relaxation while wearing the precarious crown in the final decade of his life because of the constantly pesky IRS.

To be truthful, Wortman's entire ride as a downstate gangland chief for the Chicago mob was seldom smooth. Elimination of the Shelton gang was a prerequisite for Wortman to reach his full potential, and this was accomplished through old-fashioned brutality. Hardly anyone in the know believed that Wortman knew nothing about the Shelton murders, at least those of Carl and Bernie. However, after those two were gone, Wortman had only several years to enjoy being a lord and master of downstate gambling. Governor Stevenson ensured this by bringing to an end the contradictory situation in Illinois where gambling was illegal based on the statute books, but free as a breeze where enforcement of the law was concerned. Stevenson's crackdown on wide-open gambling was punctuated convincingly in 1950 when he dispatched his suddenly less corruptible State Police to shut down flagship gaming parlors—high flyers such as the Hyde Park Club and 200 Club on the East Side, the home base of Wortman. Unrestrained gambling was the cash cow for Wortman, as it had been for Carl and Bernie, but that particular bonanza for Wortman didn't last long. Buster had to look elsewhere for dollars.

"For Wortman was a gambling man, primarily," wrote Carl Baldwin, "and when gambling had to go underground in 1950, it put a crimp in his wallet and in his aspirations. He dabbled in other fields, such as labor racketeering, trucking, jukeboxes, pinball machines, race horses, real estate developments, restaurants, nightclubs and loan companies. But income from these ventures was a trickle compared with the big money that comes from gambling with the wraps off."[5]

This did not mean that Wortman failed to rake in dough, because he did. And it did not mean that he failed to present the aura of a big-time gangster, because he did. Central and southern Illinoisans, except for those residing in caves, knew who Buster was. Youngsters growing up on the East Side thought he was the toughest man in America. Bill Nunes wasn't laying it on too thick when he recalled, in one of his books on East St. Louis, his reaction as a kid to making eye contact with Wortman one day in about 1950. Bill was searching for cigar bands at the corner of Collinsville and Illinois avenues in East St. Louis when a dark sedan paused at the corner and then slowly turned in front of him. Bill got a good look at the driver, dressed in a gray topcoat and a matching fedora.

For the "briefest of moments," wrote Nunes, "his eyes met mine. I knew the face instantly...." A chill gripped Bill, he recounted, even though Wortman "merely turned his head and drove away." Yet, continued Nunes, "for a second or two...in my own childish mind, staring evil incarnate in the face, and living to tell the tale, was like barely escaping the clutches of Dillinger or Capone."[6]

Most times when Wortman was spotted in public, he was being driven in a luxury auto by a chauffeur-bodyguard. The need for security by a man like Wortman was one of the reasons for his having built in the mid-1950s a home that arguably became the most talked-about residence in the St. Louis area. The spacious, two-story house was constructed on a large and secluded tract east of the city of Collinsville and, in a throwback to the castle world of King Arthur, a deep moat was dug around the home. The island fortress off Lemen Settlement Road was accessible only by a bridge, which curious folks venturing out to see the house dared not cross because of the always present Wortman men.

As opposed to a number of other infamous downstate gangsters, Wortman passionately hated newspaper reporters and photographers. But while they routinely saw only a scowling, cursing Wortman, others might encounter a nicer and quite charitable version when Wortman was sober. Considering himself a gourmet, Wortman often was spotted in top dining spots in Chicago and St. Louis and even, on occasion, in gang favorites like Miami Beach and Hot Springs, Arkansas. The Paddock, the lounge-restaurant run by Wortman and a brother, Ted, on St. Louis Avenue in East St. Louis, was a quality eating establishment for a time, a place where patrons could find Buster a cordial host. Gene Smith, who would become an Illinois law enforcement official and a businessman, was one who witnessed Wortman's better side when Smith, as a young man, dated one of Buster's daughters. In visits to the moated house, where Wortman's youngsters frequently threw parties, Smith found Wortman to be "a surprisingly little guy, but right out of central casting for gangsters...a fellow with a bit of the look of that tough guy actor, Lee Marvin." Yet, related Smith, "what really stuck in my mind was how smart he was; how he seemed to be almost a genius on subjects like geography. People wouldn't believe that he had a library in that house, and that it had books in it."[7] Wortman, in a generous mood, once handed Smith a book to read that was written by a widely recognized New York madam whom Buster knew.

The little known side of Wortman also included interest in early American architecture. He liked to visit restored buildings, and was intrigued by one of Daniel Boone's log cabins. He also revealed knowledge of Abraham Lincoln that went beyond the usual textbook information.

Two detriments to Wortman, his hot temper and booze, made his life more complicated than it had to be. Incident followed incident. Some were just temporary embarrassments, like the time in 1964 when he was shot accidentally in a drunken dispute with a bartender. Others plagued him much longer, but none more so than his mistreatment, when on a bender, of an internal revenue agent. It helped spur the investigation that led to his conviction and the conviction of two associates in federal district court in East St. Louis in 1962 for conspiracy to evade income taxes.

Shortly thereafter, but before sentence was passed, one of his code-fendants, Elmer (Dutch) Dowling, his chief lieutenant, was shot to death. The bodies of Dowling and a lesser hood murdered with Dowling were found near Belleville. Of course, the killings went unsolved.[8] Guesswork about the elimination of Dowling ranged far and wide, even to the extent of an assertion that Wortman may not have been in the dark about the slaying of a confidant said to be as close to Wortman as members of his family. Whatever, Dowling's death was a sign to many that all was not well in the underworld of Buster, where his grip was not what it used to be.

As it turned out, Wortman and the other still-living codefendant in the tax case were sentenced to five years in prison. However, Wortman never had to serve the time because the guilty verdict was reversed in a higher court, and he was freed at a subsequent trial.[9] By then, though, his legal expenses reportedly had weakened him financially. He also was burdened by numerous ailments, aggravated by heavy smoking, in the final years before his death in 1968 at age sixty-three. To many, his passing marked the conclusion of the era of big-league gangsters in southern Illinois.

After the departure of the Sheltons, Wortman, Birger and even Black Charlie, the criminal element in downstate Illinois was a collection of pikers. Vicious murderers, faceless crime bosses in corporate suits and drug dealers neither captured the public imagination nor inspired the widespread terror that the Sheltons and the others did in their heyday. Too, with the passing of the years and the fading of memories, harsh realities tended to gradually give way to increasingly romanticized pictures of what the Sheltons and their brethren were up to.

First and foremost, the Sheltons were an American story. Maybe not one to write home about, but nonetheless a story not only captivating, but inescapably part of the landscape in a unique country where people really have an opportunity to grow up to become what they want to be.

The realization that the Shelton story was an ignoble tale in no way subtracted from its contribution to the American experience. As was said, it took all kinds. The Sheltons desired respectability more than most. Carl hungered for it, and so, in the end, did Big Earl. They got a measure of it, and not just from those walking the darker side. But what they got a lot more of was notoriety. But then, the line between presentable and notorious easily could become blurred, depending upon who was doing the looking.

Carl, Bernie and Big Earl may not have had book learning, but they overcame their meager beginnings with the same characteristics of so many making it to the top of their chosen profession. Craftiness, pugnacity and incredible insight into greed in human nature. Like successful businessmen, the Sheltons recognized unmet desires of many people (both during Prohibition and afterward), and moved to satisfy those wants. However, the absence of civility in the ruthless fashion employed by the Sheltons to eliminate anybody blocking their paths to prosperity put them in a league of their own.

One of the more meaningful ways of defining the Sheltons was through the hundreds and hundreds of people whose lives they affected. A large number of these persons died violently, and many of those who weren't killed saw their lives tarnished. In some cases, the hurt never went away, even when there was no proof of Shelton responsibility. More than seven decades after the unsolved murder in 1926 of Mayor Jeff Stone of Colp, Carol Hicks, a resident of a town in southern Michigan and a descendant of Stone's family, was pressing the Illinois State Police for information of any kind on Stone's killing. The Shelton-Birger gang war was going strong in 1926, and Stone was thought to be disliked by the Sheltons.

"Jeff was reputedly a pretty rough character himself, and was probably playing both sides in that situation," said Hicks. "So it was maybe expected that it would end this way for him. Still, his shooting left scars and unanswered questions for his family, a not pretty legacy, through the years." Contending that "the Sheltons were absolutely responsible for the death of Jeff," Hicks added that "the failure to ever see anybody arrested or prosecuted for the killing denied the family at least some sort of closure or resolution on the subject."[10]

Historically, the Shelton boys and their gang were a bridge in Illinois between old and new. They had one foot in the past when lawlessness featured independent gunmen and their henchmen preying on society at their own will without regard to other outlaws. In that world, the Shelton brothers were very successful in defending themselves. On the other hand, Carl, Bernie and Big Earl were forerunners in the move to major organized crime, to the consolidation of far-flung criminal enterprises under the iron hand of one individual or ruling gangland clique. At their peak, the Carl Shelton-led brothers showed they didn't need a Harvard business degree to employ highly effective and lucrative organizational skills. In the end, though, the Sheltons did not have the wherewithal or staying power (especially after the killing of Carl) to withstand some of the ultimate villains in organized crime—the Capone-structured Chicago syndicate and its eventual St. Louis area allies. But the Sheltons held their own against them for years.

The Prairie State has produced many of those "poor boy finds success" scripts popularized by author Horatio Alger. The Shelton boys would have made fine material for Alger, but with a different twist. The protagonists were antiheroes. But their story was hardly that simple. The Sheltons were able to both entice and intimidate legions of folks into marching to their tune, many of them ensnared before they knew it. Few individuals perhaps anticipated such manipulative canniness from products of rustic impoverishment. The success of the Sheltons belied their origin, but, on the other hand, the success may have been greatly linked to the lessons for survival honed into them in their youth. There was just no easy explanation for the Sheltons. Carl Shelton set the pattern, and he was a Svengali, pied piper and, yes, a bit of Robin Hood all rolled into one.

Fascination with the Sheltons hardly ebbed with the passage of time. For every person who wished the brothers never had existed, there was a Harry (Gene) Stowers, an owner of a Springfield environmental laboratory who grew up in Benton, where his father knew the Shelton brothers. Gene himself saw one or more of them when he was a youngster, and that, coupled with everything he heard about them, was enough to fuel his lifelong curiosity about the Sheltons.

"Anybody can believe what they want," concluded Stowers, "but my dad and others said the Sheltons were really pretty nice people. They were actually decent, and not out to hurt normal persons. From some of the stuff that went around or was printed, you'd think that they were out to slap kids. But they didn't.

"There were a lot of people who knew them who felt they should have been put in better perspective in regard to the times and places of their lives. Memories of the Sheltons should have been recorded accurately."[11]

Little Earl was the last living Shelton who figured into part of the violence that marked his family's history. But, he shied away from talk for publication for nearly the last half century of his life, and whatever light he could have shed for the public record went with him to his grave in Orange Park, Florida, shortly before Christmas in 1998.

To be fair, Little Earl only surfaced in the tail end of the Shelton saga anyway. It was people like Ray Walker who played lead roles throughout the headline-making stuff that put the Sheltons on the map in the first place. But their lips were pretty much sealed for eternity—either through an early death spurred by their involvement or, as in the case of Walker, by fading into oblivion.

By the time of Little Earl's death, none of the children of Ben and Agnes were living. Lula died in Florida five years before the passing of Big Earl, and Hazel (a Floridian most of her life) in the years following his death.

Wayne County slowly became a distant part of the past for later generations of the family started by Ben and Agnes. With the mounting of the years, few descendants of the couple had any firsthand knowledge of the old days in Wayne.

Still, if there was a keeper of the old family flame, it was Jim Zuber. One of those enduring individuals in life who commands respect, Zuber knew what had been, and it hadn't made it easy for him.

For a young man, Zuber had his hands full back in those dark days of 1951 when he helped whisk his mother and grandmother away from the dangers of Fairfield to Florida. With his family in shambles, he could have lost Barbara, the love of his life. But Barbara was a strong woman, committed to a good man, Shelton or not, and before 1951 was out they were married. The start of their life together was delayed, though, by Jim's service to his country in the Korean War. After he returned, the Zubers did carve out for themselves in Florida a good life that included the raising of a family.

But, Jim never let go of certain keepsakes that kindled memories of his uncles, the most cherished of which were sentimental family pictures. Too, he wound up with the old, tattered family bible that had belonged to his grandmother.

Something else Zuber ended up with was the acreage that had housed the Merriam crossroads home of Agnes and Ben. Although the Zubers had no hesitation about returning to Fairfield for occasional visits, he sold the property. Visits were one thing. Living there might well have been another. When asked whether they could ever reside in Fairfield, Barbara said it wasn't likely.

"Do not forget," she said, "Jim is a Shelton."

Notes

1. Good Morning, Mr. Shelton

1. "Shelton Inquiry Stalled; Gang War Feared As Result of Killing," *St. Louis Post-Dispatch*, undated.

2. Identification of the road as Pond Creek Road was based on interviews with Wayne countians and also on widespread press accounts. However, the author was told that the road was called Beech Bluff Road by some persons in Wayne, a name related to the old Beech Bluff School along the road.

3. "Former Convict Named in Killing of Carl Shelton," *Post-Dispatch*, Oct. 24, 1947.

2. Ben and Agnes

1. James S. Zuber, interview by author, Florida, Aug. 7, 1998.

2. "Sheltons of Wayne County (Part 2)," author unknown, undated, p. 299.

3. Ibid.

4. Ibid.

5. The year of Agnes' birth was said to be 1862 by most sources. They included a Gaither family history furnished the author by Howard Gaither of Albion, Ill., and the inscription on a gravestone in Maple Hill Cemetery in Fairfield, Ill., that was provided for Agnes in event she was buried there, which she was not. Other sources, though, including a Shelton fam-

ily tree compiled by Hazel Katherine Shelton and the 1880 census records, put the year of the birth of Agnes as 1866.

6. Zuber's quote here and those in following paragraphs are taken from the interview by the author in Florida Aug. 7, 1998.

3. Destined for Trouble

1. John Bartlow Martin, *Butcher's Dozen and Other Murders* (New York: Harper & Brothers, 1950), pp. 104-106.

2. Based on records on Earl Shelton provided by the Illinois Department of Corrections.

3. Ibid.

4. James S. Zuber, interview by author, Florida, Aug. 7, 1998.

5. Ibid.

6. Records of Department of Corrections on Roy Shelton.

7. Based on records in Office of Mines and Minerals in the Illinois Department of Natural Resources.

8. Records of Department of Corrections on Roy Shelton.

9. Carl R. Baldwin, "East St. Louis," *St. Louis Commerce*, Nov. 1982, p. 68.

10. Elliott Rudwick, *Race Riot at East St. Louis* (Urbana: Univ. of Illinois Press, 1982), p. 50.

11. "Hearings before the Special Committee to Investigate Organized Crime in Interstate Commerce, United States Senate," United States Government Printing Office (1951), Part 4-A, Missouri, Exhibit No. 50, p. 812.

4. Bootlegging—The Farm Boys Hit Their Stride

1. See chap. 3, n. 11.

2. "Sheltons Allege Holdup Charge is Frameup by Foes," *St. Louis Post-Dispatch*, Nov. 22, 1926.

3. Memorandum on Sheltons, Carl R. Baldwin Collection, Bowen Archives and Special Collections, Southern Illinois Univ.-Edwardsville.

4. Ibid.

5. David Conrad, "Recreation in the Illinois Coal Town," *Concerning Coal: An Anthology* (Carbondale: Coal Research Center, Southern Illinois Univ., 1997), p. 31.

6. Gary DeNeal, *A Knight Of Another Sort: Prohibition Days And Charlie Birger* (Carbondale: Southern Illinois Univ. Press, 1998), pp. 6-7.

7. "Sheltons Divided Mail Loot in His Home, Birger Testifies: Newman Tells of Robbery Plans," *Post-Dispatch*, Feb. 1, 1927.

8. Ibid.

9. Taylor Pensoneau, "'Comic Strip' Illinois Klan Can't Get Cross to Burn," *Post-Dispatch*, Nov. 14, 1976.

10. Shelton memorandum, Baldwin Collection.

5. Flies in the Ointment—S. Glenn Young and the KKK

1. In reality, Young himself may have been the author of *Life and Exploits of S. Glenn Young*. A *Belleville Daily News-Democrat* story Jan. 27, 1925, after Young's death said that he just had finished writing an autobiography with the assistance of the Reverend Herbert Brice of Canada, an author of a number of books.

2. A Young family history by Lucile Young Bent of Oakland, Calif., in 1996 put the year of his birth as 1884. *Life and Exploits of S. Glenn Young* said on p. 251 he was born Mar. 4, 1886. On p. 157 in *Bloody Williamson*, the date of Young's birth was given by author Paul M. Angle as Mar. 4, 1887.

3. *Life and Exploits of S. Glenn Young* (Herrin: Crossfire Press, 1989), pp. 15-16.

4. Young family history by Bent, p. 242.

5. Ibid., p. 241.

6. Dickson Terry, "Big Carl Lived on Borrowed Time," *St. Louis Post-Dispatch*, Nov. 2, 1947.

7. Ibid.

8. Ibid.

9. "The Stormoguide," *Daily News-Democrat*, May 26, 1924.

10. Ray Serati, interview by author, Springfield, Ill., Aug. 26, 1998.

11. Ibid.

6. Bullets, Bombs and Tanks—And a Pile of Corpses

1. Memorandum on S. Glenn Young and Ora Thomas, Carl R. Baldwin Collection, Bowen Archives and Special Collections, Southern Illinois Univ.-Edwardsville.

2. John Bartlow Martin, *Butcher's Dozen and Other Murders* (New York: Harper & Brothers, 1950), p. 113.

3. Young and Thomas memorandum, Baldwin Collection.

4. Biennial Message of Governor Len Small to the Fifty-fifth Illinois General Assembly, Springfield, Jan. 5, 1927.

5. "Hearings before the Special Committee to Investigate Organized Crime in Interstate Commerce, United States Senate," United States Government Printing Office (1951), Part 4-A, Missouri, Exhibit No. 50, p. 813.

6. Memorandum on Sheltons, Baldwin Collection.

7. Wes Smith, "The Duchess," *Chicago Tribune,* Jan. 28, 1992, sec. 2, p. 1.

8. Gary DeNeal, *A Knight of Another Sort: Prohibition Days and Charlie Birger* (Carbondale: Southern Illinois Univ. Press, 1998), pp. 111-112.

9. Dickson Terry, "How Sheltons Battled Birger Gang," *St. Louis Post-Dispatch*, Nov. 3, 1947.

10. "Martial Law Only Remedy, Herrin Mayor Tells Governor," *Post-Dispatch*, Nov. 15, 1926.

11. "Illinois Governor Says Williamson Must Save Itself," *Post-Dispatch*, Nov. 15, 1926.

12. Dickson Terry, "Bloody Year in Shelton-Birger Feud," *Post-Dispatch*, Nov. 4, 1947.

13. See n. 9.

7. High Noon at Quincy

1. Dickson Terry, "Bloody Year in Shelton-Birger Feud," *St. Louis Post-Dispatch*, Nov. 4, 1947.

2. "St. Louis Visit of Carl Shelton Quite Eventful," *Post-Dispatch*, Dec. 16, 1926.

3. "Illinois Feudists Come to St. Louis and One Is Held," *Post-Dispatch*, Dec. 15, 1926.

4. Records at the National Archives and Records Administration, Great Lakes Region, Chicago, on Criminal Case No. 636, United States vs. Carl Shelton, Earl Shelton and Bernard Shelton.

5. Most news stories spelled the last name of the mail messenger as Mathias. However, it was spelled Methias in the federal indictment of the Sheltons for the mail robbery.

6. Information on the trial was based mainly on *Post-Dispatch* coverage of it from Jan. 31 through Feb. 5, 1927, and on records on the trial at the National Archives and Records Administration (see n. 4).

7. "Three Sheltons Become Numbers at Leavenworth," *Post-Dispatch*, Feb. 7, 1927.

8. A Crackerjack Reporter Weighs In

1. "Interesting Incidents in the Career of John T. Rogers, Reporter; Many Testimonials to His Public Service," *St. Louis Post-Dispatch*, Mar. 4, 1937.

2. Ibid.

3. "John T. Rogers of Post-Dispatch Dies Suddenly," *Post-Dispatch*, Mar. 3, 1937.

4. See n. 1.

5. "Oliver K. Bovard, Famed St. Louis Editor, Is Dead," *Post-Dispatch*, Nov. 4, 1945.

6. Irving L. Dilliard, interview by author, Collinsville, Ill., July 31, 1998.

7. See n. 1.

9. Behind the Eight Ball in Taylorville

1. Carl D. Oblinger, *Divided Kingdom* (Springfield: Illinois State Historical Society, 1991), p. 20.

2. The source for the information on the Kincaid bank robbery was the file in the Illinois State Archives in Springfield of court transcripts, abstracts of record, motions and other documents related to the 1928 trial of Carl, Earl and Bernie Shelton on a charge of committing the robbery.

3. James H. Bandy, telephone conversation with author, June 22, 1999.

4. "Selecting a Jury to Try Sheltons Proves Difficult," *St. Louis Post-Dispatch*, Jan. 4, 1928.

5. The last name of this witness was spelled Nave in the abstract of record in the case filed May 16, 1928, with the Illinois Supreme Court. But, the name was spelled Naeve in the transcript of the trial's testimony in the state archives.

6. "State Attacks Alibi Evidence of Two Sheltons," *Post-Dispatch*, Jan. 6, 1928.

7. "Shelton Boys Guilty, Given 1 Year to Life," *St. Louis Globe-Democrat*, Jan. 8, 1928.

8. Ibid.

9. "Sheltons Lose Motion for Another Trial," *Globe-Democrat*, Jan. 22, 1928.

10. "Decision May Free Shelton Brothers," *Associated Press*, Dec. 11, 1928.

10. Gangland Monarch

1. See chap. 3, n. 11.

2. Memorandum on "Gang Killings," Carl R. Baldwin Collection, Bowen Archives and Special Collections, Southern Illinois Univ.-Edwardsville.

3. Tom Duffy, "Gang Prowled in Area with Brazen Cruelty," *East St. Louis Journal*, Oct. 26, 1947.

4. Ibid.

5. Carl Baldwin, "Gangland's Pattern of Death," *St. Louis Post-Dispatch*, Jan. 2, 1951.

6. "Bombing Called Shelton Defiance of Cuckoo Gang," *Post-Dispatch*, Mar. 20, 1931.

7. Memorandum on "Shelton Gang," Baldwin Collection.

8. "2 Belleville Men Named to County Posts by Recorder," *Belleville Daily News-Democrat*, Dec. 1, 1930.

9. "Gangster Is Slain on Venice Road," *News-Democrat*, Dec. 1, 1930.

11. An Honest Sheriff

1. Leland J. Munie, interview by author, Belleville, Ill., Jan. 30, 1999.

2. From statement written for author by Shirley Munie Truttmann and received by him Jan. 30, 1999.

3. Leland Munie, interview.

4. From a paper written by Shirley Truttmann on her father, Jerome J. Munie. Undated.

5. Robert E. Hartley, "Jerome Munie: The Man Who Ran the Sheltons Out of Town," paper presented at Illinois History Symposium, 1991.

6. Ibid.

7. Hud Robbins, "Southern Illinois 'Bad Boys' Appear Rather Nice in Court," *Danville Commercial-News*, Mar. 29, 1931.

8. Document dated June 20, 1989, in which Carl Baldwin discussed his career, Carl R. Baldwin Collection, Bowen Archives and Special Collections, Southern Illinois Univ.-Edwardsville.

9. Mrs. Olney F. Otto, telephone conversation with author, June 12, 1998.

10. Carl R. Baldwin, "Gang's Early Bid for East Side Labor Control," *St. Louis Post-Dispach*, May 26, 1958.

11. See n. 8.

12. See n. 10.

13. Ibid.

14. Ibid.

15. See n. 8.

12. Strike Three in East St. Louis

1. Carl R. Baldwin, "Gang's Early Bid for East Side Labor Control," *St. Louis Post-Dispatch*, May 26, 1958.

2. "J. Schrader, Crime Foe, Rites Today," *East St. Louis Journal*, June 27, 1961.

3. "Man Who Routed Sheltons Convinced of Gang War," *Journal*, Oct. 1947.

4. Ibid.

5. Tom Duffy, "Gang Prowled in Area with Brazen Cruelty," *Journal*, Oct. 26, 1947.

6. Ibid.

7. "Shelton Pays U. S. Lien," *Journal*, July 31, 1941.

8. See n. 3.

9. See n. 5.

10. Mrs. Miki Cooper, interview by author, Springfield, Ill., July 29, 1998.

11. Ibid.

12. "Carl Shelton Reappears in City Armed with 45 Caliber Revolver; Arrested, Fined $100," *Journal*, Dec. 8, 1935.

13. Ibid.

13. A Break from the Spotlight

1. James S. Zuber, interview by author, Florida, Aug. 8, 1998.

2. Zuber's quote here and those in following paragraphs are taken from telephone conversations with the author in Nov. and Dec. 1998.

3. Margaret Bender and the year of her death were included in an obituary of Carl Shelton written by his family. She also was mentioned in Shelton family trees, including one in "Sheltons of Wayne County (Part 2)," p. 353.

4. "Sheltons of Wayne County (Part 2)," author unknown, undated, p. 353.

5. "Earl Shelton Invites Police to Visit Him," *St. Louis Star-Times*, Feb. 23, 1943.

14. Roaring Peoria

1. Cynthia Carr, "Peoria, mon amour," *Chicago Tribune Magazine*, May 5, 1974, p. 68.

2. Ibid., p. 70.

3. Editorial on Edward N. Woodruff, *Peoria Star*, Dec. 23, 1947.

4. Steve Strahler, "'The Good Old Woodruff Days'," *Peoria Journal Star*, Dec. 26, 1976.

5. Ibid.

6. Mike Kenny, "Lady for All Seasons, Jean Whalen Became Painter as a Kid of 70," *Mid-Illinois Edition, Senior Citizens News & Views*, July 1992, p. 1.

7. James S. Zuber, interview by author, Florida, Aug. 8, 1998.

8. Theodore C. Link, "How the Shelton Murders Fit into Crime Puzzle," *St. Louis Post-Dispatch*, Apr. 24, 1951.

9. "Hearings before the Special Committee to Investigate Organized Crime in Interstate Commerce, United States Senate," United States Government Printing Office (1951), Part 4-A, Missouri, Exhibit No. 50, p. 817.

10. Theodore C. Link, "Barrett's Office Advised Sheltons on Gaming Setup," *Post-Dispatch*, Sept. 14, 1948.

11. Jack W. Vertrees, interview by author, Fairfield, Ill., Apr. 24, 1998.

12. Unpublished story on Charles (Black Charlie) Harris written by Vertrees and furnished to author.

15. A Gang under Siege

1. James S. Zuber, interview by author, Florida, Aug. 8, 1998.
2. Con Kelliher, "Overflow Crowd at Shelton Rites," *St. Louis Globe-Democrat*, Oct. 26, 1947.
3. Ibid.
4. "Notes on the Funeral," *Wayne County Press*, Oct. 29, 1947.
5. Ibid.
6. David Dickey, interview by author, Fairfield, Ill., Oct. 23, 1999.
7. Richard Everett, "Story of Shelton Payoff to Leading Peorian Is Told by 'Contact Man'," *St. Louis Star-Times*, Aug. 25, 1948.

16. 1948—A Year of Upheaval

1. James A. McGill, interview by author, Springfield, Ill., Feb. 16, 1999.
2. Ibid.
3. Ibid.
4. "Peoria Was 'Right' for Sheltons Until Death Closed the Books," *Peoria Journal Star*, Apr. 17, 1956.
5. "Theodore C. Link Dies; Investigative Reporter," *St. Louis Post-Dispatch*, Feb. 14, 1974.
6. Carl R. Baldwin, "Underworld, Politics Were This Reporter's Beats," *Post-Dispatch*, Feb. 28, 1974.
7. Theodore C. Link Jr., telephone conversation with author, Aug. 26, 1999.
8. See n. 6.
9. "Ted Link's Peoria Expose That Brought On His Indictment," *Post-Dispatch*, Oct. 24, 1948.
10. Theodore C. Link, "Bernie Shelton Laid Trap to Expose 'Fixer' Seeking $25,000 for an Official," *Post-Dispatch*, Aug. 6, 1948.
11. Roy J. Harris, "Evidence of Vice, No Indictments by Grand Jury at Springfield, Ill.," *Post-Dispatch*, Oct. 21, 1948.
12. See n. 6.
13. Frederick H. Bird Jr., interview by author, Springfield, Ill., July 27, 1998.
14. Ibid.
15. "An Open Letter," *Peoria Journal*, Aug. 25, 1948.

16. Theodore C. Link, "Shelton Bribery Records Are Played for Grand Jury," *Post-Dispatch*, Aug. 25, 1948.

17. Theodore C. Link, "How the Shelton Murders Fit into Crime Puzzle," *Post-Dispatch*, Apr. 24, 1951.

18. "The Expected Happens," *Journal*, Oct. 24, 1948.

19. Jerry Klein, "End of era," *Journal Star*, July 17, 1988.

20. See n. 4.

17. Terror in Fairfield

1. Judith Puckett, interview by author, Fairfield, Ill., Aug. 14, 1998.

2. Ibid.

3. "Third of Slain Sheltons Buried Under Guard," *St. Louis Globe-Democrat*, June 11, 1950.

4. "Earl Shelton Survives Bombing of His Home," *Globe-Democrat*, Dec. 1, 1950.

5. Carl Wittmond, *Memoir* (Springfield: Sangamon State Univ. Oral History Office, 1988), p. 100.

6. William O'Daniel, interview by author, Mount Vernon, Ill., Sept. 24, 1998.

7. Ibid.

8. Lelan C. Russell, interview by author, Mount Vernon, Ill., Dec. 11, 1998.

9. James S. Zuber, interview by author, Florida, Aug. 8, 1998.

10. Ibid.

11. "Indifference Is Blamed for New Gang Warfare," *Globe-Democrat*, July 2, 1951.

12. Internal report to Michael F. Seyfrit, director of the Illinois Department of Public Safety, from James Christensen, superintendent of the department's Division of Criminal Identification and Investigation, Dec. 28, 1951.

13. Lelan Russell, interview.

14. "Shelton Building Blast in Fairfield Leaves No Clues," *Globe-Democrat*, July 16, 1952.

18. And the Years Went On

1. Jack W. Vertrees, interview by author, Apr. 24, 1998.

2. James E. Sprehe, "Conviction of Charley Harris Brings End to 20-Year Era of Fear, Hate and Vengeance in Pond Creek Bottoms Area," *St. Louis Post-Dispatch*, Nov. 7, 1965.

3. Jack Vertrees, interview.

4. Ibid.

5. Carl R. Baldwin, "Buster Wortman's Quiet Departure," *Post-Dispatch*, Aug. 11, 1968.

6. Bill Nunes, *Coming Of Age In '40s And '50s East St. Louis* (Dexter, Mich.: Thomson-Shore, Inc., 1995), p. 63.

7. Gene Smith, interview by author, O'Fallon, Ill., July 31, 1998.

8. Charles O. Stewart, "Remnants of Wortman era turned into rubble," *Metro-East Journal*, Mar. 19, 1978.

9. See n. 5.

10. Carol Hicks, telephone conversation with author, June 13, 1999.

11. Harry (Gene) Stowers, interview by author, Springfield, Ill., Apr. 3, 1998.

Select Bibliography

Angle, Paul M. *Bloody Williamson*. New York: Alfred A. Knopf, 1952.

Brownell, Baker. *The Other Illinois*. New York: Duell, Sloan and Pearce, 1958.

Casey, Robert J., and W. A. S. Douglas. *The Midwesterner*. Chicago: Wilcox & Follett, 1948.

Demaris, Ovid. *Captive City*. New York: Lyle Stuart, 1969.

DeNeal, Gary. *A Knight of Another Sort: Prohibition Days And Charlie Birger*. Carbondale: Southern Illinois Univ. Press, 1998.

Hallwas, John E. *The Bootlegger*. Urbana: Univ. of Illinois Press, 1998.

Hastings, Robert J. *A Nickel's Worth of Skim Milk*. Carbondale: Southern Illinois Univ. Graphics and Publications, 1972.

History of Wayne and Clay Counties, Illinois. Chicago: Globe Publishing, 1884.

Hossent, Harry. *The Movie Treasury: Gangster Movies*. London: Octopus, 1974.

Howard, Robert P. *Illinois: A History of the Prairie State*. Grand Rapids, Mich.: Eerdmans Publishing, 1972.

Kirschten, Ernest. *Catfish And Crystal*. New York: Doubleday, 1960.

Life and Exploits of S. Glenn Young. Herrin: Crossfire Press, 1989.

Littlewood, Thomas B. *Horner of Illinois*. Evanston: Northwestern Univ. Press, 1969.

Manchester, William. *The Glory and the Dream: A Narrative History of America, 1932-1972*. New York: Bantam, 1975.

Martin, John Bartlow. *Adlai Stevenson of Illinois*. New York: Doubleday, 1976.

_____. *Butcher's Dozen and Other Murders*. New York: Harper & Brothers, 1950.

Nunes, Bill. *Coming Of Age In '40s and '50s East St. Louis*. Dexter, Mich.: Thomson-Shore, 1995.

Oblinger, Carl D. *Divided Kingdom*. Springfield: Illinois State Historical Society, 1991.

O'Shea, Margaret N. *Oldham Paisley: A Community Editor and His Newspapers, The Marion Daily Republican and Marion Weekly Leader, 1915-1970*. Copyright 1974.

Peoria...Impressions Of 150 Years. Peoria: *Peoria Journal Star,* 1995.

Rice, Arnold S., and John A. Krout. *United States History from 1865*. New York: HarperCollins, 1991.

Rudwick, Elliott. *Race Riot at East St. Louis*. Urbana: Univ. of Illinois Press, 1982.

Swanson, Stevenson, ed. *Chicago Days*. Wheaton: Cantigny First Division Foundation, 1997.

The Kefauver Committee Report on Organized Crime. New York: Didier, 1951.

Wittmond, Carl. *Memoir*. Springfield: Sangamon State Univ. Oral History Office, 1988.

Index

A

B

Taylor Pensoneau spent twelve years as the Illinois political correspondent of the *St. Louis Post-Dispatch*. He is the author of *Governor Richard Ogilvie: In the Interest of the State*, which the *Chicago Sun-Times* called one of the ten most notable political books of 1997. He also is the coauthor of *Dan Walker: The Glory and the Tragedy*. Both books were awarded the Illinois State Historical Society's Certificate of Excellence.